Focused Issues in Family Therapy

Series Editor
D. Russell Crane, School of Family Life
Brigham Young University
Provo, UT, USA

More information about this series at https://link.springer.com/bookseries/13372

Suzanne M. Coyle

Spirituality in Systemic Family Therapy Supervision and Training

Springer

Suzanne M. Coyle
Christian Theological Seminary
Indianapolis, IN, USA

ISSN 2520-1190 ISSN 2520-1204 (electronic)
Focused Issues in Family Therapy

ISBN 978-3-030-92368-6 ISBN 978-3-030-92369-3 (eBook)
https://doi.org/10.1007/978-3-030-92369-3

This Springer imprint is published by the registered company Springer Nature Switzerland AG
The registered company address is: Gewerbestrasse 11, 6330 Cham, Switzerland

Dedicated to my past and present students at Christian Theological Seminary who make supervision challenging.

Preface

Growing up in a rural community, I became aware of the many ways that neighbors' lives overlapped and intersected. I would often say that rural neighbors know what you have done even when you have not done it. Party phone lines were a sure conduit to community gossip, as were the local gathering places: gas stations and country stores.

My father was a farmer and my mother a public school teacher. This couple arrangement was common in rural Kentucky. It seemed normal to me. However, I vividly remember a summer in our lives that gave me the breadth and depth of rural life in its storytelling.

In addition to his farming, Daddy ran a gas station/country store, and the manager of the store quit unexpectedly. Mama decided to help during her summer break from teaching. And I, around 7 years old, took seriously my job dusting the shelves lined with canned goods, bread, milk, and the everyday vittles that a rural family needed. Sometimes, I even pumped gas. Mama was known far and wide for her hamburgers flipped on an iron grill. Truckers stopped just to gobble down her hamburgers.

The vivid memory I have, however, is the storytelling that happened every day in every hour. Usually, the men of the community gathered to tell stories without end. I was fascinated. Sometimes, the men laughed and said, "You know how those women talk!" Yes, a dominant narrative of my era. Yet, to myself, I thought the men did an excellent job of talking themselves. I loved the storytelling and vowed to become a storyteller myself.

My journey began as I listened and reveled in the stories I heard everywhere. I heard of the virtues of "city life" in my hometown of 5000 people. But nothing could match in my child's mind the magic of "country life" with its stories. The beauty shop, a brief journey into city life, breathed stories. The on-the-grounds dinners and fish fries at my home church, Beech Fork Baptist Church in rural Gravel Switch, were full of stories, testimonies of being saved or, at times, not being so saved.

Both true and not so true, from these stories came a realization that my family members and I were indeed individuals. Good storytelling involved stretching the story so it became a thick description of culture. The seemingly thin stories of rural life did indeed have much diversity. We were not self-contained individuals or even a self-contained family. We lived in a community context full of values that existed through people's lives and actions.

Some of these values permeated who my family and I were, along with our neighbors. These values became nested in us.[1] Furthermore, this diversity wove itself into what we in our community believed gave us meaning. It was our diversity wedded to values that formed our spirituality, which became grounded and either grew or withered.

Through these experiences, I became convinced that spirituality is best understood through the lenses of diversity and of the self of person. Both the lenses look at what is unique about each person. These lenses are critically connected in the community and with its many systems and stories.

One might argue that the community I grew up in was not diverse. We were largely white with some Black families. Other ethnicities were not known. My family had Jewish friends in a neighboring town. They owned the clothing store where my mother, grandmother, and I shopped. I knew nothing, however, about my ethnicity.

In rural storytelling, I learned that diversity includes all our modern definitions of diversity in this age of Black Lives Matter and Gay Pride. So, it is cultural. But it also involved who we are as individuals and the ways we align ourselves to diversity even if we are white.

It was not until I moved to New Jersey and graduate school that I became aware of my Irish heritage. It was interesting to me that many of the values that have been passed down from generation to generation were now a part of who I was. Values of family, hard work, and a profound sense of tragedy permeated our family stories.

My home community has changed. Diversity now includes white families and an increase in Black families and Hispanic families. Yet, diversity existed in my growing up years as well. My family and our neighbors carried with us a sense of both who we were and what we wanted to become. Thus, our lives were founded on finding meaning in our everyday living that would carry us into the future.

The ways we found meaning focused on our values, which were woven into our very diversity. Our ethnic identity in a rural community emphasized hard work, perseverance, and independence. Though ethnic identity was interlaced with class, some of us experienced being "looked down upon" by others from a "citified" and regional perspective. I was very aware of the difference between "city kids" and "country kids." Of course, "city" was a relative term in my hometown of 5000 people.

Acquiring an education became a way for us country people to acquire status with non-rural folks. In addition, even that had its limits in academic settings. I was the speech teacher's project in graduate school to eradicate my Kentucky accent, replacing it with a more East Coast version.

---

[1] Diversity in this book describes multicultural diversities as well as the diversities with which individuals may align.

Through these experiences, other rural people and I drew strength within us to meet challenges that were the norm for adjusting to the dominant values of city/suburban life. For many of us, a spunky spirituality expressed through our unique rural ethnicity gave us the courage to stand up to small oppressions of various kinds.

As we navigated these oppressions, our spirituality became a way in which we viewed our unique diversity. Furthermore, underlying the diversity was our self of person: the ways in which we viewed ourselves and the ways in which who we were related to our spirituality. I believe for us southern rural people, our spirituality was a large lens through which we viewed our diversity, not the other way around.

I now write about spirituality from my social location of being a white, heterosexual, cisgender female who has currently has mobility challenges. My prayer is that all of us from our unique social locations can converse about our shared experiences as humans who look to the future with our hopes and dreams. It is through these hopes and dreams that generative storytelling can emerge in which liberative spirituality can foster justice in an unjust world.

Indianapolis, IN, USA Suzanne M. Coyle

Acknowledgments

Our lives are enriched by many people through our hopes and dreams. This book has been made possible by many helpers along the journey.

Christian Theological Seminary provided a generous research leave that enabled me to clear intellectual space for this project. I thank President David Mellott and the Board of Trustees for this gift.

Vice President of Academic Affairs and Dean of the Faculty at Christian Theological Seminary Leah Gunning Francis recruited peer reviewers for the manuscript. Their feedback enabled me to look beyond my limited perspective.

Jacqueline Braeger, MFT core faculty member, served as Acting Program Director while I was on research leave thinking and writing.

Kimberly King, MFT supervisor, and Christina Davis, MFT supervisor and core faculty member, joined me in conversation and practice as we integrated spirituality in supervision of students, a love that developed from our theological training.

My MFT students in MFT Live Supervision—Aaron Benjamin, Kenya Campbell, Dena Hein, Iann Matlock, Sean Oatis, Rachel Rhodes, Beth Rice, and Tierra Ruffin—taught me as I taught them.

Suzanne Midori Hanna and Shruti Singh Poulsen both challenged and supported me as I thought, practiced, and wrote.

My friend and colleague Clarisse C. Croteau-Chonka supported the editing and revision of this book. Shared stories of our graduate days gave me opportunity to laugh.

Daniela Blei, freelance editor par excellence, supported me in the writing and streamlining of this book. She started with me with the book proposal and persevered to the final product.

Hector Hernandez Marcial, a former student, lent his visual creativity to make the living web of socio-spirituality come alive.

The Springer Nature publishing team supported me through the whole writing process. Many thanks go to Judy Jones, senior editor of the behavioral sciences and team members Brian Halm, Devgun, Pradheepa Vijay, and Kala Palanisamy.

I extend special thanks to D. Russell Crane, book series editor of the Focused Issues in Family Therapy for Springer Nature. He extended both his candidness and encouragement as I struggled through topics and problem areas that resulted in this book.

Finally, I could not have finished this book without the loving support of my minister husband Peter and astrophysicist son Joel.

Contents

List of Figures

List of Tables

About the Author

Suzanne M. Coyle is an Associate Professor of Pastoral Theology and Marriage and Family Therapy at Christian Theological Seminary. She has been Program Director of the Master of Arts in Marriage and Family Therapy program since 2004. The program has been COAMFTE accredited since 1994. In addition, she is an AAMFT Approved Supervisor. Other professional credentials include her licensure as a pastoral counselor and marriage and family therapist.

Coyle has worked in various clinical settings such as directing pastoral counseling centers, childcare agencies, private practice, and church pastorates. She holds standing as an ordained minister in the American Baptist Churches USA and the Christian Church (Disciples of Christ). Her role as pastor in congregations in Pennsylvania, New Jersey, and Indiana is the foundation for integrating spirituality in life.

She holds an M.Div. and a Ph.D. in Pastoral Theology and Communications at Princeton Theological Seminary. Coyle trained at the Ackerman Institute for the Family in New York City. She also holds a postgraduate Diploma in Narrative Therapy and Community Practice from the Dulwich Centre in Adelaide, South Australia. In addition, Coyle has advanced training in narrative therapy from the Evanston Family Therapy Center and the Vancouver School of Narrative Therapy.

To expand her clinical interests in teaching, she completed the EFT Externship with Sue Johnson with further advanced EFT work in the Master Core Skills Training and additional supervision. She completed Level 1 and Level 2 in Gottman Method Couples Therapy. Her most recent clinical training focuses on Attachment Based Family Therapy.

Coyle's publishing interests focus on spiritual and systemic integration as well as liberative theologies and supervision and training. She has authored two books in addition to this book and several peer-reviewed journal articles and chapters. Coyle has presented nationally and internationally at the American Association for Marriage and Family Therapy, American Association of Pastoral Counselors, Society for Pastoral Theology, International Association for Family Therapy, and the Society for the Exploration of Psychotherapy Integration.

Abbreviations

AACC	American Association of Christian Counselors
AAMFT	American Association for Marriage and Family Therapy
AAPC	American Association of Pastoral Counselors
ACA	American Counseling Association
ACPE	Association for Clinical Pastoral Education
AMFTRB	Association of Marital and Family Therapy Regulatory Boards
APA	American Psychological Association
ASERVIC	Association for Spiritual, Ethical, and Religious Values in Counseling
COAMFTE	Commission on Accreditation for Marriage and Family Therapy Education
MAMFT	Master of Arts in Marriage and Family Therapy
MFT	Marriage and Family Therapy
NASW	National Association of Social Workers

Chapter 1
Looking at Spirituality, Supervision, and Training

My personal experience in rural Kentucky emphasized the closeness of the community where someone was always available to look over you. Sometimes that oversight was comforting; sometimes it was intrusive. It could be said that close neighbors knew what you did even if you did not do it. So, my transition to the urban Northeast was quite a shock. Never had I experienced anonymity that was sometimes exhilarating and sometimes frightening.

Supervision in marriage and family therapy (MFT) training programs shares some similarities to living in a rural community. You have many people who are interested in your progress in life. The challenge becomes how to express that interest so that the individual does not experience intrusiveness or isolation. It is a tricky balancing act to determine the nature, progress, and extent of supervision and training for the MFT student.

Spirituality described in this book reflects the personal strength of individuals living in community. It focuses primarily on lifting people up from their own strength, with that strength expanded as they gain strength from others. This type of spirituality is typically non-theistic. Another perspective on the diversities of religion and spirituality is an increasingly popular approach that is related to spiritual fluidity. This approach is a combination of theistic and non-theistic approaches. Many people combine Buddhism with some form of Christianity for a spiritually fluid spirituality. Some of this approach is influenced by the growth of yoga and mindfulness practices (Bidwell, 2018). Several forms of yoga that are practiced today originate from Hinduism as well as Buddhism.

Also carrying over from my experience growing up on a farm is the notion that all life is imbued with spirituality. This book hopes to address that concern by lifting the importance of spirituality in all supervision and training. Yet our intent is to integrate spirituality with diversities to create an inclusive spirituality that is not limited to a personalized, internalized spirituality. This discussion expands spirituality to include everyday human concerns.

S. M. Coyle, *Spirituality in Systemic Family Therapy Supervision and Training*, Focused Issues in Family Therapy, https://doi.org/10.1007/978-3-030-92369-3_1

My personal experience influences how I see the ways in which supervision is inexplicably linked to spirituality. Perhaps one could argue that all the diversity concerns listed in Core Competency #1.2.1 in the MFT Core Competencies are related but separate.

The marriage and family therapy (MFT) core competencies were developed through a collaborative effort of the American Association for Marriage and Family Therapy (AAMFT) and interested stakeholders. In addition to defining the domains of knowledge and requisite skills in each domain that comprise the practice of marriage and family therapy, the ultimate goal of the core competencies is to improve the quality of services delivered by marriage and family therapists (MFTs) (MFT Core Competencies, 2004, p. 1).[1]

This book argues that spirituality, when practiced in a non-oppressive way, is an umbrella that can link various diversities. Spirituality encompasses meaning that is larger than self and includes many diversities. It also links with who we are through the concept of self of the supervisor.

The core competencies that deal with diversity are as follows: "Recognize contextual and systemic dynamics (e.g., gender, age, socioeconomic status, culture/race/ethnicity, sexual orientation, spirituality, religion, larger systems, social context") (MFT Core Competencies, 2004, p. 2). In the MFT literature, it is for the most part understood that diversities overlap in various ways through intersectionality. Merriam-Webster (n.d.) understands intersectionality as "the complex, cumulative way in which the effects of multiple forms of discrimination (such as racism, sexism, and classism) combine, overlap, or intersect, especially in the experiences of marginalized individuals or groups."

Thus, the diversities identified in the core competencies can overlap in various ways. For example, an African American self-identified female lesbian living in a community impacted by poverty can experience the overlapping of gender, age, socioeconomic status, culture/race/ethnicity, and sexual orientation and how these experiences impact her life.[2] Her peer community at school can shun her. If she has a church, it may be that her church does not affirm LGBTQ[3] persons. At the same time, her church may affirm some aspects of her identity.

In a very different context, an aging, white heterosexual male with no family and scarce financial resources would experience intersectionality through age, socioeconomic status, and social context. The oppression he experienced would be less visible than the oppression faced by the African American female teen discussed

---

[1] The reader can access the MFT Core Competencies at https://www.aamft.org/Documents/COAMFTE/Accreditation%20Resources/MFT%20Core%20Competencies%20(December%202004).pdf.

[2] Pronouns in case studies and elsewhere in this book align with the person's gender self-identification. So, the majority of pronouns are traditional she/her and he/his. In other situations, the pronouns will be third person plural, as used by trans and fluid communities, such as they/them. The author supports this newer approach to using pronouns in the English language.

[3] Various identifiers are used for LGBT communities and their concerns. This book uses LGBTQ. This identifier does not exclude intersex and allies.

above. It would seem on one level that the urban teen would be more impacted by societal injustice than the white male. What we do not know is the level of intrapsychic and interpersonal distress that both the persons experience.

It could well be that the leveler for each of them is spirituality, and how that spirituality supports them against oppression. At this point, I would make my argument that spirituality conveys an idea more expansive and less restrictive than religion as identified in the MFT Core Competencies. Religion is understood as a system of beliefs that its adherents have followed, typically for one generation. Religion is understood to begin after two, three, or more people share a spiritual experience that they wish to carry forth. It then becomes codified.

Sometimes, this results in rigidity that people experience as oppressive and harmful. It is now not uncommon for people to talk about toxic religion. Systems of beliefs have acquired a "bad reputation." Typically, religion is classified as described by the major world religions of Christianity, Judaism, Hinduism, Buddhism, Islam, and Confucianism. It is largely theistic, with the exceptions of Buddhism and Confucianism. Moreover, recent polls indicate a decrease in the number of people who are affiliated with or practice a formal religion in the United States (Gallup, 2021).

In contrast, spirituality is generally viewed as positive. At its extreme, spirituality becomes little more than a container for thoughts and feelings. With an absence of personal connection, little opportunity exists for connecting spirituality with diversity concerns. In many conversations, one might hear people discussing spirituality that seems quite close to emotionality. At times, the two overlap and even merge with each other. Spirituality may also convey a strictly non-theistic approach to life and meaning that can relate to some holistic spiritualities that embrace the physical, psychological, and social aspect of spirituality and health (Koenig, 2012). Some holistic spiritual practices might include yoga, meditation, centered prayer, mindfulness, traditional medicine with indigenous and Asian origins, and ecologically aware engagement. Combining these holistic practices in various ways will result in multiple types of spirituality.

Spirituality as understood here tries to weave a path between theistic and non-theistic spiritualities as experienced through the self of the therapist. This notion of spirituality focuses on the way in which therapists experience themselves as they work with clients. It understands that our own religion as therapists and supervisors can never overshadow the spirituality of our clients. And, at the same time, it understands that this spirituality may eventually be a window through which to view the client's spirituality.

Yet for this book, the initial focus is on the therapist's own spirituality as developed through careful supervision. MFT literature recognizes the importance of the ways in which the supervisor works with a supervisee to appropriately respond to the client's spirituality. However, many of these approaches do not emphasize the way client's stories contribute to their spirituality. The approach developed in this book emphasizes that a flexible and applicable approach to using spirituality in supervision starts with the therapist's self of therapist and the ways in which this perspective overlaps with both the therapist and the client's own perspectives.

Focusing on the client and supervisee's emerging spiritual stories has an expressive connection with their personal spiritual stories. In contrast, more traditional MFT spiritual assessments are objective and externalized often ignoring personal spiritual stories. To give further context, the focal areas of self, systems, and spirit will be discussed.

Self as Focus

Supervisors who work with supervisees typically focus on the skills and training required to work with clients. Part of this supervision is assessing the theoretical model used to work with clients. Other components involve the client's presenting concerns and risk factors associated with the concerns. The treatment plan follows.

While the process of supervision varies from supervisor to supervisor, systemic family therapy supervision addresses self of therapist concerns. Through the self of therapist lens, the supervisor can work with the supervisee to understand better ways in which the supervisee's own personal worldview and experiences influence the work with clients.

It is from the self of the therapist that the supervisor can view deeper concerns the therapist has that can impact the work with clients. To what extent do the values that influence the supervisee create a helpful or not helpful environment for care of the client? And how does the supervisor's self of supervisor isomorphically influence working with the supervisee?

Sometimes, self of supervisee is understood primarily as being a container of developmental and psychological constructs that influence the growth of the therapist. Growth of the therapist, however, has barely any intrinsic spirituality in the literature. The view of this discussion maintains that the self of supervisee is indeed intrinsically spiritually interwoven with psychological and developmental understandings.

Systems as Focus

Systems are the interlocking webs in which we live and interact with ourselves and others. They begin with the micro system of our families and expand to mezzo systems like our work environments and macro systems such as the legal systems in which we live. As the various systems develop and grow, intersectionalities emerge such as culture/race/ethnicity and sexism. Supervisees become increasingly aware of ways in which they are oppressed by these intersectionalities, as are their clients. At the same time, systems such as families, legal systems, health systems, and religion certainly can lend support.

Self of therapist concerns can be too readily understood as relating only to the individual therapist/supervisee. However, with a systemic perspective, we recognize that all individuals are relational selves. By extension, this means that supervisees may often find themselves as part of a larger system, then another and another.

As the systems layer over each other, the self of the therapist concerns become more complicated. It becomes easy to dismiss the systemic perspective and only focus on the individual. By doing so, the depth of the self of the therapist becomes thinner. Its potential richness and resilience to dilemmas for the therapist, supervisor, and client are compromised. Sometimes as we negotiate the virtual and face to face environment, we may find it easy to just focus on the skills and interventions of supervision and therapy.

Some time ago, I was in a supervision session with one of my supervisees. He said that he wanted to talk with me about something he found troubling. The student described an interaction between us when I encouraged him to explore some self of therapist issues with his therapist around his relationship with a high-risk client. (All our students pursue their own therapy when they are in practicum.) He said that he thought that I needed to be more curious about the contributions to the self of therapist issues with his client. I then invited a conversation with the supervisee.

As our conversation continued, I began to understand more fully the student's criticism of me. As I thought through the situation, I began to see that in the environment of virtual supervision, I was too eager to focus on the skills and interventions rather than examining the student's behind-the-scenes connection with the self of the therapist issues I saw emerging in the therapeutic relationship between the student and client. I then further discussed with the supervisee specific contributions that I believed could be contributing to some stuckness with his client. We ended the supervisory conversation on a note of clarity. Certainly, in this context, I had erred on not exploring fully the self of therapist issues that could also contribute the supervisee's understanding of his spirituality.

Interactions among supervisor, supervisee, and client will emphasize the ways in which self of supervisee is interwoven with the systemic structure. The result is to create avenues for interactions between the self of supervisee and the systemic framework. By doing this, other interactions will be created that are different and unique from the back-and-forth movements of self and systems, such as unique intersectionalities that highlight unique diversities. Forming a web of connections between these movements will be spirit, or spirituality, as we will discuss in the next section.

Spirit as Focus

Spirit, in this book, understands spirituality as meaning that extends beyond self or relationships. It opens people up to meaning and connections that have a transcendent quality. This spirituality enables both theistic and non-theistic people to seek new avenues to expand their spirituality.

Sometimes spirituality is viewed as a discrete category related to the idea of religion. In turn, spirituality and religion are then understood as two related but separate types of experiences. While not experienced as a uniquely separate religion, spirituality is still sometimes seen by some people as a dispensable diversity. It may well be that spirituality for some seems like a diversity that demands belief in God or a Higher Power.

In contrast, this book's understanding of spirituality opens the search for spirit in lives of meaning to encompass many ideas. A person who understands the environment and the threat to our global ecosystems as the ultimate meaning in his life is a spiritual person. Similarly, an evangelical person who understands heaven and hell as literal places is a spiritual person, as she prays for friends to be saved by accepting Jesus Christ as Savior.

Moving from self and systems to spirit, spirit or spirituality, this interaction becomes the web that connects the various movements and connections among self, systems, and spirit. With this interconnectedness, spirituality becomes the connector of all diversities, not just one diversity. If spirituality were rigid or amorphous, this would not be a possibility. But this focus on spirit will engage with spirituality as a diversity lens with an emphasis on the self of supervisee as a relational self that supervisors and clients encounter.

Case Vignette of Supervisee/Supervisor Diverse Relational Selves

A case vignette will give a better illustration of how the aspects of self, systems, and spirit work together. The following is a case vignette of a supervisee who I supervised in the MAMFT program at Christian Theological Seminary.

Maria was a 30-year-old Latina. I supervised her for 1 year in the program. I am an ordained Protestant minister in a mainline denomination. Maria was in the process of moving toward a church-related vocation. We had the identity of female minister to share between us. We also had a love for relational systemic therapy in a postmodern approach.

Our families were not similar. I was Caucasian from the rural South and an only child; Maria was Latinx from Central America with a large family. We shared an enthusiasm for social justice as well as a need to connect to others through listening and action. In short, our demographics were quite different, but our values were similar and touched at many points.

One day, Maria reported in supervision on a Latinx family with which she was working. The family consisted of a mother, father, and two children. One of the children, Selena, had been traumatized by a drive-by shooting when a bullet lodged in the wall of her home right behind her while she was doing homework. Maria worked with the whole family around this traumatic incident.

Soon Maria proposed that Selena write a story about the incident and change the ending to the story to what she would like to see. Selena told the story of the bullet in the wall, depicting the mysterious shooter as a large, scary figure. At the end of the story, Selena showed a picture of the scary figure as a normal-sized adult. In the picture, Selena confronted the stranger. Maria reported that Selena was much less frightened. She seemed able to talk about the incident with less anxiety.

We talked about this experience in supervision and what it meant for Maria. For Maria, being Selena's therapist gave her a way to "look out for her people." Maria's viewpoint was that spirituality is a part of recognizing a client's diversity and the ways it contributes to a sense of hope. Maria believed that by offering Selena an open future through her imagining a future where she could be strong and unafraid, she had a fulfilling story. Maria said that through Selena's story, she was able to share in that story as well.

As Maria and I talked, I shared with her that I was honored to see with her, through her eyes, the story of Selena. While I possessed white privilege, I was able in some small measure to share in that story and offer back to Maria a retelling of the story. It was, for me, a story of seeking social justice. As member of the oppressor group, I could see in a moment some of the fear that oppression brings to others.

Connecting Self, Systems, and Spirit in the Case Vignette

Self, systems, and spirit are interwoven in the supervision case vignette. An interweaving of the web of spirit[4] connects with the self of supervisee/supervisor for Maria and me. We both share a spiritual identity[5] although it is not explicit. She and I both are ministers as well as therapists. We further understand spirituality to be connected with social justice. Furthermore, this spirituality relates to uses of supervisee/supervisor, despite our very different demographic identities. The personal experience of God or Other in our lives had the ability to transcend both cultural and clinical language and understandings. We were able to experience a spirituality that was bigger than us, our relationships, and beliefs.

The web of relational systemic practice then connects the selves of supervisee/supervisor as it presents seemingly disparate demographics for Maria and me. Interwoven throughout is the racial and ethnic diversity that separates us. Yet, through our similar spirituality, we can transcend some of that difference (Fig. 1.1).

[4] The web shown in this figure how a visual depiction of the ways in which the basic integrative concepts can ebb and flow. This chapter's web figure lays the foundation for the living web of socio-spirituality developed in the next chapters.

[5] Spiritual identity here refers to the beliefs, values, and culture that contribute to one's personal spirituality.

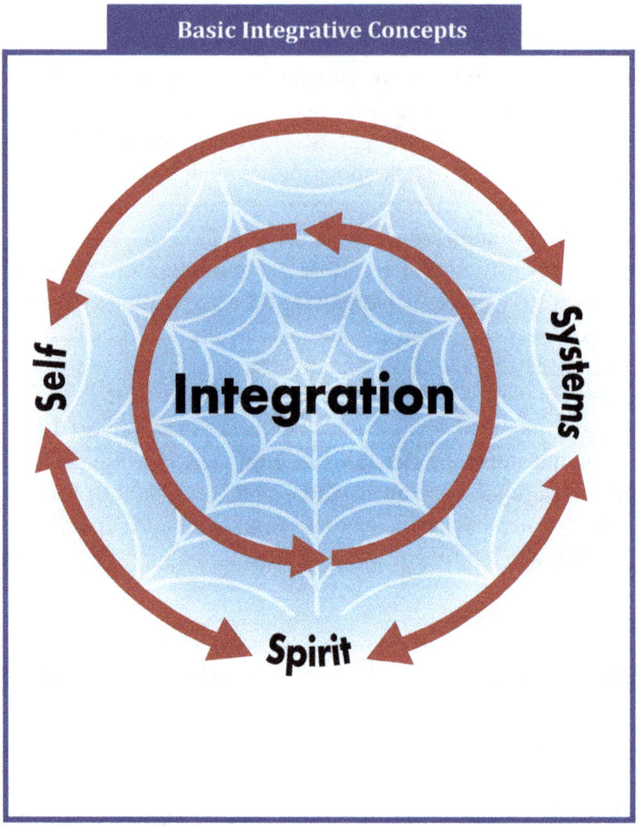

Fig. 1.1 Basic integrative concepts

Using This Book

We live in a world populated by uncertainty. Black Lives Matter and protests that cry for justice, global pandemics, environmental crises all are societal outcries that will not be resolved soon. Some will never be resolved. We will need to determine how to live in a world filled with inequities. Finding ways to infuse people's lives with spirituality can be a viable approach forward in addressing these challenges. The ideas and practices explicated here may enrich such a way forward.

This book focuses on theory and practice and the dynamics between them. Chapters 2–4 focus on theory that underlies the concepts of self, systems, and spirit. Chapter 2 lays out the use of spirituality in contemporary systemic practice as well as connections to and differences with religion. The case is made that spirituality needs to become a more vital part of family therapy compared to spirituality's status in other mental health professions.

Shifting from this focus, Chap. 3 moves spirituality into a context of diversity using a religious/theological methodology connected to a social science methodology. The beginning of the living web of socio-spirituality is introduced here, which begins to illustrate the integration of spirituality and social justice. Building on the living web of socio-spirituality, Chap. 4 deepens diversity concerns and social justice in a spiritual context. The living web of socio-spirituality is enhanced with liberative theologies and spirituality in a postmodern clinical practice.

Chapter 5 and the remainder of the book emphasize practice that emerges from this theoretical perspective. Chapter 5 integrates spirituality in individual, tandem, and group supervision, giving some directions for both supervisor and supervisee. The full development of the chapter provides a framework based on the living web of socio-spirituality that allows for different MFT modalities to be utilized in supervision. Chapter 6 bounces from foundational supervision to provide a case study of a COAMFTE accredited MFT program where spirituality is integrated into the curriculum through the concepts of immanence and transcendence. Suggestions for creating a spiritually integrated curriculum for both faith-based and secular programs are offered. Closely aligned with a spiritually integrated curriculum, Chap. 7 offers a case study of a course, "Integration of Self, Systems, and Systems," that can serve as an example of using the focal point of spiritual integration.

Chapter 8 provides a bridge between theory and practice in an exploratory research project on spirituality in an MFT live supervision group focused on ways to make spiritual interventions with clients. Students read didactic material about self, systems, and spirit as well as discussing suggested questions to lay the foundation for spiritual interventions. Then, Chap. 9 moves from the counseling room and classroom into the community setting, offering new directions for spiritually integrated practice. Here social justice can powerfully address challenges such as poverty, racism, sexism, gender exclusion, agism, and ableism. Examples of ways in which collective narrative practice can be used in community settings are offered.

Following the discussion in Chap. 9, Chap. 10 offers some unique faith-based and secular internship placement contexts that provide a bridge between family therapy and community outreach and care. Storytelling is highlighted as a method to be utilized in these settings along the lines of spiritual practice in a systemic perspective. Chapter 11 closes the book with some thoughts about imaginative and innovative future possibilities for spiritual integration.

Masters and doctoral MFT students can learn from Chaps. 1 to 4; doctoral students, faculty, and supervisors can profit from the entire book. A self, systems, and spirit practice exercise is offered at the end of Chaps. 2–11 that can be used in several ways. They can be used as an experiential follow-up to a discussion of the chapter in an academic setting, in agency setting, or in a non-academic residential training program.

Systemic practitioners from family therapy, mental health counseling, professional counseling, family psychology, social work, and psychiatry can find material in this book that will address spirituality in a systemic context for their own profession. Suggestions for their applications conclude each chapter. Sometimes these applications are detailed and, at other times, suggestive. Finally, the appendices offer some examples of practice products that can be adapted to spiritual integration in systemic family therapy supervision and training. Footnotes throughout the text will direct the reader to those adjunct appendices.

References

American Association for Marriage and Family Therapy. (2004). *Marriage and family therapy core competencies*. Author. Retrieved from https://www.coamfte.org/Documents/COAMFTE/Accreditation%20Resources/MFT%20Core%20Competencies%20(December%202004).pdf

Bidwell, D. R. (2018). *When one religion isn't enough: The lives of spiritually fluid people*. Beacon Press.

Jones, J. M. (2021). *Church membership falls below majority for first time*. Gallup. Retrieved from https://news.gallup.com/poll/341963/church-membership-falls-below-majority-first-time.aspx

Koenig, H. G. (2012). Religion, spirituality, and health: The research and clinical implications. *International Scholarly Research Notices, 2012*, 278730. https://doi.org/10.5402/2012/278730

Merriam-Webster. (n.d.). Intersectionality. In *Merriam-Webster.com dictionary*. Retrieved August 13, 2020, from https://www.merriam-webster.com/dictionary/intersectionality

Chapter 2
Spirituality in Contemporary Systemic Practice

For systemic family therapists, spirituality and religion invite lively conversation. General concerns emerge about the tendency to ignore spirituality and religion and avoid the imposition of personal beliefs in the therapy session. Here, the reader will be introduced to generative approaches to spirituality that can enrich individual and family life.[1]

Importance of Religion and Spirituality in Americans' Lives

Reviewing Americans' degree of preference for religion and spirituality lays the foundation for this book. Religion and spirituality are complex constructs that may largely depend on the varying cultural and spiritual values of individuals and specific groups. Therapists and supervisors will be supported in their work with clients and supervisees by understanding the difference and overlap between these two concepts. Research published by *Gallup* and the Public Religion Research Institute provides the reader with important demographic data.

In 1999, one half of Americans who identify as Christians were church members of a formal denomination. In 2019, a *Gallup* poll found that church membership had declined to 41% of all Americans. Of that number, 68% were recorded as traditional (born before 1945); 57% as baby boomers (born between 1946 and 1964); 54% as Generation X (born between 1965 and 1979); and 42% as millennials (born between 1980 and 2000) (Jones, 2020).

[1] The terms used in systemic practice—such as clinician, therapist, marriage and family therapist, and family therapist—refer to the professional identities of systemic therapists in general. Similarly, systemic practice, systemic family therapy, marriage and family therapy (MFT), and family therapy all refer to the psychotherapeutic profession.

S. M. Coyle, *Spirituality in Systemic Family Therapy Supervision and Training*, Focused Issues in Family Therapy, https://doi.org/10.1007/978-3-030-92369-3_2

In 2017, a *Gallup* poll found that 87% of Americans responded "yes" to the question: "Do you believe in God?" (Hrynowski, 2019). That same year, the Public Religion Research Institute found that 29% of respondents described themselves as "both spiritual and religious;" 18% as "spiritual but not religious;" 22% as "not spiritual but religious;" and 31% as "neither spiritual nor religious" (Raney et al., 2017). When the percentages are tallied, 69% of Americans identify as spiritual or religious in some form.

In 2018, a *Gallup* poll discovered that religion ranked as important for 72% of Americans, of whom 51% ranked religion as "very important" to them (Brenan, 2018). At the same time, there is a downward trend when it comes to membership and participation in a formal organized religion. Twenty-one percent of Americans do not have a formal religious identity (Newport, 2016).

From this data, we can conclude that spirituality in some form is significant for most Americans. Our role as systemic therapists and supervisors is to discover what kind of therapeutic response can address spiritual concerns for our clients and supervisees. Then, we must determine how we bring spiritual literacy and spiritual sensitivity to systemic practitioners. In this discussion, systemic practice refers to a therapeutic approach, in marriage and family therapy for example, that looks at interconnecting patterns of belief, thought, and behavior affecting families and other larger systems.

Development of Spirituality and Religion in Systemic Family Therapy

Marriage and family therapy has a storied history of responding to families' needs. In the postwar World War II years, the American economy flourished with new housing and educational opportunities for returning veterans. This boom continued into the 1950s, and interest in improving family life continued for decades. Marriage enrichment through church paragroups emerged, such as the Association for Couples in Marriage Enrichment, founded by David and Vera Mace in 1973 (Better Marriages, n.d., http://www.bettermarriagesdc.org).

In contrast to other mental health disciplines that focused on the individual, interest in family life for marriage and family therapy was novel from the 1950s to the 1970s. Psychotherapists such as Bowen, Minuchin, Whitaker, and Satir nurtured the development of marriage and family therapy as a separate profession, resulting in a veritable golden age of MFT in the 1970s (Coyle, 2015). In its systemic view of families as a distinct area in the profession, marriage and family therapy developed a unique niche in the psychotherapy community.

Between the 1970s and 1990s, little interest in spirituality in systemic practice is evident in the MFT literature. But then, spirituality emerged as a critical component of a comprehensive treatment plan for individuals, couples, and families in relational systemic practice. MFT literature does not seem to specifically address this emergence of spirituality. My personal thinking is that perhaps clients themselves were sharing their spirituality with their therapists. In turn, it makes sense that therapists became more interested in spirituality. In 1963, the American Association of Pastoral Counselors was founded to support the new field of pastoral counseling that had emerged in seminaries and schools of religion (Pastoral Counselors, New York Times, 1963). Pastoral counseling began integrating theology and clinical practice. Perhaps, this new field planted a seed for receptiveness to spirituality in clinical practice.

The 1990s began to see an increase in peer-reviewed articles in MFT journals. During this period, other mental health professions in addition to family therapy, such as psychology, social work, and mental health counseling recognized the value of addressing spirituality in the lives of clients (Adams, 1995; Anderson, 1987; Anderson & Worthen, 1997; Brownell, 2014; Carlson et al., 2002; Erickson & Carlson, 2014; Gambrel & Keeling, 2010; Prest & Keller, 1993; Walsh, 2007). For clinicians and supervisors, this historical development offers a holistic view that explains the orientation of the MFT field in comparison to its peer psychotherapeutic professions. This bird's-eye view points to some of the ways that the systemic approach of MFT can enrich the lives of families. This overview may also give marriage and family therapy some insights into how we may better integrate spirituality into clinical practice (Anderson, 1987).

Currently, MFT training programs do not dedicate a great deal of attention and training to spirituality when compared to other clinical skills. In contrast, psychotherapists from the ministry stream of counseling have focused their clinical training to emphasize competency in spirituality to the same extent as clinical skills. Family therapists, true to their interdisciplinary origins, could learn from this psychotherapeutic group as well as offer critiques. MFTs might also consider the integration of spirituality in our clinical practice to better understand the belief system that informs family functioning. Such integration of spirituality into family therapy would respond to people's growing interest in spirituality that is shown by recent researchers (Hrynowski, 2019; Raney et al., 2017; Brenan, 2018; Newport, 2016).

Organizations relating to marriage and family therapy do not have any subgroups that focus on spirituality in systemic practice. The American Association for Marriage and Family Therapy, the professional organization representing MFT, does not have topical interest groups that focus on spirituality. Other cognate groups, such as the American Family Therapy Academy and the International Family Therapy Association in the United States, do not have any special groups focusing on spirituality.

Interest in spirituality in clinical practice has grown since 1990 (Adams, 1995; Anderson, 1987; Anderson & Worthen, 1997; Brownell, 2014; Carlson et al., 2002; Erickson & Carlson, 2014; Gambrel & Keeling, 2010; Prest & Keller, 1993; Walsh, 2007). More recent interest is cited in an article on integrating spirituality in MFT training (Coyle, 2017; Williams-Reade et al., 2018). Despite growing interest from clinicians and the public in spirituality, marriage and family therapy does not have a specialized group that deals with spirituality. MFT does provide workshops focusing on spirituality at annual conferences, and MFT literature in professional journals does publish articles about the importance of spirituality in clinical practice. Innovation in developing an integrative model of spirituality with systemic practice, however, is largely missing.

Thus, in discussing the role of spirituality in systemic practice, it is important for MFTs to create an integrative model of spirituality that can respond to public interest in spirituality. To this end, it will be important to address the following concerns: (1) how to create a unique systemic methodology for spirituality; and (2) how to determine the role of special interest groups on spirituality in MFT. After accomplishing these tasks, spirituality in supervision and training can be adequately addressed. The first step is to arrive at a definition of spirituality that informs systemic family therapy.

Distinctions Between Religion and Spirituality

To better understand spirituality in contemporary systemic practice, this discussion will now define religion and spirituality. Distinctions between religion and spirituality in systemic practice will be explored. A view of family spirituality will be offered. Finally, the current practice of spirituality in systemic family therapy will be addressed.

Religion and spirituality are related and different. Spirituality is generally understood as individual religious sentiment and as a practice preceding the establishment of a formal religion. The study of religion assumes that spirituality is shared by more than one person and then by a group of persons that wishes to transmit that experience to others (Bowker, 1997). This beginning of a communal spiritual experience then becomes codified, so that it can be passed down to other believers through sacred writings, rituals, and beliefs. Common examples of this institutionalization can be seen in the establishment of world religions such as Confucianism, Buddhism, Taoism, Hinduism, Judaism, Islam, and Christianity. The major religions then break down into sub-groups, which in Christianity are Protestant, Catholic, and Eastern Orthodox; in Islam, Sunni and Shiite; and in Judaism, Orthodox, Conservative, and Reform.

The belief systems of each major religion are not specifically addressed in most systemic family therapy literature. Some books identify differences in specific beliefs and their impact upon the lives of clients (Onedera, 2008). Some attention to the differences between theistic and non-theistic belief systems is also mentioned as helpful to systemic and non-systemic clinicians (Pargament, 2011).

For the purposes of this discussion, a basic definition of religion is sufficient to understand its purpose in the work of systemic family therapy. Prest et al. define religion as "the formal institutional contexts for spiritual beliefs and practice" (1999, p. 64). This understanding focuses upon religion as codifying beliefs as well as the practice of specific behaviors. An ethical framework can then develop into a canon of what is right and what is wrong (Carlson et al., 2002). This discussion is limited to the function of religion in clinical practice. However, decades of culture wars in this country may have some impact on the often-polarizing effect of religion in people's everyday lives. It is also important to understand the impact of institutionalized religion when working with clients who express their spirituality within the church (Kelly, 2002; Onedera, 2008).

Reviewing the differences between religion and spirituality, scholars typically refer to religion as the field of academic endeavor. A study of the development of religions, however, posits that a desire to maintain a spiritual experience is the purpose of establishing a religion. As religion attempts to both maintain and develop such experiences, it can become a sterile cocoon of what was once robust and vibrant. Religion can be absent of spirituality, a personal and emotive expression of transcendence. At the same time, religion can have expressions of spirituality to provide vibrancy (Coyle, 2009). Religion and spirituality can thus be connected or separate.

Distinctions between religions are well known in world cultures. Different religions are understood to incorporate difference(s) in beliefs and values. At the same time, spirituality has many different expressions that are sometimes overlooked. Helpful distinctions can inform the reader about various kinds of spirituality:

1. *Religious spirituality* is the sense of devotion to the sacred presence that religious societies have determined.
2. *Humanist spirituality* is the belief in the sacredness of humanity. Generally, it is feeling close to a group of people and the state of affiliating with and making sacrifices for them.
3. *Nature spirituality* is defined as believing in the sacredness of nature and the tendency to establish connections with it. Responses of awe that are experienced in the face of natural events or feelings of wonder during an exquisite view are examples.
4. *Universal spirituality* is a personal stance related to creation. It consists of thoughts that are related to humans' search for their place in the universe, the struggle for self-discovery within the endlessness of the universe, or the splendor of the universe (Worthington & Aten, 2009).

Each of these categories could be a part of psychotherapeutic work with a client. In focusing on relational systemic work, I am particularly attracted to religious spirituality and universal spirituality.

They both address the typical distinction between religion and spirituality without artificially separating the two. Religious spirituality provides a grounding for work with a client who adheres to a formal religion while connecting to a spiritual sensitivity to God and others as critical to being a faithful member of his or her religion. Universal spirituality seems a good fit for clients who are atheist, agnostic, or self-identify as "spiritual but not religious."

Let us see how attention to these two categories can provide different perspectives for a supervisor supervising a therapist with similar presenting problems but quite different spiritualities.

Your supervisee Heather has Matthew and Joseph as her clients. Each just heard that his father has stage IV cancer and is not expected to live more than 2 months.

Matthew, a Reform Jew, attends synagogue. As he frames his anticipated loss in his Jewish faith, he shares with Heather that his personal belief is to respect life and that he views death as part of life. He is angry and scared but reaches within to find some support in this personal spirituality. Heather and Matthew decide to explore this impending loss through his spiritual resources. Yes, Heather is struggling with his understanding of life after death. Reform Judaism does not understand heaven as place for believers after death. Heather is a fundamentalist Christian who sees life in heaven after death as a way of framing what happens in this life.

Joseph identifies as an atheist. Heather is mindful of his love of life and generosity toward his family and friends. As she talks with Joseph, he reflects upon his connection with some close friends. Joseph shares with Heather that the support of his spirit will come from the intangible hope he always gets from human connection. He sees that connection as the ultimate value in true spirituality. Heather struggles to connect with Joseph. For her, it would be quite difficult to accept a loved one's death without believing in heaven.

Clearly, Heather as a therapist will approach each client quite differently due to her own spirituality and remaining true to her theoretical orientation. The difference in Heather's therapeutic approach will emerge from the ways in which her clients, not her, see their spirituality. Explicitly, Matthew would be closer to religious spirituality and Joseph to universal spirituality. Yet, Heather as a therapist will need to assess her own spirituality and the way in which it influences her work with each of her clients. To some degree, the presenting problem is not the most important consideration. What is critically important is the way that each client creates meaning out of his life. You, in turn, as Heather's supervisor will need to attend to your own spiritual stance while challenging her to attend to her own spirituality. You will need to lift up isomorphic experiences that can illumine helpful paths for Heather to work with Matthew and Joseph.

Spirituality in Systemic Practice

How, then, do family therapists define spirituality as they ponder systemic practice? An overview of definitions in MFT literature is helpful for this discussion. Spirituality is "the human experience of discovering meaning, purpose, and values which may or may not include the concept of God or transcendent being" (Prest & Russel, 1995, p. 4). Other scholars see spirituality as a process that continues through life (Pargament, 2011). Generally, spirituality can be understood as an individual's journey, beliefs, and connectedness with others (Miller et al., 2004).

Looking at spirituality in a clinical context can emphasize emerging concerns from scholarly understandings. Spirituality generally comes from the Latin word "spiro," which means "to breathe" (http://www.etymonline.com/word/spirituality). To breathe certainly implies a dynamism of life that energizes the person. Spirituality, by its word origin, is not static but life-giving. By further expanding spirituality, people can experience life in its fullest.

Spirituality, as referenced by Holmberg et al., can be a universal human experience as well as specifically expressed in history, culture, and social interactions (2017). It can also be quite different for others (Swinton, 2001). These understandings provide encompassing contexts for spirituality. At the same time, spirituality can be related to those things that share a specific secular or religious context. As Kütük emphasizes, spirituality is not always explicit but can be implicit (2020). It is this subtlety that therapists need to remember as their clients share their life journeys. For example, a person can engage quite deeply in environmental concerns as expressed in their membership in the Sierra Club. On a religious level, a person can practice a quiet personal connection with the Spirit as evidenced at a non-programmed Quaker meeting.

In distinguishing between religion and spirituality, an in-between area will always be present. In general, religion is understood in social science circles as that which restricts and limits, while spirituality engages with the individual (Pargament, 1999). This discussion sees such constraints as sometimes valid but mostly unnecessary.

Even for practitioners and scholars, the understanding that religion is rigid may hold true with professional groups. Such was my experience in a postmodern training group I participated in several years ago. The group initially met for a period of 6 weeks. Then, due to group interest, they met for a few years after that initial 6-week experience. My interactions with those professional colleagues were cordial and deeply engaging. We discussed life, its limitations, and the role of postmodern practice as a possibility for mitigating such rigid constraints. I also shared my profession as an ordained minister and MFT professor.

One day at lunch, I sat by Mary, a European colleague, with whom I had never had an in-depth conversation. As we talked about a current social dilemma, I expressed my concern about how a particular religious and spiritual perspective had limited a population's options for self-governance. She turned and looked at me in astonishment and said: "I knew you were a minister so I naturally believed that you would take a rigid position to social issues."

For the next 30 minutes, we discussed our mutual understandings of religion, spirituality, and social issues. Her astonishment continued throughout our conversation. Despite her liberal arts education and broadly liberal social positions, Mary found herself clinging to the notion that anyone connected to religion would surely harbor a limiting viewpoint for people's understanding of the world. Here was an educated person who believed that I, as a therapist, could keep my clinical and religious beliefs so separate that one could be open-minded and the other limiting. This understanding may be more prevalent than one might think. It certainly highlights the need to explore more closely the ways in which spirituality can be both life-enhancing and life-limiting.

The distinctions between religion and spirituality raised here are all important. Taken together, they give the practicing systemic family therapist a holistic view of spirituality as it functions within their own lives and the lives of their clients. For the purposes of this book, spirituality is defined as "the expansion of something that is larger than self or relationship" (Coyle, 2013). This broad definition includes both theistic and non-theistic expression of one's beliefs as well as supporting a system that recognizes the role of emotion in spirituality but sees it as separate. In addition, the role of thinking or cognitive reflection is also an important part of this definition. In the subsequent discussion on methodology, an underlying approach that connects spirituality with systemic family therapy will become evident. Its foundation is based on a wholly different but related discipline that can support the clinician. This surprising discipline is theology. Theology is understood as "faith-seeking understanding" (Coyle, 2017).

While spirituality/religion is part of the context here, this book practices a theological method that emphasizes critical reflection on one's own belief system, whether theistic or non-theistic. This approach will also integrate a behavioral science methodology. Two types of theology will influence this discussion as it unfolds. One is embedded theology and the other intentional theology. Embedded theology is implicit beliefs that are a part of our lives: values and understanding that we act upon each day. Intentional theology is the critical reflection and analysis of these implicit beliefs (Stone & Duke, 2013).

Developing Spirituality in Clinical Practice

Understanding how to use spirituality with clients and supervisees requires a grasp of the current MFT literature on spirituality in clinical practice. References to spirituality encompass a broad spectrum of spiritual practices. General understandings of spirituality in clinical practice focus on its significance in people's lives and the need to pay attention to how clients understand spirituality in their own lives. Furthermore, therapists need to understand their role in responding to that need from clients (Brownell, 2014; Erickson & Carlson, 2014; Prest & Keller, 1993; Walsh, 2007).

Other understandings of spirituality focus on the historical division between science and spirituality (Adams, 1995). The post-World War II world saw the rise of science as a cultural source of wisdom. Scientists became respected arbiters of truth. Clergy increasingly became arbiters of religious and spiritual matters that were not recognized as applying to everyday matters in society. The 1940s and 1950s, however, still saw clergy as influential in America, but fissures in the society's respect for religion and spirituality began to emerge. Many Americans saw the dawning of this scientific renaissance as a relief from sometimes rigid understandings of religion and spirituality. Fact, not emotion, was looked to as a source of wisdom.

Of course, not all Americans took up science. Some faithful religious people saw this surge of science as a threat to "things that are not seen" in the words of Paul the Apostle. Thus began a slow division between groups of people of faith and religion. Other believers saw science as help for human dilemmas, not a challenge to religion and spirituality.

A helpful typology of responses to the connection between the behavioral and the theological is offered by Townsend. He posits four positions for relating the behavioral sciences and religion. His use of religion, however, is compatible with the use of spirituality in this chapter. The first position is independence, whereby psychotherapists assume that science and religion are entirely independent and autonomous. Science asks questions about objective observations while religion probes human meaning (Townsend, 2009).

The second position is a dialogue that expects that a mutually informing conversation between science and religion is possible. The argument is that both ask similar questions and use similar philosophical methodologies (Townsend, 2009).

The third position is integration, which looks for a direct relationship between the content of theology and the content of science. Whereas dialogue maintains a firm boundary between science and religion, integration softens this boundary (Townsend, 2009).

The fourth position is conflict that is the least prevalent position in contemporary practice. This position understands that science and religion can be connected in many ways. This approach would be more likely to be held by a theologically conservative therapist (Townsend, 2009).

From these examples, applications can be made to contemporary systemic practice. The dialogical and integrative approaches seem to offer promise for their application to systemic family therapy. The word used in MFT literature is integration. However, an actual explication of a methodological approach to integrating spirituality in MFT is largely absent (Wendel, 2003).

Using spirituality in a focally systemic setting became more prevalent in the 1980s. Efforts to apply spirituality to couples and family therapy began to blossom and show increasing sophistication (Anderson, 1987; Anderson & Worthen, 1997). Then, beginning in the 2000s, research studies were conducted to better understand the actual attitudes of family therapists (Carlson et al., 2002, 2011; Çetintaş & Ekşi, 2020; Prest et al., 1999).

Spirituality can be expressed through multiple definitions. An early approach utilized a quantitative sharing of spirituality inventories that focused on spiritual areas. Clients responded to inventories that indicated which spiritual themes fit them best (Pargament, 1997). This kind of spiritual assessment focuses on the explicit dimensions of spirituality. Also, a sense of history and relationship for clients is utilized using spiritual genograms (Dunn & Dawes, 1999; Frame, 2001; Hodge, 2001; Şahin, 2017: Willow et al., 2009; Wiggins, 2000). Other uses include the use of spiritual ecomaps (Hodge, 2005; Hodge & Limb, 2009, 2014) and a combination of the spiritual genograms and spiritual ecomaps (Rempel et al., 2007; Şahin, 2017).

The current scene acknowledges the impact of less modernist concepts as applied to spirituality. These include both postmodern practices (Coyle, 2013, 2014; Griffith & Griffith, 2002; Moules, 2000; Neden et al., 2011; Waldegrave, 2003) and the practice of mindfulness in systemic family therapy (McCollum & Gehart, 2010; Gambrel & Keeling, 2010; Gehart, 2012). These clinical approaches emphasize the client taking responsibility for his or her own spiritual perspective. It is an open-ended clinical approach as opposed to the constrained approach of the client fitting into specific spiritual categories that are utilized in spiritual inventories. Both the approaches have their place in clinical practice. This book will explore the open-ended approach of postmodernism and mindfulness (Coyle, 2015; Gambrel & Keeling, 2010).

In these past decades, the notion of spirituality as oppressive and limiting for clients has softened. Most scholars understand that spirituality can be both limiting and growth-producing. The therapist's role is to nurture the growth-producing function of spirituality. In working with families, developing family rituals between members can increase family cohesiveness (Mahoney, 2013; Pargament, 1997). An example of such a spiritual ritual for families might be engaging family members in the practice of hospitality (Coyle & Davis, 2017). Sociologists note that in our contemporary society, families often isolate themselves and neighborly visits are rare.

Before I began my doctoral studies, I lived in a high-rise apartment in Philadelphia. My ministry was set in that area as I worked to develop a new church start. As part of that ministry, I began to visit people who lived in my high-rise apartment, which was difficult. Some rejected my visits. Still others appreciated the initiative.

Sarah, one of my neighbors, said that she had lived in the apartment building for over a year. I was the first person who had reached out to her in a friendly manner. We connected as friends and had several conversations. As she shared about her loneliness in the apartment, the conversations quite naturally moved into sharing about spirituality. Sarah was not a strictly "religious" person. She was, in today's parlance, "spiritual but not religious." Our spiritual friendship developed over 6 months to the point of her inviting me to attend Midnight Mass on Christmas Eve at the Catholic Cathedral.

I was not a therapist to Sarah. However, the encounter does illustrate the lack of hospitality in our society. Families can engage in rituals of hospitality by connecting with non-related families that are only connected to them in a spiritual sense (Coyle & Davis, 2017). Hospitality can extend to therapeutic relationships with our clients and supervisees as therapists and supervisors in the way in which we "set the table" of therapy to be open to the spiritual experiences they may bring to therapy.

As we focus on the content of such conversations, it can be helpful to identify the spiritual issues that are being discussed in therapy sessions. One helpful approach is outlined by Brownell in specifying some broad issues that a therapist can use (2014). What follows is a brief description. While they are conceptualized from a Christian perspective, other devotees to such religions as Judaism, Islam, Buddhism, and so forth can apply their specific religious orientation to the general spiritual perspective.

Brownell presents the issues as follows: (1) living in the present; (2) truth as an ultimate reality; (3) faith and uncertainty; (4) communal belonging; (5) dissatisfaction with God; (6) rigidity and legalism; (7) abuse; (8) spiritism, spiritualism, and the Occult; and (9) endings, death, and person eschatology (2014). In identifying these issues, the therapist could focus on them with the client without naming them as such during the counseling session. Or the therapist could respond to the client with some broad question around that particular issue to see how the client might respond.

Some of these issues also focus on larger existential questions of living that all therapists and clients must decide about how to engage. These include living in the present, truth as an ultimate reality, faith and uncertainty, communal belonging, rigidity and legalism, and death and personal eschatology. As the therapists listen to their clients, these issues are broadly implicit. The client may speak directly about the concern. Or the client may speak around the issue while the therapist is thinking about the focal issue as they understand it.

Other issues are more explicit, such as dissatisfaction with God, rigidity and legalism, abuse, and spiritualism/the Occult. These themes are also connected to focused religious issues, or the emotional and physical consequences of abuse. The therapist or supervisor would likely choose to deal with abuse in a direct manner and then focus on the emotional as well as spiritual repercussions.

The categories that are existential are more applicable to spirituality as the therapist and supervisor encounter them with the client or supervisee. Let us focus on how the therapeutic approach to living in the present might work. Juan comes to you for therapy as a 24-year-old Latinx male who is currently unemployed following the first job he had after graduation as a teacher in a public elementary school. The school district was forced to lay off some non-tenured teaching staff due to budget cuts.

Another young Caucasian teacher hired at the same time was not laid off. The school is predominantly Caucasian.

Juan can find work as a coffee barista. The salary pays his rent and essentials. Plus, he enjoys the camaraderie with his co-workers. But he is eager to get on with a life that includes getting a job as a teacher, his chosen vocation.

As you talk with Juan, he is both discouraged and angry about his lot in life. Juan was raised Catholic in a first-generation Mexican American family. His growing up years included many challenges. He was the only family member who spoke English. His family always encouraged him to succeed in life. They saw America as a land of opportunity.

So, upon graduation and his hiring at an elementary public school in a high achieving school district, Juan really believed in the American dream. Now, with his layoff, he no longer sees his place in American society as what he really deserves after all his hard work. Juan wonders aloud if he was laid off because of his race. Furthermore, he drifted from his family roots as a Catholic. Juan now self-identifies as spiritual but not religious.

You, as a therapist or supervisor, could go in many directions with your treatment of Juan.

Several spiritual factors may be considered. Focusing on spirituality, you could talk explicitly about his disappointment with Catholicism. One could also encourage an implicit discussion around Brownell's category of living in the present. Certainly, Juan is experiencing quite a bit of frustration about living in the present.

At the same time, some troubling issues regarding racial injustice are lurking in the background. What should you do? Looking at the overarching concern about not living in the present could be a profitable path to take with Juan. At the same time, as the therapy progressed, you or your supervisee might address the focal spiritual issue of his self-identifying as spiritual but not religious. Certainly, that is not a negative category of spirituality in itself. But it would be helpful to better understand how this new identification connects with his family religion of Catholicism.

This interesting hypothetical case boosts our sense of the close connection between spirituality and racial identity. How do they influence each other? Does one take priority over the other? Does one rule out the other? Or how can they be recognized as they interact with each other? The answer to these questions is certainly foremost in my thinking as this discussion of spirituality develops. In the next chapters, the direction about the relationship between spirituality and diversity will be more fully developed.

Another approach that can address broader spiritual conversations in systemic therapy is posited by Larner. He presents an appealing concept of "spiritual dialogues," which he defines as "what transcends or takes us beyond our everyday experience of self and world" (2017). Coyle similarly presents spirituality as "that which is larger than self and relationships" (Coyle, 2014). Focusing on this way, spirituality becomes an inclusive means of conversing about how spirituality can provide openness for our clients to the interactions of the world that lift us all above the gritty day-to-day realities of life. Larner's case illustrates a curious and encouraging therapeutic approach that invites clients to explore all facets of life. I find my own outlook on spirituality quite compatible with Larner's. As our discussion of religious engagement becomes more nuanced, I will present my own spiritual approach before proceeding to the next chapter.

An Approach to Integrating Spirituality in Systemic Practice

It is my understanding that a spiritually integrated approach is certainly in keeping with the introduction of the spiritual but not religious category. Recent decades have seen the development of the term "spiritual but not religious" to describe part of the population. This researcher did not find any MFT literature that addressed "spiritual but not religious" as a part of this conversation about religion and spirituality. Our culture is indeed divided. But at the same time, a brief overview of "spiritual but not religious" can give some vibrancy to this volume's understanding of spirituality.

Certainly, the term "spirituality" has become more distinct from religion during the last decade, as the "spiritual but not religious" has gained prominence in a cultural conversation about personal religiosity. It does not, however, totally separate spirituality from religion. Rather, it opens therapeutic awareness about spirituality so that therapist and client understand that process as embracing both the implicit and explicit dimensions of spirituality that both connect and separate from religion. The meaning that a client draws from stories may inform their spirituality despite the explicit content of the story being related to religion as the following example describes.

One of my supervisees counseled a 65-year-old African American man who told the intern that he had moved forward from the Pentecostal religion in which his parents raised him. He said that he never missed Sunday worship or a midweek prayer meeting when growing up. To do so would mean that he was not faithful.

For years, Bob has periodically attended a United Church of Christ congregation. He told Fred, the intern, that his spirituality was now free of his growing up years. Two months into the counseling relationship, Bob told Fred that he discovered that he had Parkinson's Disease. Fred and Bob talked. At the end of the conversation, Fred suggested that he continue in his chosen spirituality.

At the beginning of the next session, Bob said he found himself at his "rigid" old Pentecostal church praying mightily. He said that the religion he experienced in that church gave him more peace than his newfound spirituality.

Unknown to Bob, the stories of Pentecostalism gave him stability that he needed, despite the rigidity. From that religion came Bob's spirituality of peace that connected him to a God who was all-knowing and all-powerful. He was surprised. But Bob said he needed that religion now.

Spirituality in these therapeutic relationships is not about religious preferences, but about beliefs and meanings that clients assign to their spiritual experiences (Çetintaş & Ekşi, 2020). Such experiences in therapy are important and should be a "no blame" zone. As Smith and Harkness stress, clients may be worried about the therapist evaluating the quality of their spirituality. One way to diffuse this type of worry is to simply encourage sharing their spiritual stories (2002).

As clients share more deeply about their stories, the discussion may trigger spiritual questions (Smith & Walsh, 2009). By their very nature, spiritual questions are given meaning through asking as well as answering. During this process of questioning, clients reflect upon the nuances of their feeling and thinking in life. The implicit quality of spirituality rises to the surface of the conversation between therapist and client.

Refocusing spirituality for a world of multiple realities, Holmberg et al. present a diagram depicting a process to develop spiritual literacy. Spiritual literacy embraces the following concepts: (1) recognition of clients' spiritual and religious experiences, practice, and culture; (2) working systemically in dialogue; (3) using clients' resources and language; (4) bridging linguistic uncertainty; (5) increasing personal awareness and competency; (6) working with personal hindrances; and (7) breaking the silence in the public space (2020). While one may begin by recognizing clients' experiences, this spiritual literacy process need not be a linear pattern, but a therapist and client beginning, where the client's story is thickest before proceeding.[2]

[2] Narrative practice contends that most problem saturated stories need a richer description rather than boiling them down to basics. Thus, this book believes that clients' stories need to be "thicker" or more richly described.

Case Study

In presenting my approach to spirituality, I share my work with a client from many years ago. All identifying information has been changed. My private work during this time was a blend of individuals, couples, and families, with most clients being individuals. Throughout this book, I will present my personal therapy with clients, supervision with supervisees, and community work with specific populations to illustrate my understanding of spirituality, beginning with Beth.

Beth was a 20-year-old Caucasian university student who found my name in a Yellow Pages listing (this alone identifies the time as long ago). She set up the appointment with my receptionist, who alerted me to Beth's arrival in the reception area. At this time, I was only seeing clients in a private practice with some private supervision and no teaching.

One day, Beth entered my office looking around as she sat in the chair opposite me. She was a student at the local university majoring in English. She told me that she was not sure what she wanted to do. English seemed like a dead-end. Beth indicated that she really was not interested in exploring her vocational possibilities in counseling. She suggested that she wanted to understand herself better. Furthermore, she said she wanted to control her anxiety better but was not interested in any medical referral.

I then introduced myself as a pastoral counselor and marriage and family therapist who was an ordained minister. Beth and I then talked about any questions she had about me and the basics of counseling. Beth picked up on my being a minister and said, "I want you to know that I'm not religious."

I then asked her if it was problematic that I was a minister. She responded no, and then repeated that she was not religious. Beth wondered if I would be able to work with her. I indicated that I could work with her. She agreed that we could see how things went.

Over the next few months, Beth made good progress. Her anxiety lessened. She seemed calmer and more confident. Our therapy was marked by dialogical conversations focusing on meaning in life. Beth talked about what made her fulfilled as well as the challenges she encountered. We discussed various dilemmas in life and how she responded to them.

After a few months, Beth decided that her therapy had done what she had hoped. She felt more confident and ready to approach life's challenges. Most important, she told me that she was able to reach deep within herself for resources she did not know she had. Then, before we ended the last session, Beth looked directly at me. She said that remembered that at the first session, she had said that she was not religious. Then, with a pause, Beth said, "I am not religious today. But now I know that I am a deeply spiritual person. Thank you for helping me realize that."

Our conversations were never explicitly religious. I did not pray with her. We did not read any sacred scripture. I never used the word "spiritual." We did engage in deeply reflective conversations. I did offer open questions. We talked about what Beth found engaging. In short, we explored the immanence of life as having an implicit transcendence. This is how I understand spiritual systemic therapy. It is an engaging of immanence and transcendence, which the therapist reflects on through an inner dialogue with the self. This engagement of immanence and transcendence produces the possibility of hope. Furthermore, this engagement encourages the telling of stories and asking curious questions.

Uniqueness of Spirituality in Family Context

My therapy with Beth did not focus on a family context. She and I did engage in conversations around immanence and transcendence—both the earthly and the divine. Through those conversations, I saw how her family stories influenced who she was as an individual. My unique perspective as a family therapist enabled me to focus our therapeutic interaction on storytelling about her values. As she further developed her own sense of spirituality, Beth was able to see herself through a lens of family. Despite the therapeutic modality being individual, spirituality became a context in which her family stories gained life. MFT can develop a systemic methodology for spirituality that offers a unique perspective alongside mental health disciplines. Responding to spirituality with family stories is something that therapists who work with families try to do every day. Justice challenges are often lying just underneath a seemingly simple story. Developing an integrative model of spirituality that envelops the whole of human experience, including social concerns, could provide a valuable systemic resource for MFTs in academic, community agencies, group practice, and private practice settings.

The true uniqueness of spirituality in a family context is to focus on the systemic understanding of family as an entity. This chapter discussed research focused on participants' views of spirituality. Yet no study has focused on spirituality in the family, only on individuals' understanding of spirituality. While some studies did examine spirituality through a systemic lens, no research has defined or studied *family spirituality* as a special type of spirituality.

In this book, family spirituality is defined as a shared narrative of a family's life that connects individual family members with stories of belief and values. These family stories can be thickened and co-created to offer hope for the future. Family spirituality listens to individual family members' voices as they seek unity through diversity.

Our earlier foci of self, systems, and spirit can be utilized to bring the uniqueness of systemic family practice as we understand the family context as an environment where spirituality can flourish. Spirituality as understood in most other psychotherapeutic professions focuses on individual spirituality. The model of spirituality in this book is applicable to individuals. However, it also has a distinctness that can be applicable to families, most notably through family stories of belief and values.

Spirituality in family life needs to recognize the spirituality of individual family members in the same way that family therapy recognizes the individual clinical concerns of distinct family members. In a similar way, spirituality for individual family members can be thickened through the enriching of family narratives or stories. Also, spiritual family stories may at times not be nurturing for all the individual family members.

How do we as systemic family therapists respond to spirituality, for both the family entity and its family members? We start with the basics of self, systems, and spirit in our care of the family, which will be illustrated through the following case study of an intern and his supervisor.

Case Study

Deepa and Amar Patel are a young Indian American couple, both born in the United States after their parents immigrated to the United States. Deepa was the oldest of three daughters and longed to pursue a career in medicine. Amar was the youngest of three sons and also wanted to pursue a career in medicine. They met in medical school and immediately sensed a kinship. Deepa became a neurologist, Amar a neuroscience researcher. Both shared an appreciation for Indian culture while seeing themselves as participants in American culture and society.

Deepa and Amar came for counseling at the campus clinic. A beginning MFT intern, Aaron, was assigned to them for couples counseling. Deepa expressed her love and connection with Amar, which she believed was still strong after 3 years. Amar agreed with Deepa. Yet, they were both deeply troubled by their contrasting understanding of the role of Indian culture and religion in their lives.

Amar was proud of his separation from traditional Indian culture. He wanted to pursue an American lifestyle, and despite his appreciation for tradition Indian religions and culture, he did not see them as a viable option for him. Amar self-identified as "secular," not religious. Deepa, in contrast, still believed in traditional marital roles. This presented challenges for her in her desire to be a mother as well as a medical professional. She also actively practiced Hinduism.

Aaron was quite distressed in his supervision session with his supervisor after his intake session with the Patels. He said he did not see any way that a couple could have a spiritually rich relationship with different religions. Christine, Aaron's supervisor, began talking with Aaron about his own religious beliefs and how that might influence his counseling the Patels. As the supervision sessions continued, it became clear that Aaron had conflicts with his family about religion. While he considered himself spiritual, he did not attend synagogue as did his family who were Orthodox Jews.

After more supervision sessions, Aaron decided that he would focus on how Deepa and Amar could co-create a spirituality to support them both. He presented the idea to Deepa and Amar. At first, they were both against it. Then, they began to talk with each other about what values were most important to each of them. For Deepa, she valued Hinduism for its belief in truth and quest for truth. For Amar, he valued love of all humans as a truth that transcends everything. They began to talk about focusing on what might connect them above what separated them. Deepa was not sure that this approach would work. Aaron agreed to travel with them on this path.

We do not know if this co-creation of spiritual values will be a strong enough connection for Deepa and Amar. However, it does honor the self, systems, and spirit foci that MFT brings to spirituality. Deepa and Amar will work toward honoring their individual selves as well as their relational selves, which is who each partner is when a connection is made to the other. Systems emphasize the importance of who they are as a couple, while spirit recognizes that spirituality is an overarching value that supports the individual partners as well as the couple.

In addition to their concerns as a couple, Deepa and Amar live in a culture rife with stories and norms that they are challenged to respond to as second-generation Americans. Discrimination against them both as persons of color can be both explicit and implicit. From this type of discrimination, social injustice can arise. As the couple experiences social injustice, the pain from that injustice can then systemically affect Deepa and Amar as a couple and as individuals. Responding to this pain, they will likely reach for their inner resources, which will draw on their spirituality.

Moving toward an integrative model of spirituality, the couple and therapist, and perhaps the therapist's supervisor, will explore avenues that contribute to a model we will name the living web of socio-spirituality.[3] Let us look at the basic foundations of the living web of socio-spirituality.

Fig. 2.1 Living web of socio-spirituality basic foundation

[3] This living web of socio-spirituality will be developed in Chap. 3. For now, the web serves as a flexible container of spirituality and social justice. This model shown in Fig. 2.1 illustrates the foundations of this living web of socio-spirituality.

In looking at this diagrammatic web, the therapist and supervisor can intervene with the client at any point through social justice or spirituality. This kind of intervention demonstrates how the systemic concept of equifinality can work. As a circular process, the model affords the clinician flexibility, just as the web is flexible yet strong in responding to the clients. Further possibilities exist as the systemic clinician may choose to explore a section of the web representing the family or the whole web representing the client(s) and the ecological context.

MFTs need to identify our own unique approach to spirituality and religion. For example, we do not have a formal professional group that focuses on spirituality as some of our sister professions. Reviewing the connections of other mental health disciplines will help us as we determine how to integrate spirituality in systemic family therapy.

Awareness of Spirituality Across Mental Health Disciplines

Spirituality in a comprehensive spectrum recognizes both immanence and transcendence. As this book explores spirituality in a systemic family therapy context, I want to encourage participation of other mental health disciplines in the development of this integrative model of spirituality. So, at the end of most chapters in this book, a section will be dedicated to ways in which other mental health disciplines can collaborate with marriage and family therapy in this model of socio-spirituality. So, now we will look at ways in which different psychotherapy professions have become aware of spirituality.

A cognate psychotherapy organization, the American Association of Pastoral Counselors (AAPC), was established in 1963. This organization saw its mission as integrating psychotherapy and spirituality. AAPC credentialed its members through a rigorous training process with required supervision hours (Walker et al., 2012). In recent years, the AAPC has relinquished its formal organization and become a part of the Association for Clinical Pastoral Education (ACPE), an organization primarily for chaplains.

ACPE now has a psychotherapist category for former AAPC members. Several states now license pastoral counselors. Recognizing pastoral counselors through state licensure offers a place at the table, alongside other mental health professions, for those whose primary focus is integrating spirituality and clinical practice.

Psychologists, social workers, and mental health clinicians meet spirituality with mixed responses. For some clinicians, spirituality is viewed as a part of a client's life that needs to be separated from therapeutic issues. These mental health professionals see their religious clients as needing to consult with their minsters or chaplains. Other clinicians might understand their atheist and agnostic clients as not having any spiritual issues that require exploration. Of course, a holistic understanding of spirituality would purport that all people have a spiritual reality, whether a client self-identifies as atheist, agnostic, or a believer.

The response in some mental health professions regarding spirituality has been to organize their own organizations within their profession. The American Association of Christian Counselors (AACC) was organized over 30 years ago for mental health professionals. Whereas AAPC (now ACPE) was originally designed for ministers with seminary training, AACC was founded with licensed therapists who are Christian (American Association of Christian Counselors, 2020).

Other organizations have emerged with their membership, limited by their professional licensure. In 2009, the American Psychological Association (APA) founded the Society for the Psychology of Religion and Spirituality. As an APA division, this group meets during the APA Conference (Society for the Psychology of Religion and Spirituality, 2020). Social workers have different organizations that address spirituality as a theme for their members' work. The oldest group is an independently incorporated organization: the North American Association of Christians in Social Work (NACSW), which incorporated in 1954 following a series of meetings at Wheaton College, an evangelical institution (North American Association of Christians in Social Work, 2020).

In 2011, the Council on Social Work Education (CSWE) organized the Religion and Spirituality Work Group in 2011, "to promote social workers' knowledge, values, and skills for ethical and effective practice that takes into account the diverse expressions of religion and spirituality among clients and their communities" (Council on Social Education, 2020). Another social work professional organization, the National Association of Social Workers, does not have any affiliated subgroup that focuses on religion and spirituality.

The American Counseling Association (ACA) has a division called the Association for Spiritual, Ethical, and Religious Values in Counseling (ASERVIC). This division promotes "spiritual, ethical, religious, and other human values within the discipline of counseling" (American Counseling Association, 2020). Meetings are held during the ACA conference and at other times throughout the year.

A strength of these mental health disciplines is their inclusion of sub-groups that specifically focus on spirituality. Thus, each profession has the ability to discuss spirituality in these sub-groups as they work to deepen the role of spirituality in their discipline.

Professionals in these sub-groups on spirituality could discuss the living web of spirituality presented in this book in their regular meetings. An MFT could be invited to the group discussion to present the model and then have a brainstorming session about ways in which the model fits and does not fit their particular discipline. Or the group could discuss the model without any marriage and family therapy professional. In either case, the model could be used to stimulate approaches to spirituality that lift up that mental health discipline's uniqueness. The result could be a contribution to the role of spirituality in all psychotherapy.

Movement Toward Method

Moving toward methodological considerations in future chapters, a model of spirituality that is accessible to both theistic and non-theistic students will focus on conversations between self, systems, and spirit. Immanence and transcendence will be presented as theological concepts that non-theologians can practice with success. This method will be enhanced by a theological foundation that recognizes the writings of Freire and liberation theology, with a clinical emphasis on postmodern narratives that honor the stories of clients as they emerge in everyday life. Finally, connecting diversity and culture will be integrated with spirituality to create a lens of culture and spirituality that can serve all those who identify with diversity issues.

Self, Systems, and Spirit Practice

What Is Spirituality?

This practice is designed to generate a series of questions about spirituality. Those questions will be used to create a collaborative environment for therapeutic encounters. The different perspectives that emerge are expected to enrich one another. This naming exercise is related to narrative practice. The process of naming carries the potential for giving hopes and dreams a name that brings our present into the future.

Naming the Group

The group divides into sub-groups of four to six people. The first step for each subgroup is to gather together with the purpose of assigning their group a name that conveys some aspect of spirituality to the individual members of the group and then to agree upon a name that conveys the collective understanding of a quality of spirituality.

- The facilitator determines the length of time for the group to select its name. It is suggested that a one-and-a-half to 3-h timeframe be set.
- For example, people could suggest the name of a spiritual leader like Buddha, Jesus, Confucius, etc. Another example would be to identify a quality of spirituality like peace, love, etc. Finally, another example would be to select a random word like Lake Placid, etc.
- The group then shares their group name with the other groups.

Naming Spirituality

- The facilitator asks each individual of each sub-group to write a definition of spirituality that speaks to them.
- The individuals of each sub-group share their definitions with the whole group.
- Then, each sub-group works with their individual members to come up with a definition on which the whole group can agree.
- The sub-groups meet in a large group to discuss the outcomes of their collaboration.

Naming Possibilities

- The facilitator asks each sub-group to discuss Chap. 1. The question for consideration: "What catches your attention?"
- The sub-groups summarize their answers for discussion.
- Finally, the sub-groups and then the whole group identify some possibilities for their group from the definition of spirituality and discussion of the chapter.
- Some suggested possibilities might be the following: (1) Discuss how the definition of spirituality could impact the curricular structure itself; (2) Work to integrate an awareness of the understanding of spirituality in the clinical practicum experience; and (3) Students might study different religions and discuss how spirituality could emerge from that study.

References

Adams, N. (1995). Spirituality, science and therapy. *Australian and New Zealand Journal of Family Therapy, 16*(4), 201–208. https://doi.org/10.1002/j.1467-8438.1995.tb01060.x

American Counseling Association. (2020). American Counseling Association. www.counseling.org

American Psychological Association. (2020). Division 36: Society for the Psychology of Religion and Spirituality. Retrieved from https://www.apadivisions.org/division-36

Anderson, D. A. (1987). Spirituality and systems therapy: Partners in clinical practice. *Journal of Pastoral Psychotherapy, 1*(1), 19–32.

Anderson, D. A., & Worthen, D. (1997). Exploring a fourth dimension: Spirituality as a resource for the couple therapist. *Journal of Marital and Family Therapy, 23*(1), 3–12. https://doi.org/10.1111/j.1752-0606.1997.tb00227.x

Better Marriages. (n.d.). *History of better marriages*. Author. Retrieved from https://www.better-marriages.org/about/history-of-better-marriages/

Bowker, J. (Ed.). (1997). *The Oxford dictionary of world religions*. Oxford University Press.

Brenan, M. (2018). *Religion considered important to 72% of Americans*. Gallup. Retrieved from https://news.gallup.com/poll/245651/religion-considered-important-americans.aspx

Brownell, P. (2014). *Spiritual competency in psychotherapy*. Springer Publishing Company.

Carlson, T. D., Kirkpatrick, D., Hecker, L., & Killmer, M. (2002). Religion, spirituality, and marriage and family therapy: A study of family therapists' beliefs about the appropriateness of addressing religious and spiritual issues in therapy. *American Journal of Family Therapy, 30*(2), 157–171. https://doi.org/10.1080/019261802753573867

Carlson, T. S., McGeorge, C. R., & Anderson, A. (2011). The importance of spirituality in couple and family therapy: A comparative study of therapists' and educators' beliefs. *Contemporary Family Therapy, 33*(1), 3–16. https://doi.org/10.1007/s10591-010-9136-0

Çetintaş, Ş., & Ekşi, H. (2020). Spiritually oriented couple, marriage and family therapies. *Spiritual Psychology and Counseling, 5*(1), 7–24. https://doi.org/10.37898/spc.2020.5.1.096

Council on Social Work Education. (2020). *Members of the spirituality and support group*. Author. Retrieved August 10, 2020, from https://www.cswe.org/Education-Resources/Religion-and-Spirituality-Clearinghouse/Members-of-the-Religion-and-Spirituality-Work-Group

Coyle, S. (2009). Spiritual narratives: Hope and healing through stories of faith. In H. J. Ellens (Ed.), *The healing power of spirituality: How faith helps humans thrive* (pp. 189–201). ABC-CLIO.

Coyle, S. M. (2013). *Re-storying your faith*. John Hunt Publishing.

Coyle, S. M. (2014). *Uncovering spiritual narratives: Using story in pastoral care and ministry*. Augsburg Fortress Publishers.

Coyle, S. M. (2015). From systems to narrative family therapy. In F. B. Kelcourse & K. B. Lyon (Eds.), *Transforming wisdom: Pastoral psychotherapy in theological perspective* (pp. 214–230). Cascade Books.

Coyle, S. M. (2017). Integrating spirituality in marriage and family therapy training. *Australian and New Zealand Journal of Family Therapy, 38*(1), 142–155. https://doi.org/10.1002/anzf.1195

Coyle, S. M., & Davis, C. J. (2017). Christian couples and families. In S. Kelly (Ed.), *Diversity in couple and family therapy: Ethnicities, sexualities, and socioeconomics* (pp. 203–230). Praeger.

Dugan, G. (1963). Pastoral counselors organize group to establish standards. *New York Times*. Retrieved from https://www.nytimes.com/1963/04/21/archives/pastoral-counselors-organize-group-to-establish-standards.html

Dunn, A. B., & Dawes, S. J. (1999). Spirituality-focused genograms: Keys to uncovering spiritual resources in African American families. *Journal of Multicultural Counseling and Development, 27*(4), 240–254. https://doi.org/10.1002/j.2161-1912.1999.tb00338.x

Erickson, M. J., & Carlson, T. (2014). *Spirituality and family therapy*. Routledge.

Frame, M. W. (2001). The spiritual genogram in training and supervision. *The Family Journal, 9*(2), 109–115. https://doi.org/10.1177/1066480701092004

Gambrel, L. E., & Keeling, M. L. (2010). Relational aspects of mindfulness: Implications for the practice of marriage and family therapy. *Contemporary Family Therapy, 32*(4), 412–426. https://doi.org/10.1007/s10591-010-9129-z

Gehart, D. R. (2012). *Mindfulness and acceptance in couple and family therapy*. Springer Science & Business Media.

Griffith, J. L., & Griffith, M. E. (2002). *Encountering the sacred in psychotherapy: How to talk with people about their spiritual lives*. Guilford Press.

Hodge, D. R. (2001). Spiritual genograms: A generational approach to assessing spirituality. *Families in Society, 82*(1), 35–48. https://doi.org/10.1606/1044-3894.220

Hodge, D. R. (2005). Developing a spiritual assessment toolbox: A discussion of the strengths and limitations of five different assessment methods. *Health & Social Work, 30*(4), 314–323. https://doi.org/10.1093/hsw/30.4.314

Hodge, D. R., & Limb, G. E. (2009). Establishing the preliminary validity of spiritual eco-maps with Native Americans. *Clinical Social Work Journal, 37*(4), 320.

Hodge, D. R., & Limb, G. E. (2014). Spiritual assessment and Latter-day Saints: Establishing the preliminary validity of spiritual eco-maps. *Journal of Social Service Research, 40*(3), 367–380. https://doi.org/10.1080/01488376.2014.893947

Holmberg, Å., Jensen, P., & Ulland, D. (2017). To make room or not to make room: Clients' narratives about exclusion and inclusion of spirituality in family therapy practice. *Australian and New Zealand Journal of Family Therapy, 38*(1), 15–26. https://doi.org/10.1002/anzf.1198

Holmberg, Å., Jensen, P., & Vetere, A. (2020). Spirituality–A forgotten dimension? Developing spiritual literacy in family therapy practice. *Journal of Family Therapy, 43*(1), 78–95. https://doi.org/10.1111/1467-6427.12298

Hrynowski, Z. (2019). *How many Americans believe in god?* Gallup. Retrieved from https://news.gallup.com/poll/268205/americans-believe-god.aspx

Jones, J. B. M. (2020). *U.S. church membership down sharply in past two decades*. Gallup. Retrieved from https://news.gallup.com/poll/248837/church-membership-down-sharply-past-two-decades.aspx

Kelly, E. W., Jr. (2002). Religion in family therapy journals: A review and analysis. In L. Burton (Ed.), *Religion and the family: When god helps*. Haworth Press.

Kütük, H. (2020). The spiritual approach to systemic family therapies. *Spiritual Psychology and Counseling, 5*(1), 25–43. https://doi.org/10.37898/spc.2020.5.1.100

Larner, G. (2017). Spiritual dialogues in family therapy. *Australian and New Zealand Journal of Family Therapy, 38*(1), 125–141. https://doi.org/10.1002/anzf.1207

Mahoney, A. (2013). The spirituality of us: Relational spirituality in the context of family relationships. In K. I. Pargament, J. J. Exline, & J. W. Jones (Eds.), *APA handbooks in psychology. APA handbook of psychology, religion, and spirituality (Vol. 1): Context, theory, and research* (pp. 365–389). American Psychological Association. https://doi.org/10.1037/14045-020

McCollum, E. E., & Gehart, D. R. (2010). Using mindfulness meditation to teach beginning therapists therapeutic presence: A qualitative study. *Journal of Marital and Family Therapy, 36*(3), 347–360. https://doi.org/10.1111/j.1752-0606.2010.00214.x

Miller, M. M., Korinek, A., & Ivey, D. C. (2004). Spirituality in MFT training: Development of the spiritual issues in supervision scale. *Contemporary Family Therapy, 26*(1), 71–81. https://doi.org/10.1023/B:COFT.0000016913.62876.86

Moules, N. J. (2000). Postmodernism and the sacred: Reclaiming connection in our greater than human worlds. *Journal of Marital and Family Therapy, 26*(2), 229–240. https://doi.org/10.1111/j.1752-0606.2000.tb00292.x

Newport, F. (2016). *Five key findings on religion in the U.S*. Gallup. Retrieved from https://news.gallup.com/poll/200186/five-key-findings-religion.aspx

Onedera, J. D. (Ed.). (2008). *The family therapy and counseling series. The role of religion in marriage and family counseling*. Routledge/Taylor & Francis Group.

Pargament, K. I. (1997). *The psychology of religion and coping. Theory, research, practice*. Guilford Press.

Pargament, K. I. (1999). The psychology of religion and spirituality? Yes and no. *The International Journal for the Psychology of Religion, 9*(1), 3–16. https://doi.org/10.1207/s15327582ijpr0901_2

Pargament, K. I. (2011). *Spiritually integrated psychotherapy: Understanding and addressing the sacred*. Guilford Press.

Prest, L. A., & Keller, J. F. (1993). Spirituality and family therapy: Spiritual beliefs, myths, and metaphors. *Journal of Marital and Family Therapy, 19*(2), 137–148. https://doi.org/10.1111/j.1752-0606.1993.tb00973.x

Prest, L. A., & Russel, R. (1995). *Spirituality in training, practice, and personal development*. Unpublished paper.

Prest, L. A., Russel, R., & D'Souza, H. (1999). Spirituality and religion in training, practice and personal development. *Journal of Family Therapy, 21*(1), 60–77. https://doi.org/10.1111/1467-6427.00104

Raney, A., Cox, D., & Jones, R. P. (2017). *Searching for spirituality in the U.S.: A new look at the spiritual but not religious*. PRRRI. Retrieved from https://www.prri.org/research/religiosity-and-spirituality-in-america/

Rempel, G. R., Neufeld, A., & Kushner, K. E. (2007). Interactive use of genograms and ecomaps in family caregiving research. *Journal of Family Nursing, 13*(4), 403–419. https://doi.org/10.1177/1074840707307917

Şahin, Y. (2017). Using spiritual genograms in family therapies. *Spiritual Psychology and Counseling, 3*(1), 47–60. https://doi.org/10.12738/spc.2018.1.0030

Smith, A. L., & Harkness, J. (2002). Spirituality and meaning: A qualitative inquiry with caregivers of Alzheimer's disease. *Journal of Family Psychotherapy, 13*(1–2), 87–108. https://doi.org/10.1300/J085v13n01_05

Stone, H. W., & Duke, J. O. (2013). *How to think theologically*. Fortress.

Swinton, J. (2001). *Spirituality and mental health care: Rediscovering a 'forgotten' dimension*. Jessica Kingsley Publishers.

The North American Association of Christians in Social Work. (2020). Retrieved from https://www.nacsw.org/

Townsend, L. (2009). *Introduction to pastoral counseling*. Abingdon Press.

Waldegrave, C. (2003). *Just therapy – A journey: A collection of papers from the Just Therapy team, New Zealand*. Dulwich Centre Publications.

Walker, K. R., Scheidegger, T. H., End, L., & Amundsen, M. (2012). The misunderstood pastoral counselor: Knowledge and religiosity as factors affecting a client's choice. In *American Counseling Association Annual Conference and Exposition, March 23–25, San Francisco, CA, USA*.

Walsh, F. (Ed.). (2007). *Spiritual resources in family therapy*. Guilford.

Wendel, R. (2003). Lived religion and family therapy: What does spirituality have to do with it? *Family Process, 42*(1), 165. https://doi.org/10.1111/j.1545-5300.2003.00165.x

Wiggins, M. (2000). The spiritual genogram in family therapy. *Journal of Marital and Family Therapy, 26*(2), 211–216. https://doi.org/10.1111/j.1752-0606.2000.tb00290.x

Williams-Reade, J. M., Lobo, E., & Gutierrez, G. (2018). Integrating spirituality into MFT training: A reflexive curriculum and qualitative evaluation. *Journal of Marital and Family Therapy, 45*(2), 219–232.

Willow, R. A., Tobin, D. J., & Toner, S. (2009). Assessment of the use of spiritual genograms in counselor education. *Counseling and Values, 53*(3), 214–223. https://doi.org/10.1002/j.2161-007X.2009.tb00127.x

Worthington, E. L., & Aten, J. D. (2009). Psychotherapy with religious and spiritual clients: An introduction. *Journal of Clinical Psychology, 65*(2), 123–130. https://doi.org/10.1002/jclp.20561

Chapter 3
Spirituality in a Thick Context of Diversity

Spirituality is sometimes understood as a transcendent experience that may have little to do with the earthly everyday concerns of human life. Yet many people experience spirituality as an anchor when worries arise. Spirituality needs to connect with the everyday world. It is through that bond that spirituality is helpful for dealing with human concerns.

Spirituality's Connections to Culture and Diversity

Spirituality connects us as humans to our deepest beliefs and values. Some people might understand spirituality as synonymous with emotions and even feelings. This book's understanding of spirituality takes a different view. The discussion here prioritizes deep beliefs and values that transcend our earthly humanity. But it also understands who we are as humans—our earthly existence—as an inescapable dimension of our spirituality.

Some family therapy scholars have indicated that in any holistic understanding, culture is connected to spirituality. In Holmberg et al.'s diagram of spiritual literacy, clients' spiritual and religious experiences, practice, and culture are identified as one of seven perspectives (2021). Furthermore, the authors, citing Elkins (2013), understand spirituality as "a way of being in regard to self, others, culture (sic), nature, life and includes a transcendent dimension" (2021, p. 3).

Focusing on this holistic view of human life, spirituality cannot be experienced every day without connecting to the constraints of birthplace, community, the shape of our lives, the color of our skin, and our socioeconomic resources. But not all MFT scholars hold this perspective. They may see spirituality as a diversity issue that is quite separate from human diversity; as the old saying goes, "heavenly minded and no earthly good." Still others, such as Stander et al., contend that

S. M. Coyle, *Spirituality in Systemic Family Therapy Supervision and Training*, Focused Issues in Family Therapy, https://doi.org/10.1007/978-3-030-92369-3_3

spirituality is like any other aspect of culture, such as race, gender, or sexual orientation (1994).

Indeed, spirituality is related to various dimensions of culture. But it differs from other aspects of culture and inhabits a different sphere of what is human and what goes beyond the human. A spiritual practitioner may sense it, and yet the same person may find it difficult to specify its qualities. It is challenging to identify discrete qualities that are value laden. The intensely personal nature of spirituality may seem to connect only with an individual and not with a relationship or community.

Traditional definitions of religion and spirituality rely on spirituality as a precursor to the formation of a formal religion. When a particular spirituality attracts more adherents, the desire may grow among those believers to create a formal religion. Thus, the institutionalization process occurs (Coyle, 2017). People's increasing connection to the "spiritual but not religious" category, however, has a different perspective than traditionally understood religion or spirituality.

This chapter introduces a connection between spirituality and culture, or more accurately defined, diversity concerns. Spirituality means a holistic understanding that lifts diversity concerns: individual effects such as race, gender, and sexual orientation. With the 1969 publication of James Cone's *Black Theology and Black Power* (2018), these diversities and the spirituality that comes with them burst into the world of culture and theology.

Diversity concerns and their accompanying spiritualities have been identified in the MFT Core Competencies in CC# 1.2.1 (MFT Core Competencies, 2004). Liberation theologies such as queer, gay, lesbian, transgender, Black, Latinx, Asian, and ableism theologies understand the need for acknowledging one's diversity as part of deepening one's spirituality.[1] In addition, the social justice movement addresses the challenges of persons impacted by socioeconomics through theological groups. Broadly understood, liberation theologies support all these groups of persons with diversity-related challenges.

Relational systemic therapists are always interested in their clients' connections and interactions with family and societal systems. The liberation theologies referenced above also share these concerns. There is also an understanding that our clients need to be enabled to find a way to live with the problems they bring to counseling. For example, the therapist needs to battle for the structure of the counseling session (Whitaker & Ryan, 1989). This could look quite different for a therapist who uses CBT, EFT, solution-focused, or narrative approaches.

As the therapy progresses, the client needs to win the battle for initiative and forge an individual or family path forward (Whitaker & Ryan, 1989). As that occurs, the therapist works to support that process. In a similar way, liberation theologies can lift the spirituality of the person oppressed by societal injustice. Another possibility is that a more livable life is possible, even with oppression. Liberation

[1] Liberation theology is a general category that includes many different theological approaches such as Black, womanist, feminist, Latina, queer, etc. Liberation theologies are sometimes used to indicate that different theologies emphasizing liberation exist. Liberative theologies often refer to an integrative approach used in pastoral theology. See Coyle and Townsend.

theologians would not stop there. Transformation for individuals and families only occurs with societal transformation. Thus, a circular pattern of supportive spirituality in the face of diversity challenges is required to lead to each level of transformation.

The partnership between spirituality and diversity develops a response to clients' problems. The result of such a dialogue would be an umbrella of spirituality and diversity/culture sheltering thc therapeutic enterprise. Some MFTs do see spirituality as a holistic, inclusive dimension of life. Aponte points to universal implications for "secular and religious" spirituality that "speak to morality, meaning, and the nature of the individual's relationship to the world, whether or not it is supernatural" (2002, p. 16).

In this sense, the problems that clients bring to us as therapists rest upon an understanding of spirituality that is life-giving and not limiting. Aponte writes: "However personal an issue may be, its existence and solution touch on the lives of others. These ties, with all of their social and moral implications, exist at the levels of marriage, family and community" (2002, p. 17).

The purpose here is to express that our clients' lives are not sharply compartmentalized into a predominant spiritual quality while a preponderance of diversity concerns, such as race, gender, and other diversity matters keep us tethered to the earth. For example, Angie, a young, white woman in her twenties living in Appalachia and impacted by poverty attends an evangelical church every Sunday. This congregation has specific directives about what behaviors she is to follow. Angie is quite faithful in this practice. Yet, she experiences an emptiness that just will not go away.

In our first counseling session, she said, "I do what the preacher tells me to do in his sermons. I read my Bible daily and pray. Yet, I feel like I'm always at the bottom. Women are at the bottom in these parts. I'm going to nursing school now to make something of myself. But my husband gets with his buddies, and they laugh at me."

During our sessions, we discussed her mild depression that impeded her concentration as well as her belief in herself. Yet, what came up again and again were the obstacles she faced as a woman. In addition to the gender bias, she contended with were obstacles created by poverty. Angie further shared with me that her personal spirituality was stunted because despite her interest in the Bible, the men in the congregation said that she needed to share her thoughts in a women's Bible study group.

Angie's dilemma illustrates how spirituality inhabits the earthly and heavenly worlds in a symbolic way. Angie yearns to have an experience that nurtures her in the here and now while giving her a taste of something that is not limited to human reality. She wants to take in a breath of the transcendent. Angie's world is what Aponte (2002) was referencing.

Angie and I addressed this spiritual emptiness in our sessions. The language sometimes explicitly fit her theological context, not mine. At times, implicit understandings framed the process. Of great importance was my awareness of my own spirituality. Aponte refers to the spirituality of the therapist that must be recognized by the therapist (2002). But my spirituality as a therapist who was Christian was not important for Angie. And yet it was critical because I was aware of the boundaries of my own spirituality and sensitive to Angie's. A therapist who was non-theistic and aware of his or her own spirituality could also have worked with Angie.

For Angie, spirituality had the potential of enriching her life as opposed to the "rigid religion" she found in her church. This spirituality was not limited to praying, reading the Bible, and having moral values. It had the potential for her to connect with her culture as an Appalachian woman who wanted "to better" herself. Through our conversations, Angie said, "God loves me as I am as a woman. I'm not going to listen to what everyone says I should do. I'm going to do what God tells me and be a strong woman." My experience with Angie lives out Helmeke and Bischof's understanding of spirituality as a culturally rich experience that allows clients to see societal roles in different ways through therapy (Helmeke & Bischof, 2002).

Spirituality is an overarching concept that covers the whole of human life. This spirituality is "our cultural heritage, racial identity, politics, everyday philosophical views and our religious convictions" (Aponte, 1998, p. 38). Like Aponte, see spirituality similar to specific diversity concerns (2001). Race and gender for people may seek spirituality as diversities are lived out in everyday life. As the therapeutic process continues, a dialogue between diversity and spirituality will ensue.

It is challenging to adhere to a dialogical process with differing diversity and spirituality. In therapy, it can be easy to leave out one area and overemphasize another. And when dealing with culture/diversity, most of our clients have several diversity concerns that are important, as in Angie's case. For her, gender was a focal issue, as was socioeconomics. Many times, areas of diversity overlap in what we therapists now understand as intersectionality.

Intersectionality is "the interconnected nature of social categorisations (sic) such as race, class, and gender, regarded as creating overlapping and interdependent systems of discrimination or disadvantage" (Oxford Dictionary of Human Geography, 2013).[2] While some people experience intersectionality as discrimination, others may experience it as privilege. For example, a white woman in Angie's community who owns a real estate company may experience socioeconomic privilege that blunts gender discrimination. Intersectionality is composed of complex interactions between and among overlapping diversities. For a therapist, it can be quite difficult to pick up its nuances in the therapeutic process.

Acknowledging that spirituality is part of culture, a client's values likely also have a spiritual connection (McNeil et al., 2012). By recognizing both spirituality and diversity, the therapist may see their intersectionality in the clinical process. A therapist may be less likely to miss something as the therapy moves along through the recognition of intersectionality. Furthermore, the engagement of spirituality and culture/diversity is likely to make mutually informing changes to the way clients see them both.

[2] On the history of "intersectionality," see Merrill Perlman (2018, October 23). On the meaning of intersectionality, see Bridie Taylor (2019).

Socially Transformative Practice in a Diverse Context

Reviewing the last two decades, a growing emphasis on cultural competency has emerged. We now have many new terms to define as we try to determine the differences and commonalities between them. The following are just a few: cultural competence, multicultural awareness, diversity concerns, social justice, cross-cultural responsiveness, and even more. COAMFTE Standards Version 12.5 notes rigor in assessing students' sensitivity and skill in responding to clients who are challenged by the increasing burden of intersectionalities in their lives (COAMFTE Standards, 2017, Version 12.5).

Understanding "culture" as an overview of diversities may help us make sense of the many terms that relate to multiculturalism and diversity. We need to discover or create a term that can function as a sheltering umbrella to understand spirituality better therapeutically. We can then move to unravel the tangled ball of yarn called culture. Focusing on our need as therapists to honor both our clients' culture and spirituality may culminate in a clinically responsive practice for us and an example for our students.

Moving from an emphasis on multi-cultural competence (Sue & Sue, 2012), we can now lift some boundaries between culture, diversity, and spirituality. In this book, we shelter culture and diversity under an umbrella of social justice that can transform the worlds that we, our clients, and supervisees inhabit. By doing so, spirituality and social justice can work toward action. Two practices in recent MFT scholarship can aid us in that journey. One approach advanced by St. George and Wulff is systemic practice that can incorporate social justice with everyday family therapy (2016). Another approach by Poulsen and Allan is to integrate cross-cultural responsiveness with family therapy (2018). The following discussion will draw out contributions from each approach. Then, we will integrate those approaches with spirituality to generate a robust methodology that will eventually lay the foundation to supervise and train masters and doctoral students in an inclusive expansion of traditional notions of spirituality.

First, let us turn to the socially transformative MFT approach of St. George and Wulff (2016). Social justice is utilized here to address the changing picture of our society and the ways in which we now work with families as opposed to older models of systemic family practice. Previous decades of family work focused only on familial dynamics. While one might address some outside influences, the primary focus was within the family system.

The emergence of the feminist movement in the 1960s and the civil rights movement of the 1960s and 1970s set the stage for social change. Various populations have sought adjustments within their families as well as their communities. Interest in change is broad, but it draws on social justice that looks for growth within individuals and families, as well as the community context. St. George and Wulff contend that such attention to life inside and outside the family demands attention to social justice. It has been quite difficult, however, to apply this idea to our everyday work (St. George & Wulff, 2016).

MFT burst onto the psychotherapy scene with a great deal of radical enthusiasm to change the psychotherapy world. The field, however, moved into larger systems in small fits and starts. It did not remain in the larger systems but rather abandoned larger systems to social work. Now is the time for family therapists to truly recognize the challenges to changing the systems that impinge upon the lives of families: racism, sexism, poverty, and more. Merely looking at discrimination from these systems is not enough. It is insufficient to simply apply "common sense" and activism to making systemic changes. MFTs have a sophisticated skillset that involves knowing how to activate change in systems of all sorts. That is who we are.

Social justice moves toward action. Social justice talk with our clients engages with social action (Snyder et al., 2016). We are not tethered to a state of being in the therapy room. Our engagement with social justice makes it imperative for us to act. Yet, the process is a delicate balance between social justice, spirituality, and clinical challenges.

Support for social justice recognizes the power and privilege that permeate the larger social systems of our client families. It also is a part of what we do as therapists and supervisors. All of us have power. All of us have privilege. The degree to which we have power and privilege depends largely upon our social location and the intersectionalities that make up who we are as humans. Thus, we need to be aware of our many selves as well as our capacity to act as needed for the well-being of clients.

This ability to act infuses Poulsen and Allan's work (2018). The discussion in this book elects to use a different term, rather than cross-cultural, to identify the many diversities that typically fall under the term "cultural." The powerful word in this work is "responsiveness," since we systemic therapists often know what should change for our clients in the world beyond their families. We, however, lack the courage to carry it out. We need to be responsive rather than merely observing the environmental limits of our clients.

Our responsiveness to social inequities is enabled by phenomena that are invisible even to the clinically trained eye, and yet prove so perceptible to many of our clients. Class is one of these invisible diversity opponents that we would prefer to leave alone. Yet, as Dadras and Daneshpour contend, classism has contributed to the birth of multiculturalism in therapy. That class background can impede the systemic transformation of larger systems that hurt and impair some families (2018).

This blockage of systemic change comes from a view of multiculturalism that is determined by a white perspective (Dadras & Daneshpour, 2018). White scholars created assumptions about what should change, culturally, and what should remain the same, culturally. Indigenous or marginalized people were for the most part, not consulted. Under the guise of doing good, white researchers often, perhaps unintentionally, defined cultural competence. Norms were set for achieving cross-cultural awareness that were usually on white terms.

So, despite "wanting" good for clients, it is also possible for us as therapists and supervisors to forget our prejudicial class norms that dictate what we do. To this end, we need to continually examine our own class, political, and personal perspectives, and assumptions, whether they are conservative or liberal. Not examining these perspectives can result in our becoming masters of otherness (Dadras & Daneshpour, 2018). Put differently, the scholarly class with privilege constructs the norms by which multiculturalism is assessed. Furthermore, it sets the stage for the privilege and power of the dominant group to determine what are desirable outcomes for our work as therapists and supervisors with our disenfranchised clients and supervisees.

This kind of social analysis is critical to family therapy practice. Social theories such as critical race, neo-Marxist, feminist, queer, and decolonizing frameworks can be applied to dismantle the normative structures of family therapy practice (McDowell, 2015). While effective, this approach still sets up someone to be "in charge." The approach here will focus on putting the client "in charge" through a postmodern approach.[3] Narrative practice applicable to therapy, supervision, and training will be viewed through an MFT lens that is not limited to postmodern approaches. The methodology will lend itself to strengthening the clients' voices in different theoretical contexts.

Foucault was aware of this challenge of orienting the method toward the client in his examinations of social institutions such as prisons and asylums. His interlocking concepts were power and knowledge. People who hold knowledge in any society also hold power. It is only when knowledge is shared with others that people can gain power and exercise some control over their future so that social transformation can occur (Foucault, 2000).

We who have knowledge have power and privilege. While all people have privilege, the degree to which individuals enjoy privilege depends on their social location. In that social location, we decide how we will use our privilege. The pertinent question here comes from Jack, a white male student from rural Indiana, who said one day in group: "Now that I know what white privilege is, what do I do with it?" Indeed. What do we do with our privilege, whether racial, gender, sexual orientation, or socioeconomic?

Implementing Socially Transformative Practices

Understanding what social transformation is demands intellectual rigor and respect for others' perspectives. However, this type of understanding is just the first step for both therapists and supervisors as we work to weave an awareness of social challenges for clients through our clinical skills. The exceedingly difficult step is how we find accessible interventions that can enable changes in our clients' lives.

From the previous discussion, we know that all of us have social challenges that originate from our social location. Both power and privilege are situated in each person's social location whether it is recognized or not. People in a higher

[3] The approach utilized in this book is influenced by my training at the Evanston Family Therapy Center, the Dulwich Centre in Australia, and the Vancouver School for Narrative Training, where I studied narrative therapy and collective narrative practice.

socioeconomic context may not fully recognize their power and privilege. They are afforded access to many things in our society due to their privilege. In contrast, people in lower socioeconomic contexts often cannot help but recognize the social injustice they experience daily.

So, how do therapists and supervisors find interventions that can transform our clients' everyday experiences? Socially transformative practice can be implemented through recognizing people's diversity concerns and their stories about how those injustices impact their lives. Then, we explore with clients how their spiritual stories sustain them in the face of such challenges. Finally, we engage with clients in dismantling these metanarratives so that people can work toward a new, generative story for their future. Let us look at a case study of an MFT intern who is counseling a graduate student who has encountered several challenges.

Case Study

Paula self-identifies as a trans woman and uses the pronouns they, them. They are a 24-year-old white doctoral student in anthropology at a local university. Paula self-identifies as an agnostic. George is a 25-year-old, African American, cisgender male who is in the marriage and family therapy program at a different university. He is a member of the African Methodist Episcopal church.

Paula's story starts with their beginnings in a small southern town where they never felt like they fit in. Entering a public research university was so exhilarating. There they were able to engage in lively debates that Paula was not able to have in their small town. During their master's program, they began the transition to becoming a transwoman. Now in their doctoral program, Paula feels that their gender identity supports all that they wanted in life.

Yet, things are not all well. Paula tells George that they have two sets of relationships: those people who agree with their gender and political perspectives and others who are the exact opposite. As a result, Paula feels quite separated from most of their family and friends back home in Greenville. They feel like they have two lives. Paula asks George what can be done to respond to the experienced social injustices.

George is quite interested in his role as a systemic family therapist in addressing social injustice while also exploring a client's inner world. He himself experiences living in different worlds as he pursues a degree at a university that has quite different values than his hometown in rural Colorado. Black Lives Matter continues to be a social movement in which he is quite active. So, he seeks to help Paula explore where their different worlds sometimes collide.

In a session, George first asks Paula in what ways society and cultural values impact their life. Paula responds that they find that it is difficult to reconcile a sense of truth with themselves and have a truthful relationship with others in their life. George and Paula determine that the injustice comes from a conflict with Paula's inner peace and the way they interact with significant people in their life.

Then George asks Paula to share a story in which their spirituality sustained them through difficult times. Paula said that they vividly remember a time as they were transitioning when a conservative woman in Paula's hometown wrote them a brief note. In the note, the woman said that although she did not agree with Paula's transition, she knew Paula and her family to be "honorable" people. So, the woman continued that she thought perhaps there was something Paula knew that she did not know and wished her well.

Paula said to George that this story is one they carry with them—the meaning of life is never "one note," but many notes. George and Paula talked about the value of perseverance, which Paula said is a spiritual quality that they try to keep daily. At this juncture in the therapy, George and Paula began to weave Paula's experience of injustice with their spiritual sustenance of perseverance. Periodically in therapy, George and Paula go back to the story of perseverance and social injustice to determine where Paula's journey is headed.

This brief case study highlights some interventions that employs social justice and spirituality. Later in this chapter, the diagram of the living web of sociospirituality will be presented as a visual tool to guide the therapist and supervisor.

Moving to a Creative Approach for Spirituality and Diversity

Social justice demands equity for persons whose identities are connected to race, class, ethnicity, culture, gender, sexual orientation, ability, and socioeconomics. Acting on behalf of our clients who experience injustice is onerous. Working toward justice within the counseling room is a great challenge. Add to that action for systemic change as the therapist works with the client to encourage and engage outside the therapy room. It is a heavy task!

This task means that systemic family therapy must develop a creative approach that engages both the therapist and client, and in an educational setting, the student. Some methodological considerations map out a process that can be followed step by step. This map provides direction for the therapist and client through the journey so that progress can be identified. A drawback is that both therapist and client may easily assume that following the map is all that is needed. That success is sure to follow is an uncertain assumption.

Another methodology, in contrast to systemic family therapy, is to travel the social justice road wherever it may take both therapist and client. The challenge in this case is that we are lured by the illusion of success when really, we may be blindly following our desire to right the wrong. A possible outcome to this approach may be that the process in the counseling room does not have the needed specificity for therapeutic change for the client along with their everyday communities.

Underlying this social justice-focused methodology is the well-known analysis of Paulo Freire, who in *Pedagogy of the Oppressed*, dismantles top-to-bottom learning. Freire discusses the culture of silence that corners marginalized people into accepting the knowledge that is passed down to them. Freire advocates for the creation of knowledge by the marginalized—to have many voices heard (Freire, 2018).

Another often overlooked volume by Freire is *Pedagogy of Hope*. In it, Freire and Freire contend that without hope, any release from oppression is impossible for the marginalized (2021). Thus, we, as family therapists, must use the quest for hope to infuse a healing approach. With a systemic focus, we identify both social justice and spirituality that listens to voices from disenfranchised families. Then, we train our students to be competent in this area.

The intent of integrating social justice/diversity and spirituality is to draw from their unique strengths. Rivett and Street contend that "spirituality is viewed in the same way that we might view race and gender issues in therapy" (2001, p. 461). Drawing from this understanding, creating a methodology utilizing approaches from both spirituality and diversity would be beneficial for both dimensions. The result would be a robust approach affording both breadth of systems and robustness of content. So, we begin with an image that can encompass both.

Creating a Spirituality Diverse Model

In the twentieth century, clinical chaplaincy in psychiatric hospitals was influenced by an image created by Anton Boisen: the living human document (Dykstra, 2005). The medical model approach prevalent in hospitals was to diagnose patients and focus treatment on that diagnosis. Physicians assessed patients based on interviews. However, the diagnostic category was primary. As a psychiatric patient and chaplain, Boisen began to look at the world of diagnosis in a different way. He saw the human patient as containing all that the practitioner needed to read to create a treatment plan. The diagnosis was embodied in the patient. Prior to the living human document image, chaplains typically met in small groups to discuss patients. Part of that group case conference was to review a written case study (Hiltner, 1958).[4] The use of the living human document encouraged chaplains to interact directly with patients to "read" the person as you would a document. The report form of supervision is reminiscent of an MFT report as the basis for supervision. Consequently, the interpersonal interaction of supervisee with client was processed in supervision.

For decades, the living human document was a prevailing image in pastoral care for the assessment of care-seekers under the minister and chaplain's umbrella. It fit well with the prevailing psychoanalytic approach of the individual. New social norms emerged in the 1950s and 1960s, ushered in by the civil rights movement. As more systemic concepts emerged, the image of the living human web, first coined by Miller-McLemore, modified the living human document image. Unlike the document, which is readable, the web cannot be read. Individuals within the web who

[4] Seward Hiltner was my residency doctoral advisor during my Ph.D. studies at Princeton Theological Seminary.

have not yet spoken must speak for themselves (Miller-McLemore, 1993). No longer can professionals speak for others, regardless of the good intent. Individuals in a privileged social location must turn power to the underprivileged, the outcasts, the underclass, and the silenced by sharing knowledge.

By the early 1990s, family therapy was largely influenced by postmodern models of therapy. Pastoral counseling, despite a growing affinity for the living human web, still clung to psychoanalytic models. Ironically, despite a connection with churches, pastoral counseling did not work much with families. Both the fields recognized the importance of public social concerns or social justice in different ways. At the same time, the two fields did not formally engage in interdisciplinary conversations. Perhaps the pastoral counselors were too religious for the MFTs and the MFTs were too systemic for the pastoral counselors.

Increasingly, fields endeavor to have some interdisciplinary conversations to address many societal challenges. Conferences of psychotherapy organizations periodically invite speakers from different fields to address societal and cultural injustices. In recent years, the American Association for Marriage and Family Therapy has invited interdisciplinary speakers to address current social injustices. The 2021 annual conference sponsored by AAMFT is titled the Systemic Family Therapy Conference 2021. Its purpose is "providing systemic thinkers with personal and professional development, cutting edge clinical skills and training, this event will examine the role of systemic therapy in communities and institutions, and its impact on global society."[5] Such an invigorated approach could result in increased conversation between mental health professions about systemic therapy.

Other organizations currently engage in interdisciplinary conversation. Such an example is the Society for the Exploration of Psychotherapy Integration (SEPI) (2021). "The Society for the Exploration of Psychotherapy Integration (SEPI) is an international, interdisciplinary organization whose aim is to promote the exploration and development of approaches to psychotherapy that integrate across theoretical orientations, clinical practices, and diverse methods of inquiry."[6]

The image of the living human web will be used to provide the structure for a spiritually systemic model. First, an exposition of the current state of the image of the living human web is needed. Several changes in pastoral counseling have moved the image to the forefront of the field. Increasingly, the audience for pastoral counseling is the public, not the academic guild. The public yearns for day-to-day connections with spirituality to heal their brokenness because of social injustice. Some of these injustices are exacerbated by social and economic isolation. These marginalized voices need to be heard. The same can be said for family therapy. While ensconced in academia, it is imperative that research and teaching are utilized to connect with the marginalized, not only the guild.

The public's voices were heard through the rise of the liberation movements, including the feminist and Black movements, which have now expanded to include

[5] Available at https://networks.aamft.org/conference/home.

[6] See Mission Statement at https://www.sepiweb.org/page/3.

other marginalized groups (Miller-McLemore, 2018). The evolving nature of these movements in response to social injustice can be seen in contemporary society. The living human web image is also used in interdisciplinary fields such as bioethics to emphasize the need for marginalized voices to be brought into the conversation (Carlin, 2019). This dimension brings into play the social systems or larger systems that can enrich MFT as it seizes on this opportunity to go beyond the family system. Larger systems such as legal systems, medical systems, church systems, corporate systems, mental health systems, and social services systems need to be assessed to determine the ways they enrich or hinder people's lives. Such an approach would realize the "interconnectivity of social systems and the systemic nature of pastoral care" (Miller-McLemore, 2018, p. 316).

Another focal area for this image is the congregation. Of course, this is not the purview of relational systemic therapy. A possibility is that the image of the living human web could be more fruitfully re-named the web of life. Such a shift would move the emphasis to the role of interconnectedness to help provide robustness in challenging social injustice in contemporary life (Osmer, 2007).

So, what image best captures the integration of spirituality and social justice? The image for this methodology will be a web to indicate the systemic, interactive flavor of spirituality and social justice. It needs to do more than the "human" in the living human web, however. We need to recognize the larger systems that can both help and hinder social justice. Humans are a part of this web, but larger systems include both humans and the concretizing of human action. These systems become an entity in themselves. The web must also recognize life (Osmer, 2007). But it needs to realize that the web of life in this context could profit from specificity about spirituality. An image that emphasizes living or life is also needed.

This image of the living human web can connect to family therapy's image of the web of human experience, which originally emerged from the web of constraints within the Meta frameworks perspective. This construct was designed to incorporate knowledge from family therapy that could transcend specific theoretical models (Russell, 2019). It was based on Bateson's concept of negative explanation (2000). The concept of constraints was then developed from Bateson's thinking to understand the factors that prevented families from solving problems (Breunlin, 1999). Constraints such as sequences, organization, culture, gender, development, and mind were found at multiple levels to constitute this barrier to making change. The intersecting entities are society, community, family, and the individual (Russell, 2019).

This web of constraints was revised and incorporated into the Integrative Systemic Therapy model but can also be used as a standalone device for hypothesizing. With the addition of biology and spirituality to the constraints, it was renamed the web of human experience (Pinsof et al., 2018). The image of a web for systemic family therapy provides a diagram that conveys the interconnectedness of larger systems and aspects of human life.

An image that can best integrate the dimensions of social justice and spirituality can be called the living web of socio-spirituality. It will emphasize socially

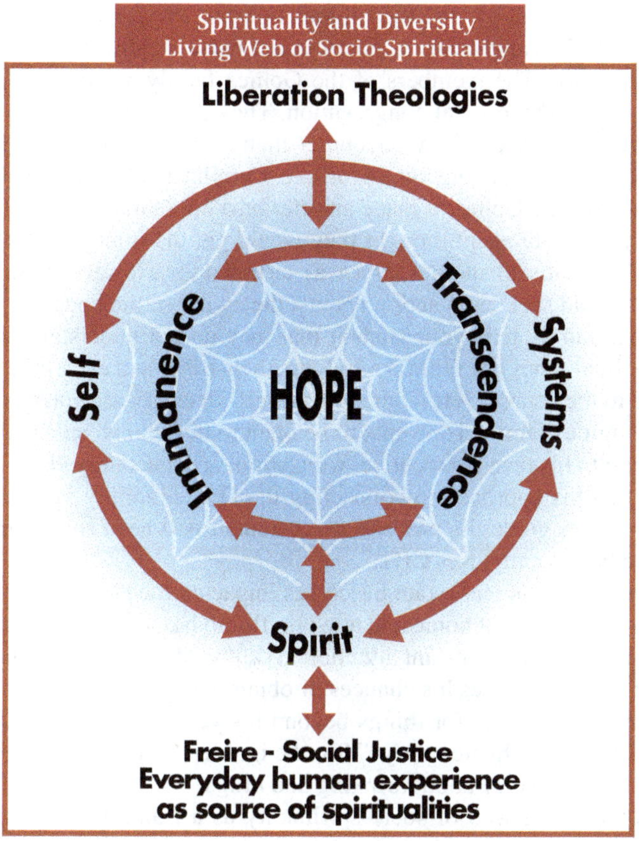

Fig. 3.1 Spirituality and diversity living web of socio-spirituality

responsive spirituality. The web imagery offers a model that would interconnect social justice and spirituality. The image of a web conveys systemic movement that offers social justice and spirituality the freedom to retain their distinctiveness as well as their capacity to integrate with the other focus: social justice or spirituality. Figure 3.1 is a diagram of the living web of socio-spirituality that will illustrate with a case study that follows the diagram.

Case Study

Both humans and larger systems engage in this web. As the interaction goes back and forth, the therapist and/or client has the option to identify what beliefs and values interact in this process. For example, the Gomez family begins therapy with a trainee in your MFT program. The family includes Camilla, 43 years old, and her husband, Rubio, who is 44, and their three children: 18-year-old Marcos; 16-year-old Hector; and 15-year-old Silvia. Camilla is a nurse's aide while Rubio is a construction supervisor. The members of the Gomez family are faithful churchgoers who attend a large Pentecostal congregation. They are documented so they do not have immigration worries. They encounter many other dilemmas, however. They rent their home, which is being put up for sale. Camilla and Rubio have worked hard and saved money. The Gomezes made an offer on a house that was above the asking price. Their real estate agent thought they would get the offer, but it was rejected. The real estate agent said another offer was accepted for a lower fee. She added that the Gomezes could seek legal action against the owner of the house.

The Gomez family tells your student that they do not understand why this has happened to them. They are faithful, studying their Bible and even tithe a portion of their income to the church. Jeff, your student, self-identifies as agnostic and was not raised in a religious family. He wants to be open to his clients' spiritual viewpoints while adhering to his own perspective, which you have encouraged. Jeff told you in supervision that his approach to counseling the Gomez family is to listen closely and let their voices guide the process. Your student will need some support in this process since he typically uses CBT.

The fallout from this real estate fiasco has impacted the entire family. Camilla is constantly stressed, both at home and at work. Rubio has a difficult time concentrating in a job that demands constant attention to safety. Marcos's grades have dropped at school, which jeopardizes his chances of obtaining a college scholarship. Hector has assumed responsibility for things beyond his years. Silvia looks at the family disarray and thinks, "Why not party?" So, she ignores her curfew and goes out with friends. Her parents worry about drinking and drugs.

Jeff uses the living web of socio-spirituality as a frame for his work with the Gomez family. In the beginning, he works to make a place for all the voices of individual family members. Jeff goes around the family asking them what they would say to the real estate unfairness. This illustrates Freire's notion of the marginalized speaking out. Camilla says, "Go away, unfairness. I have worked awfully hard. This is not right." Rubio says, "Real estate laws don't do anything for me and my family. I'm angry and feel so helpless." Marcos says, "I should be able to help my dad. But, I have too much. I'm just giving up." Hector speaks up, "Hey, Marcos, I can help out." Silvia adds, "I have a life. I'm just going to be with my friends."

In a session, Jeff talks with the entire family and encourages each member to speak out even more. The next few sessions develop this conversation. As Jeff reflects upon his work with them, he identifies some diversity concerns that are limiting them in everyday life. The following list emerges: racism, socioeconomic concerns, and perhaps gender. In a tentative start, he brings up racism. Many stories tumble out. They work to process all this information.

He then moves to address specific diversity concerns that affect the entire family. Racism is a big concern for them all. Since Jeff is white, he self-identifies his white privilege and invites the family to respond. After they discuss racism's presence in the room, in their lives, and larger systems, Jeff then wants to focus on their individual challenges.

At this point, Jeff wants to employ a theoretical orientation in supporting the family. He could continue this more postmodern approach. But Jeff thinks he needs to practice something familiar. So, he goes back to CBT. He takes the family's voices and crafts interventions that address each member's dilemma: Camilla—stress, Rubio—lack of concentration, Marcos—feeling overwhelmed, and Silvia—feeling overwhelmed.

The sessions continue for several weeks until the family experiences less stress. The family system is functioning better. However, they must now face the larger systems that have stressed them their entire lives. They begin a careful course of speaking up whenever they believe they can without extreme repercussions. Jeff, although enjoying white privilege, is now considering getting involved in social justice in the larger systems in which he is a member.

Jeff moves to the spirituality of the Gomez family. He once again invites them to voice their understanding of spirituality. Maria expresses her disappointment with her congregation. She says that when she told her Bible study group about their problems, they told her to pray more. Rubio supports the church's position on prayer and just says that he needs to pray more. All the teens agree with their mother's criticism of the church. They all agree that they are not yet ready to attend a different church. Jeff suggests that they explore in session how their spirituality connects with their real-life experiences with real estate and racial discrimination. The diversities of race and socioeconomic difference overlap with each other as the family members seek a spirituality that offers both realism and hope.

Integrating Spirituality with Social Justice

Up to this point, our journey has taken us to define spirituality, observing its differences with religion, as a concept and a reality, as well as its commonalities. Then, we moved to the everyday grit of larger systems as they impact our clients. Diversity concerns such as race, class, culture, ability, religion, spirituality, gender, sexual orientation, and socioeconomics affect us all daily.

We have argued that arbitrarily separating spirituality from diversities is a treacherous path. However, when we embark upon that journey, we may miss the richness of each focus that can support our clients. Certainly, we need to attend to each focus. The spirituality in this book encompasses the more traditional idea of spirituality lifting us to transcendence and the immanence of acknowledging our human limitations.

Religion sometimes presents human limitations as a flaw that must be overcome. Yet in many major religions, the divine is connected to the earthly. Judaism espouses a holistic view of the human person. Christianity understands God to be incarnate in Jesus Christ. Hinduism humanizes deities with animal companions. By recognizing the human in ourselves, we can form our spirituality to speak to our humanness as we hope for a glimpse of the divine.

Now we come to the further thickening of the living web of socio-spirituality. Diversity, social justice, and Freire's methodology support this endeavor. As we move forward, we will weave liberative theologies with the concept of hope in the web as well as postmodern approaches, particularly narrative practice. How then do these everyday experiences of injustice and spirituality also apply uniquely to other mental health professions?

Spirituality in Diversity Across Mental Health Disciplines

Acknowledging diversity is a focus that all mental health disciplines see as critical to responsible therapy. Spirituality, in a similar way, is increasingly viewed as an essential part of psychotherapy. At the same time, different psychotherapeutic professions have unique practices where diversity and spirituality can be utilized. Family psychologists perhaps represents the closest practitioners in psychology to systemic family therapists. Using the living web of socio-spirituality, family psychologists could draw out the diversity and spirituality of the whole family. Then, each family member could be invited to place the family's story on the living web of socio-spirituality.

Social workers could identify the community in which they work with their clients. As they do case management with the family, the social worker could spend a considerable amount of time on the community context. Where in the community do their clients find spiritual resources? Where in the community do clients seek resources to address social injustices?

Mental health counselors may find themselves in a community agency where directly addressing spirituality is a sticky issue. A way of connecting their clients with spirituality would be to start with the social injustices that the client experiences. As that story is expanded, the counselor could ask the client, "What sustains you through these hard times when injustice comes to you?" The client's answer may be a way to explore spirituality in the client's own words.

Self, Systems, Spirit Practice

Diversity and Spirituality in the Living Web of Socio-Spirituality

This practice is designed for peer groups of students and/or supervisors. According to a pre-assigned rotation, participants bring a clinical case for discussion and supervision. As an alternative, pre-practicum students can select a clinical case from a systemic family therapy textbook. The process for the session is as follows:

- The facilitator distributes copies of Fig. 3.1 living web of socio-spirituality to all participants.

- The session may begin with the discussion of this chapter. An alternate approach is for the facilitator to summarize the chapter contents.
- The group participants identify the aspects of diversity/social justice and spirituality they see in the clinical case.

Then, the facilitator asks either sub-groups or individual participants the following questions:

1. As you make a treatment plan for the clients in the case study using the living web, what topic would you first engage the client in considering during the session?
2. How would you move from that point to a proximate goal for the session and to a contribution to a longer-term therapeutic outcome?
3. How would you respond to the client's problem story?
4. How would you use the living web to encourage the client to develop a future story using spirituality to address social injustice?

Group Feedback: Sub-groups discuss their experience of the process in the large group.

References

American Association for Marriage and Family Therapy. (2004). *Marriage and family therapy core competencies*. Author. Retrieved from https://www.coamfte.org/Documents/COAMFTE/Accreditation%20Resources/MFT%20Core%20Competencies%20(December%202004).pdf

American Association for Marriage and Family Therapy. (2021). *Systemic Family Therapy Conference 2021*. Author. Retrieved September 20, 2021, from https://networks.aamft.org/conference/home

Aponte, H. J. (1998). Love, the spiritual wellspring of forgiveness: An example of spirituality in therapy. *Journal of Family Therapy, 20*(1), 37–58. https://doi.org/10.1111/1467-6427.00067

Aponte, A. (2001). Love, the spiritual source of forgiveness: An example of spirituality in therapy. *Therapie Familiale, 22*, 337–359.

Aponte, H. J. (2002). Spirituality: The heart of therapy. *Journal of Family Psychotherapy, 13*(1–2), 13–27. https://doi.org/10.1300/J085v13n01_02

Bateson, G. (2000). *Steps to an ecology of mind: Collected essays in anthropology, psychiatry, evolution, and epistemology*. University of Chicago Press.

Breunlin, D. C. (1999). Toward a theory of constraints. *Journal of Marital and Family Therapy, 25*(3), 365–382. https://doi.org/10.1111/j.1752-0606.1999.tb00254

Carlin, N. (2019). *Pastoral aesthetics: A theological perspective on principlist bioethics*. Oxford University Press.

Commission on Accreditation for Marriage and Family Therapy Education. (2017). *COAMFTE Accreditation standards: Graduate & post-graduate marriage and family therapy training programs Version 12.5*. Author. Retrieved from https://www.coamfte.org/documents/COAMFTE/Accreditation%20Resources/2018%20COAMFTE%20Accreditation%20Standards%20Version%2012%20May.pdf

Cone, J. (2018). *Black theology and black power: 50th anniversary edition*. Orbis Books.

Coyle, S. M. (2017). Integrating spirituality in marriage and family therapy training. *Australian and New Zealand Journal of Family Therapy, 38*(1), 142–155. https://doi.org/10.1002/anzf.1195

Dadras, I., & Daneshpour, M. (2018). Social justice implications for MFT: The need for cross-cultural responsiveness. In S. Poulsen & R. Allen (Eds.), *Cross-cultural responsiveness & systemic therapy* (pp. 1–20). Springer. https://doi.org/10.1007/978-3-319-71395-3

Dykstra, R. C. (Ed.). (2005). *Images of pastoral care: Classic readings*. Chalice Press.

Elkins, D. N. (2013). *Beyond religion: A personal program for building a spiritual life outside the walls of traditional religion*. Quest Books.

Foucault, M. (2000). *Ethics: Essential works of Foucault 1954–1984* (Vol. 1). Penguin.

Freire, P. (2018). *Pedagogy of the oppressed*. Bloomsbury.

Freire, P. (2021). *Pedagogy of hope: Reliving pedagogy of the oppressed*. Bloomsbury.

Helmeke, K. B., & Bischof, G. H. (2002). Recognizing and raising spiritual and religious issues in therapy: Guidelines for the timid. *Journal of Family Psychotherapy, 13*(1–2), 195–214. https://doi.org/10.1300/J085v13n01_10

Hiltner, S. (1958). *Preface to pastoral theology*. Abingdon Press.

Holmberg, Å., Jensen, P., & Vetere, A. (2021). Spirituality – A forgotten dimension? Developing spiritual literacy in family therapy practice. *Journal of Family Therapy, 43*(1–2), 78–95. https://doi.org/10.1111/1467-6427.12298

Intersectionality. (2013). *Oxford dictionary of human geography*. Oxford University Press.

McDowell, T. (2015). *Applying critical social theories to family therapy practice*. Springer.

McNeil, S. N., Pavkov, T. W., Hecker, L. L., & Killmer, J. M. (2012). Marriage and family therapy graduate students' satisfaction with training regarding religion and spirituality. *Contemporary Family Therapy, 34*(4), 468–480. https://doi.org/10.1007/s10591-012-9205-7

Miller-McLemore, B. J. (1993). The human web: Reflections on the state of pastoral theology. *The Christian Century, 110*(11), 366–369.

Miller-McLemore, B. J. (2018). The living human web: A twenty-five-year retrospective. *Pastoral Psychology, 67*(3), 305–321. https://doi.org/10.1177/154230500806200102

Osmer, R. R. (2007). *Practical theology: An introduction*. Wm. B. Eerdmans Publishing.

Perlman, M. (2018, October 23). The origin of the term 'intersectionality'. *Columbia Journalism Review*. Retrieved from https://www.cjr.org/language_corner/intersectionality.php

Pinsof, W. M., Breunlin, D. C., Russell, W. P., Lebow, J. L., Rampage, C., & Chambers, A. L. (2018). *Integrative systemic therapy: Metaframeworks for problem solving with individuals, couples, and families*. American Psychological Association. https://doi.org/10.1037/0000055-000

Poulsen, S. S., & Allan, R. (2018). Cultural responsiveness in family therapy: Integrative and common factors lens. In S. Poulsen & R. Allen (Eds.), *Cross-cultural responsiveness & systemic therapy* (pp. 69–77). Springer. https://doi.org/10.1007/978-3-319-71395-3

Rivett, M., & Street, E. (2001). Connections and themes of spirituality in family therapy. *Family Process, 40*(4), 459–467. https://doi.org/10.1111/j.1545-5300.2001.4040100459.x

Russell, W. P. (2019). Web of human experience in couple and family therapy. In J. Lebow, A. Chambers, & D. Breunlin (Eds.), *Encyclopedia of couple and family therapy* (pp. 3145–3150). Springer.

Snyder, L. J., McIntosh, S., & Gosnell, F. (2016). Learning to speak social justice talk in family therapy. In S. St. George & D. Wulff (Eds.), *Family therapy as socially transformative practice* (pp. 57–68). Springer.

Society for the Exploration of Psychotherapy Integration (SEPI). (2021). Mission statement. Retrieved from https://www.sepiweb.org/page/3

St. George, S., & Wulff, D. (2016). Family therapy + social justice + daily practices = transforming therapy. In S. St. George & D. Wulff (Eds.), *Family therapy as socially transformative practice* (pp. 1–7). Springer.

Stander, V., Piercy, F. P., Mackinnon, D., & Helmeke, K. (1994). Spirituality, religion, and family therapy: Competing or complementary worlds? *The American Journal of Family Therapy, 22*(1), 27–41. https://doi.org/10.1080/01926189408251295

Sue, D. W., & Sue, D. (2012). *Counseling the culturally diverse: Theory and practice* (6th ed.). John Wiley & Sons.

Taylor, B. (2019). *Intersectionality 101: What is it and why is it important?* Womankind Worldwide. Retrieved from https://www.womankind.org.uk/blog/detail/our-blog/2019/11/24/intersectionality-101-what-is-it-and-why-is-it-important

Whitaker, C. A., & Ryan, M. O. (1989). *Midnight musings of a family therapist*. W. W. Norton.

Chapter 4
Methodological Considerations for Integrating Spirituality in Socially Just Systemic Training

Spirituality is ill served through a limiting understanding of what constitutes the individual's beliefs, practices, and values. As we move forward, spirituality is understood as a lens through which we can see all the diversity concerns that MFTs currently apprehend through multiculturalism. Many diversity concerns are illuminated by spirituality. Gender orientation is an example of a diversity that one's spiritual values greatly impact. Social justice and spirituality engage with each other to create socio-spirituality.

Moving from Social Justice to Inclusivity

In this chapter, we continue to thicken the living web of socio-spirituality. The diversities that bind us to our earthly existence offer a door to open ways to experience a breath of transcendence. Even a brief glimpse of transcendence can help therapists, clients, and supervisees live life amid social injustice. Many times, we all can see and identify transcendence. Living transcendence, however, means that we must be immersed in the experience, deeply feel it, and act from it.

A Freirean methodology that involves social justice as well as spirituality facilitates a counter-story to a hierarchical approach.[1] Paulo Freire was a Brazilian educator who believed that only by acting on social issues can change, and development occur. He encouraged oppressed people to be involved in their liberation from injustice. Social justice and spirituality are voices that inform each other. At the same time, a spirituality that truly engages both the immanent and the transcendent can

[1] The use of counter-story here comes from narrative practice, which encourages people to discover a generative story or counter-story that challenges a problem-saturated story.

S. M. Coyle, *Spirituality in Systemic Family Therapy Supervision and Training*, Focused Issues in Family Therapy, https://doi.org/10.1007/978-3-030-92369-3_4

respond in multiple ways: (1) by participating in a spiritual process that engages transcendence so that marginalized people can breathe, looking first to the liberation of the spirit; (2) by uncovering the spiritual qualities that are embedded in social diversities, focusing on the social; and (3) by weaving the spiritual qualities back into both the mystical and social.

Such a Freirean foundation can integrate both the social and spiritual. As an educational pedagogy, Freirean theory is used in critical social analysis as well as in liberative theological approaches. Its trust in the voices of marginalized people strengthens its relation to social and theological approaches. In turn, people can begin to envision a more transcendent existence that thickens stories of despair into stories of hope.[2] An overview of social analysis by Freire can sometimes turn into a grim journey of overcoming injustice and despair. At times, the social reconstruction introduced by the therapeutic advocate experiences little joy in the arduous path to justice.

These experiences of righting wrongs, however, can create moments of joy that engender hopefulness for both social justice and spiritual growth. A story of hope can then result for families, offering them a spiritual reservoir to confront daily dilemmas. Supporting spiritual values necessitates acknowledging our ecological identities. We are tied to a world in which increasing natural disasters influence our everyday lives. It is difficult to ignore the effects of these disasters as well as a global pandemic in our lives. Our ecological identities are who we are.

Hence, our immanence can connect to a hopeful future. Here in the United States, we may be too captive to our geographical mobility that neglects the role of place in cultural values. Moving for a job or abandoning our hometown for other reasons can lead to an empty spirituality that relies too heavily on accomplishments and economic prosperity. Place is tied to who we are. The stories we tell are set in a geographical context.

When studying at the Dulwich Centre, I was introduced to the work of Just Therapy, a group in New Zealand that is firmly rooted in the values of the land. Their work honors the land they inhabit as well as justice for all people. Waldegrave and his colleagues believe that therapists need to advocate for political and public health conditions that mitigate barriers to good health for their clients (Waldegrave et al., 2003). Consequently, when therapists advocate outside the therapy room, the outcomes of such action flow back into the therapy room. The traditional diagnostic process of situating the problem within the client and family is challenged by an alternative perspective where clients can recognize the pathology that lies with "power discourse and social injustices" (Dadras & Daneshpour, 2018, p. 15).

In societal realms, power discourses can create norms that are harmful for some families. As therapists consider what is life-giving socially and spiritually for clients, it is critical to discover a bridge that can dismantle destructive paradigms of power and privilege. An alternative construct to address the complexities of

[2]The word "thicken" is used here in a narrative practice sense. As people understand the painful and joyful parts of their stories, they are better able to develop their own resilience to life's challenges.

identities in family work through social justice is cultural equity (Almeida et al., 2011). "Cultural equity addresses the multiplicity of personal, social, and institutional locations that frame identities in therapeutic practice by locating these complexities within a societal matrix that shapes relationships: power, privilege, and oppression" (Almeida et al., 2011, p. 44).

This Freirean-influenced approach contrasts with the cultural competence training movement, where it is assumed that a dominant cultural/ethnic group can "learn" about various diversities and then work to "do" the helpful thing for oppressed groups. Progressive liberal professionals need to guard against thinking that they may instinctually know how to help others. In fact, help easily can turn into hindrance. Such an approach can quickly deteriorate into colonizing a group of people. One can then identify some people as an Other, and in doing so, patronize them. Cultural equity takes the Other and transforms it into Otherizing to indicate the need for a new paradigm (Almeida et al., 2011). This discussion will continue to use the Other with the understanding that new paradigms are needed.

Self in the Living Web of Socio-Spirituality

In the last chapter, we discussed the weaving of social justice and spirituality into the living web of socio-spirituality. Layers of relations were created by emphasizing diversities and the social environment in which humans experience them with a grounding of spirituality supporting it all. In this chapter, the goal is to continue weaving dimensions of spirituality into the dimensions of diversity. By the end of the chapter, the web will be created as it reaches a trinity of relational systemic experience: self, systems, and spirit.

The concept of self has introduced a rich source for MFT throughout its history of emphasizing the need for therapists to understand themselves in the consultation room with their clients. Self of therapist has its origins in part in Bowen theory. As we focus on ourselves and our clients, this theory lifts the necessity of differentiating from our families of origin. The desired outcome for therapist, supervisor, and client is to remain emotionally connected and at the same time non-reactive. We become a non-anxious presence. This is so difficult. At most times in our lives, it is impossible. Our modern world is full of anxiety. Perhaps, we can try for less anxious.

Bowen's theory calls on the therapist and supervisee to always be aware of his or her family of origin dynamics. We need to continually "work" on our family of origin issues so that these do not harm our families or our clients. With some psychodynamic connections, the outstanding feature of Bowenian work is to find out how to be emotionally connected with our families but not emotionally reactive. It is not that we work through these issues. It is that we are on a lifelong journey.

Family of origin work found its translation into intergenerational therapy modeled by Philip Guerin. From Bowen's intergenerational approach to family work, the notion of self of therapist has permeated the mainstream of MFT theory and work. Some therapists weave this reflexive process into peer groups and their self-reflections. Training programs often integrate reflecting on self of therapist issues in clinical supervision as well as examining didactic components from the curriculum.

Perhaps it can be argued that no one is better known for self of therapist training than Harry Aponte and his colleagues. The model flourished at Drexel University as the Person of the Therapist, or POTT. This approach assumes that the more the therapist and client can be present in the process of therapy, the greater access the therapist has to self, and the client to therapy. Being present then adds "clarity of insight, depth of sensitivity and potency of effectiveness to the therapist's clinical performance" (Aponte & Kissil, 2016, p. 1).

Pursuing this understanding of self requires associating with three aims: (1) knowledge of self: self-insight involving the psychological and relational aspects of our lives as humans and our role as therapists, along with personal worldviews, values, morality, and social location; (2) access to self: the therapist moves beyond intellectual exploration to examine the inner self and philosophical/spiritual perspectives that shelter memories, emotions, spirituality, and social consciousness in the moment of therapy; and (3) management of self: whatever therapists know of themselves must involve discernment and discipline. It is not just a whim of the moment but a rigorous process of self-examination (Aponte, 2016).

The purpose of POTT is to expand effectiveness in the therapist's therapeutic work. Recent research on POTT indicates that those changes to the therapist's professional life extend to other areas of the therapist's life. Participants in the study reported experiencing changes in self-awareness and self-acceptance, self-access, and proactive use of self in therapy. At another layer, the participants reported that they attributed POTT to enable them to have more self-acceptance and better manage personal relationships (Kissil et al., 2018).

The study did not focus on the direct correlation between the professional self of therapist and the personal self of therapist. However, the assumptions of POTT are that all humans have a core woundedness that we need to recognize. Only by managing that core issue can therapists be able to work with their clients to achieve the client's therapeutic goals. The study's researchers hypothesize that an isomorphic process is likely to have been at the core of POTT work contributing to personal aspects of the participant's life. An implication from the study is that it is helpful to conduct self of therapist work with the supervisee's peers in a group setting (Kissil et al., 2018).

The foundation of this model is spirituality as defined in this book's opening chapters. This, however, is a different type of spirituality that connects with determinants of being human and all the attendant diversities. As such, spirituality here connects intimately with the whole person who is experiencing spirituality. Of course, some people may profess that they are engaging in spiritual practices when it is merely some intellectual exercise. This does not describe this notion of spirituality. It is about going to the depths of immanence in human experience so that transcendence can be experienced.

To this end, socio-spirituality must have an awareness of one's self that enables the therapist and supervisee to delve deeply into the therapeutic process in the room.

At the same time, the therapist must be open to engagement in the outside world. Some types of activism on behalf of social justice may not offer the therapist an opportunity for robust social action. That prescriptive perspective is a rather shallow model of social justice that says, “do as I say,” not “do as I do.” Spirituality in this book is engaged in holistic care of person and world. To this end, it is important for therapists and supervisees to know who they are and how that awareness of both self and relationships affects the way they approach and implement social justice with spiritual depth.

Reviewing the POTT model, several dimensions of self-awareness stand out that fit in our developing model of socio-spirituality. Self-insight in POTT involves personal worldviews, values, morality, and social location. Furthermore, awareness of self involves a spiritual perspective that oversees memories, emotions, spirituality, and social consciousness (Aponte, 2016). This notion of spirituality connects well with a spirituality that is driven by concerns for social justice. To adequately engage in social justice, one must be aware of one’s capacity for moral, spiritual, and social engagement so that effective change can be made. Moreover, the holistic engagement of self in the spiritual impetus for social justice cannot be made without thorough self-examination. Only through such self-examination can one develop the kind of resilience necessary for this hard work.

Certainly, in systemic training, the development of self-awareness for novice therapists is considered an important component of work that has social transformation as its goal (Ashbourne et al., 2016). Of course, the novice therapist has a long journey before challenging diversities that they can address personally. Typically, responding to LGBTQ diversity is challenging for many beginning therapists. Those students having a conservative religious point of view may experience such engagement as particularly challenging. McGeorge et al. suggest that doing important self of therapist work is necessary in these situations so that the supervisee’s beliefs can be reconciled through their self-awareness (2014).

This self of therapist work need not be solitary. As POTT contends in a research study, group work provides the support that such transformation requires. In fact, it may be helpful to think of such group work as a multiple-selves team (St. George & Wulff, 2016). Training programs could consider ways to incorporate this name into their self of therapist groups so that it will not be understood by trainees as being ripped from limb to limb. Such groups need to balance comfort and confrontation. Further recommendations about applying this concept to training programs will be explored in later chapters.

For now, we focus on the first component of self, systems, and spirit. Self in this discussion is understood as an individual’s awareness of his or her inner thoughts, feelings, and spiritual sense. It is grounded in the immanence of the human person. It does not, however, limit itself to the experience of the human body. It can reach both inward and outward to the transcendent in life. Self is generally understood as a stable collection of thoughts, feelings, and spirit that is recognizable to the individual and others with whom he or she is in relationships. However, that stable self can change to some degree in different relationships. For example, an individual might experience herself differently with her husband—that core collection—than with her children. A single male might experience himself differently with his parents who live across the country than with his close friends in immediate proximity in ways that are quite distinct from familial connections.

Mutter and Neves stress that cultural awareness must be connected to a differentiation of self as well as spirituality. Such an interconnectedness mitigates against the therapist applying spirituality as an abstract concept in the therapy room without a connection to the client's self (2010). In this discussion, self is also understood as the inner sense of who one is that gives direction to beliefs, values, and actions. Thus, self becomes a moral compass but not without limitations. To give self-awareness total power over one's spiritual identity and social choices without any discernment would be irresponsible. At the same time, self is that inner expression that expresses spontaneity for the client's decision-making, which is based on personal history.

Self of therapist concerns in MFT training are often addressed and supervised through a broad understanding of how one accesses self through family of origin themes. Such identifying themes emerge in the trainee's work with clients. The formation of personal values from this training has outcomes in the socially transformative choices therapists make. Self of therapist training does not, however, make a direct connection to social action. It has more of an indirect connection to spirituality.

Dadras and Daneshpour contend that self of therapist in MFT literature lacks a broad explication of identity from a sociopolitical perspective. To this end, a socially responsive sociopolitical differentiation of self needs to be implemented (Dadras & Daneshpour, 2018). We then move to this book's model of spirituality embedded in social justice. It is imperative that some aspects of giving students access to self will understand this kind of self-work also to be embedded in social justice and spirituality.

Up to this point, the foundation for the living web of socio-spirituality is grounded in a Freirean methodology that advocates accessing knowledge from those marginalized people who have had that knowledge kept from them. One technique for acquiring this knowledge is helping the supervisor and student both understand the ways they themselves perceive they are marginalized. This foundation is utilized by both social justice and theology in their quest to right the wrong. Thus, both the areas can draw from that emphasis.

Bookending that foundation are the concepts of immanence and transcendence which have a spiritual focus. Immanence grounds the human, while transcendence aspires to the divine, whether theistic or non-theistic. A human experiences diversities of all types based upon his or her social location. Then, we present social justice as that engagement of immanence and transcendence that calls upon spirituality to act as the thread that weaves together everything.

We come to where we are now. What is missing? Essential to implementing such a model is the ability to both discern and act. Self is that inner experience of the human who has earthly dimensions such as race and gender and connects with spirituality. Spirituality that is disembodied is merely a nod to the transcendent without any effect on human existence. Spirituality must be tethered to the human. We move forward to explore a trinity that gives voice to the living web of socio-spirituality. This development will be completed in this chapter. Then, we will explore the practice of this systemic family therapy model.

While spirituality is important in systemic work, one cannot impose their spiritual values on clients. A deterrent is to provide opportunities for self of therapist work. As the student engages in this work, they are better equipped to avoid both blending with and imposing their spiritual values on those of their clients (Carlson et al., 2014). Such is the focus on self as we move toward the connections between self, systems, and spirit.

Systems in the Living Web of Socio-Spirituality

Moving from self to systems expands our earlier discussion about cultural awareness/diversities and their connection to spirituality. In this living web of socio-spirituality, we begin identifying the various systems that are addressed in this methodology. Diversities constitute a need for cross-cultural responsiveness as the identity of the therapist is explored through privilege, power, and social justice (Poulsen & Allan, 2018).

Various intersectionalities inhabit self, systems, and spirit. A systemic view of the diversities of race, gender, sexual orientation, culture, class, ability, age, and socioeconomics understands that these diversities can function independently. Humans identify themselves through these diversities. Many naming schemes are determined by people with power and privilege who marginalize others. In turn, engagement through social justice is necessary to effect change for appropriate knowledge exploration.

So, in weaving together these systems, diversities are identified and responded to through social justice or a lack of social justice. The larger systems that social justice seeks to engage are typically ensconced in entities such as educational institutions, medical networks, mental health systems, legal structures, social services, and businesses. Dismantling and/or making systemic changes to such entities is incredibly difficult. A niche in family therapy is a systemic approach to understanding larger systems, which can be illustrated by this dimension of the living web.

Another approach to change is, of course, the various MFT modalities that embody these systemic principles. The chosen MFT modalities in this discussion are postmodern collaborative and narrative theories with an emphasis on narrative practice. Although not a strictly systemic approach, narrative found a home in MFT in its early years (Freedman, conversation, 2007). Instead of using more traditional systemic and integrative models, narrative practice in this methodology will be applied to change systemic marginalization.

Such a theoretical model can offer a broad critique of social injustice. In his critique of the colonization of western society, Akinyela offers a movement toward post-colonial therapy that is closely related to narrative therapy though four principles: (1) storytelling and witnessing: creating meaning through call and response;

(2) interpretation of meaning: discerning meaning through sharing of texts or stories; (3) a non-expert stance: the owner of the stories resists others' interpretation of the story; and (4) building upon testimonies of hope (Akinyela, 2002).

Story has an honored history in African culture. Stories are told at the palaver, where the community comes together for conversation about problems. As the community comes together to engage in problem-solving, stories are shared (Mucherera, 2010). Other narrative-related approaches to therapy from African culture emphasize the value of intercultural counseling. In contrast to multiculturalism, intercultural counseling emphasizes the uniqueness of different cultures. An intercultural phrase responds to us as humans: "Like no other, Like all others, Like some others" (Lartey, 2003). This nod to African heritage provides context to consider narrative practice as connected to a particular culture. Other non-western and marginalized populations here in the United States could utilize this cultural context given that dominant discourses both hinder and heal marginalized people.

Stories that make meaning from a person's story and stories of hope for a family or community are dimensions of narrative practice that will be utilized in this methodology. The family's stories or narratives that shape their intra-family lives as well as their public lives provide a unique way to infuse spirituality in storytelling. Several narrative practices can be used in therapy and supervision.[3] However, a general approach in narrative practice used here is the story and counter-story (Madigan, personal conversation, 2018). In story and counter-story, a client shares a story that has meaning for their lives. The story could be problem-saturated or nurturing. In either case, people always have stories that stand in contrast to the story they live by. And underneath any story are multiple stories. A single story does not exist. For example, a family theme encapsulated in a maxim can be a springboard to a family story. We turn to that storying process now.

In my counseling practice, I worked with a woman in her twenties named Jessie. She had a master's in computer science and yet worked in a low-paying customer service department. Jessie was unable to have the confidence to live out her vocational dreams. One day I asked, "If there were a cross-stitched motto hanging above your family's living room couch, what might it say?" Without hesitation, she replied, "It's too much trouble." We then thickened the family story behind this motto. Jessie said that her family was usually lethargic and never tried to change things. They just accepted whatever happened, with the results often prompting a family depression. Jessie indicated that she followed her family's example in usually thinking that she was powerless to change things in her life. We began to look for undiscovered stories in her life, moments when she departed from her family by acting with intention. Slowly, we began to thicken these thin stories into different narratives to strengthen her sense of agency. Jessie's thickened stories enabled her to set limits

[3] Several narrative practices can be used in therapy and systemic supervision such as externalizing, re-authoring or re-storying, the absent but implicit, or relative influence questioning. For a detailed description of these practices, see Stephen Madigan, *Narrative Theory*, APA series or the Dulwich Centre website at http://www.dulwichcentre.com.au. For the purposes of simplicity, this book uses the general practice of story and counter-story.

with her sisters who often took advantage of her, getting her to do all the care for their aging parents. Finally, Jessie was able to discover a counter-story that challenged the family story of "It's too much trouble."

A related but different understanding of spirituality in this book is Michael White's categorization: immanent, ascendant, and immanent-ascendant. Immanent refers to how a person relates to their self and identity as they explore their own deeper inner spaces. Ascendant spirituality focuses on those things, prioritizing them over the everyday, and connects with the Sacred in whatever way one conceives of that. Immanent-ascendant combines elements of the first two spiritualities; it includes an experience of the Divine deep within oneself as well as a relationship with a god that is transcendent. These are non-material, in contrast to the concept of spiritualities of the surface, or material spirituality. White defines the ways people construct their own identities in contrast to taking what is given to them as spiritualities of the surface (Hoyt & Combs, 1998).

This discussion will continue to use immanence and transcendence in a narrative while departing somewhat from White. Immanence and transcendence are drawn from a theological framework that has as its assumption the existence of God. Despite that orientation, immanence and transcendence also assumes a progressive theological position in a theistic frame that can invite atheist and agnostic people in conversation. According to this understanding of immanence and transcendence, both exist on a continuum, not in distinct categories as was the case for White. White's material spirituality figures in this discussion of immanence but also transcendence. To be human is to have that capacity for touching a transcendent God.

Both the categories move back and forth in a rather perspectival method, like that used by Hiltner (1958). When I wear my trifocals, for example, I have the option of different corrected visions. I do not take off my glasses and put on my readers. The reading function of my trifocals is there and available as I move my eyes to the field of vision I need. This is also true of this perspectival approach as applied to narrative practice (Coyle, 2014).

The desired outcome is for the family to create a future story of hope (Coyle, 2010). By creating new stories or narratives about their lives, families can have personal agency and put words to their spirituality (Pearson, 2017). As new narratives emerge for families, postmodern therapy and narrative theory convey a deep respect for diversity and socially constructed cultural practices (McDowell, 2015). This approach alone helps to connect our living web as a methodology with dominant public discourses on self and systems and their effects.

Another narrative practice not widely known here in the United States is collective narrative practice (Denborough, 2008; Denborough, 2018). I delved into this approach during its inauguration during my training at the Dulwich Center in 2008. This approach is influenced by both Foucault and Freire, through its notion is that much is to be learned from folk psychology—the wisdom of people from their native culture. Put quite simply, it focuses on gathering the voices of many so that the collective story is told from multiple points of view with no intent to distill these voices into one, unified whole.

Cheryl White and David Denborough of the Dulwich Centre became quite interested in how narrative practice might bring about social change. They both interviewed Paulo Freire in 1997. At that time, Freire talked with great passion about the deleterious effects of liberal capitalism. Freire died the following day (Denborough, 2008). The Freirean maxim, "Unity in diversity" is experienced in a chorus of voices. This approach integrates spirituality with effecting justice, according to everyday people rather than those who hold power. Examples of collective narrative practice will be discussed in a later chapter that focuses on community projects that engage social justice and spirituality.

Immanence and transcendence create the structure of the living web of socio-spirituality. As participants weave their stories of spiritual emptiness and social injustice through this web, connecting with their humanness as well as their capacity for a relationship with the divine, several outcomes are possible. One can experience despair or emerge with stories of hope. We now turn to that and the task of liberative theologies.

Spirit of the Living Web of Socio-Spirituality

Several theological approaches are possible in a postmodern systemic context. Traditional theologies can be integrated into the narrative frame. Furthermore, a common theological perspective that systemic practitioners integrate is narrative theology (Finger, 1983; Cook & Alexander, 2008). Narrative theology sees story as the link between people's own life stories and the Bible. This theological approach is based on the understanding that just as people use stories to make meaning of their everyday lives, so can they use stories in the Bible to see how the Biblical witness interacts with their everyday stories.

Using narrative theology in a limited way to encourage people to first identify their life stories is a path to spirituality. In a Christian context, favorite Scripture and Bible stories connect with changing stories of faith (Coyle, 2013). Religions such as Judaism, Islam, Buddhism, and Hinduism have similar literature in their sacred canons. Other narrative approaches focus on identifying stories of communities of faith, to enable change in communities of faith, and to lead communities of faith (Goleman, Finding Our Story, 2010a; Goleman, Living Our Story, 2010b; Goleman, Teaching Our Story, 2010c).

In my journey to find theological/spiritual connections, I have always been struck by the spiritual "feel" of narrative practice. And when I attend training in the use of stories in supervision and therapy, I always see a variety of people: ministers, therapists, community organizers, and many others. What might they all have in common? My very unscientific observation suggests that participants at narrative gatherings are enthralled with the power of story to make meaning out of life. They see this generating of meaning as a spiritual process in itself. Furthermore, they have a commitment to righting social wrongs.

In narrative practice, I participated in postgraduate training in 2010 at the Dulwich Centre, where I explored some of my thoughts with peers and faculty. Up to that point, my thoughts had focused on the potential value of linking liberation theologies and narrative. One day, I talked with David Epston to hear his thoughts on such a connection. I knew he was interested in working with South American narrative therapists. It seemed like a natural question. His response was simple and to the point. David indicated that he thought that liberation theology was a solid fit with narrative practice (Epston, personal conversation, 2010b).

Prior to that conversation and since then, I have practiced and researched that connection. Narrative theory is clearly the one MFT theory that has a political as well as religious theoretical foundation. Narrative has been characterized as having three overarching foci: politics, ethics, and poetics (Epston, Dulwich lecture, 2010a). Its political orientation connects to its demand that therapists and clients examine dominant discourses in society that lift up an expected norm. In other words, it freely sees social justice as part of therapy in the room. It brings to life the narrative maxim, "All personal problems have their origin in social concerns." So, this integrating of narrative with liberation theologies is a thickening of the stories that make meaning of people's lives. Both narrative therapy and liberative theologies participate in the quest for social justice (Coyle, 2014).

Our discussion will refer to liberation theologies such as Black, womanist, feminist, queer, *Mujerista*, and so forth as liberative theologies. This means that our essential dimension of self, system, and spirit engages with liberative theologies, and with the support of Freirean and Foucauldian philosophies. The three theological/philosophical methodologies challenge social injustices that marginalize many populations. Liberative theologies as well as narrative practice understand that privilege occurs in every life in both marginalized people and others in culturally dominant communities. The question is then not whether privilege exists, but what we do with the privilege we have.

Privilege is understood by liberative theologies as that human dimension where we hold the power that privilege provides. Those persons who marginalize others also marginalize themselves. They do not, however, often recognize this marginalization because they are intoxicated with a desire for power, which is deified in the human, political, and material worlds. Liberative theologies show that the way for all persons to escape oppression is identifying what blocks their compassion for others. Another major barrier to personal development is what stultifies the instinct to engage with the spiritual so that the transcendent can present different possibilities for those suffering social and spiritual injustices.

The first step in the spirit of the living web of socio-spirituality is to open the human self to the immanence of the world to then experience transcendence while a person is firmly grounded in the immanent. From a Christian perspective, then, Jesus is seen as the liberator of persons from oppressive political structures that block social justice. Of course, understanding Jesus as the liberator may limit access to this methodology if one is not a Christian. To expand this approach, one can turn to other religions to determine who or what deity offers freedom to humans. For an agnostic/atheistic perspective, a spirituality larger than self and relationships that offer a freeing of spirit can be utilized. One example is an environmental cause that infuses the grandeur of the universe into people.

One can also look to liberative theologies in a way that opens possibilities to both theistic views from other spiritualities and non-theistic spiritualities. To do that is to understand the "spirit" in self, systems, and spirit. Spirit can be understood as the Sustainer, or who or what endures. With its feminine word origin, Spirit offers an interesting connection to people with diversities who might be oppressed by masculinized images from dominant discourses. "Sustain" is also a word commonly used in narrative practice to refer to stories and communities that support people during hard times.

Combining Spirit as a compatible notion with feminist, womanist, and *mujerista* theologies emphasizes inclusivity and relationality. As the Spirit interacts with us, we become renewed to life (Poling, 2011). It is only when we are empowered in a generative way that we can truly be liberated or freed from oppressive structures. At this point, we are better able to pick up the gauntlet for the hard work of challenging systemic social injustice.

Here we find the powerful and freeing concept of hope. Hope emerges from the spectrum of immanence and transcendence. There it is: anticipation and sustenance. Hope is a concept that spans the spectrum between the forms and embodiment of self, systems, and spirit. Just as narrative practice asks, "What are your hopes and dreams?" hope draws on liberative theologies. Since we are rooted in the present, which is often rife with injustice, we also look to the future. As we re-story our spiritual narratives to find renewed power to not conform our lives to oppressive narratives, we engage in remembering past moments when we did experience the transcendent while in our human immanence.

Reweaving of the Living Web of Socio-Spirituality

In the previous chapter, we began the weaving of our living web. Now, we add to that structure and move to a case example. The building of the web began with a Freirean foundation of opening power and knowledge to those people who will live out their experiences. We move from the immanent level to the human. Then, we acknowledged that this web must be in touch with the everyday challenges all people experience, but especially the socially marginalized.

By weaving these threads into the web, the traditional notion of spirituality limited to an internalized sense is now thickened to include a call for the person to respond to social injustice. It is not possible to be socially responsive and not engage oneself. As the self is involved, the individual becomes aware of his or her limitations and aspirations. Awareness of self then motivates the person to look for glimpses of the transcendent.

Through the connection with transcendence or God, the individual believes that a future may be possible. Understandings from other religions about the transcendent can also be applied such as One, Allah, or Higher Power. Hope breaks through the despair of oppression. At this juncture, the individual can decide to look to the future and follow hope. Or the individual can decide to stay in oppression. Hope, then, is the springboard for stronger spirituality and the motivation to take on challenges. Communities of liberative theologies can sustain the hope that is gained through greater self-awareness and the inspiration of societal transformation. Following now is the complete living web of socio-spirituality.

Dynamic Description of the Living Web of Socio-Spirituality

The living web of socio-spirituality has self, systems, and spirit as its foundations. The practitioner who uses the model can start at any of these concepts. True to the systemic concept of equifinality, no prescribed entry point exists. Multiple avenues are present to engage with socio-spirituality. At the core of this model is the understanding that all humans are spiritual in an inclusive way. All humans participate in immanence—earthly rooted being—as well as transcendence, or unbounded spirituality. Both immanence and transcendence may be present in a person's stories at the same time.

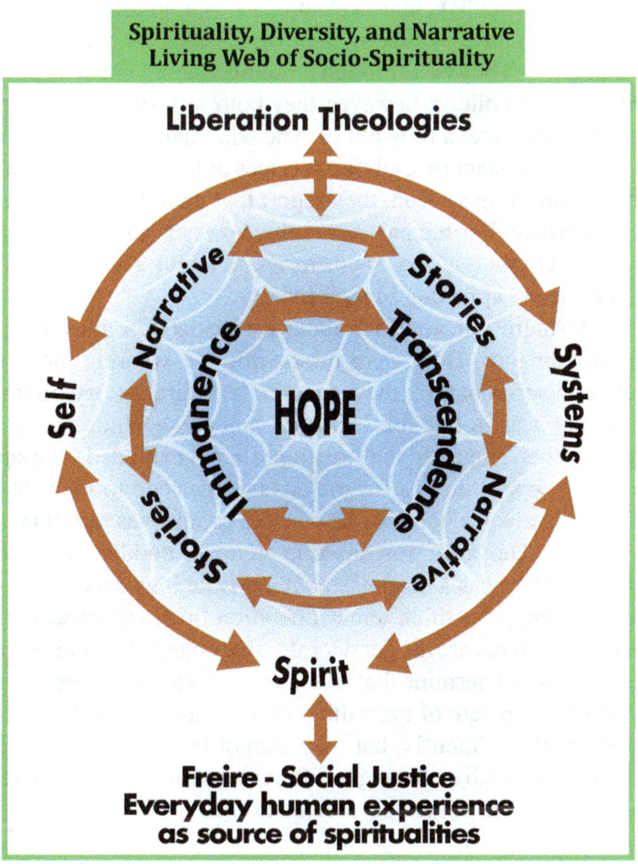

Fig. 4.1 Spirituality, diversity, narrative—living web of socio-spirituality

As the clinician alongside the client explores the client's narratives, attention is paid to the story and counter-story as well as the effects of those accounts on the client. Questions may emerge. How does this story create meaning for the client and their spirituality? Does the client experience immanence or transcendence primarily in their spirituality? Both? None? What are the client's hopes and dreams?

Girding all these facets of the model, the goal of social justice is intimately attached to hope that is in some ways the critical task of all therapy. For clients who never experience social justice, be it associated with race, culture, age, ability, gender identity, or sexual orientation, this model offers a therapeutic plan that progresses bit by bit. For clients who are privileged, this model demands that they become aware of social justice and involved in its realization. Let us now see an application of the living web of socio-spirituality.

Applying the Living Web of Socio-Spirituality

The Smiths are an African American couple who have been married for 3 years. Emma, 28 years old, is a CPA, and DeAndre, 29, is a middle-school teacher. They have no children. Both have worked in their professions for 5 years since receiving their master's degrees. They met through an online dating site. Both were raised in religious homes. Since college, however, they both self-identify as spiritual but not religious. At times, they feel a little out of sync with many of their friends who typically attend either Protestant or Catholic services at least a few times a year.

At your first counseling session, they report that up to this point, they have been happy in their marriage. For the past 6 months, however, they bicker and then have difficult resolving conflicts. They seem to argue about everything. You begin to explore what has been happening in their lives.

Emma and DeAndre tell you that about 6 months ago, they both applied for advancement at their jobs. Both were turned down. Exploring the possibilities of racial and gender discrimination, they each had a different story. Emma said that a man got the job she was in line for. DeAndre said that a White man got the job he wanted. As you further discussed the situation, Emma exploded. She said that in the field of accounting, opportunities for job advancement go to men. She lashed out saying that DeAndre always got what he wanted. Emma was raised in a community impacted by poverty. DeAndre was raised in an upper middle-class suburban community where his father was a headmaster at a private high school.

Spiritually, you begin to think about liberation theology, especially Black and womanist theologies. What are the gender roles that emerge for Emma and DeAndre? Our cultural discourses determine that Black women should do everything. They are assigned socially to take care of everything in the black family. In contrast, the cultural discourse for Black men is that they cannot be trusted. Liberative theology speaks to both discourses by offering a different discourse or narrative that speaks to freedom that is not constrained by societal norms.

In talking to them you hear that many of the issues that arose primarily concerned the couple and their different experiences with closeness in their families and previous relationships. You choose EFT to focus on their issues. However, you are wondering how to avoid missing any spiritual or diversity concerns. It is possible that those dimensions are affecting their lack of emotional closeness. In any case, you as the therapist may believe that connecting with a client's spirituality enables emotional closeness as well.

So, you look at the living web of socio-spirituality. Given the bookends of immanence and transcendence, you discern that the Smiths are always self-reflective. So, you talk with them about the ways in which each views what gives their life meaning. Emma and DeAndre both say that they dedicate themselves to social projects. Emma works as a volunteer at a center for abused children. DeAndre is an active member of the Sierra Club. Their families would say these foci are important but would never get personally involved. Emma and DeAndre both say that their involvement in advocacy gives them a sense of meaning and a connection to something beyond themselves.

You move forward with the living web as a visual guide. You can start at any point in the web diagram because it is a recursive process that understands that systemic interventions can punctuate a cycle at any point. So, given what you know about the Smiths, you begin to use their advocacy groups as an embodiment of the Freirean philosophy that encourages marginalized populations to have a voice.

For Emma, you and she discern the agency the abused children could have at the center. You then support Emma in her work with an exercise the children can do outside the therapy room at the community agency. For DeAndre, you and he think about how he might empower some of his peers in the group to connect with others who are local and excited about the environment. He moves forward outside the therapy room.

Periodically, you listen to Emma and DeAndre talk about the effect of their advocacy work as a form of spirituality. They both describe that their individual connections with others have unexpectedly helped them be more open to emotional closeness with each other. You then begin with their Emotionally Focused Therapy work, which seeks to develop emotional connection between partners. The EFT process brings them both to an emotional experience that flourishes with a desire to work with others outside the counseling room. Hope is flourishing. You begin to identify hope with them through the EFT process.

After a few months of therapy, Emma and DeAndre say they believe that they are ready to terminate therapy. As you talk with them, you become aware of the power of the socio-spirituality that enabled both Emma and DeAndre to work toward emotional closeness with each other through your preferred theoretical modality: EFT's emphasis on emotion can encourage the couple to share deeply with each other. The result can be as a deeper spirituality of their identity as both individuals and a couple. Their stronger relationship may then engage them more closely with the advocacies they endorse. In turn, they may experience spiritual meaning in their lives. You look over the living web of socio-spirituality. The impactful aspect of the web for you and your clients was immanence, which led to hope based on the Freirean foundation. Despite using EFT, you, as a therapist, could say that their individual stories were co-created through a process of story and counter-story. Their stories of distance became a story of connection.

Finding Spirituality in Social Justice Across Mental Health Disciplines

All mental health disciplines are interested in some way in spiritual experiences. The ways in which spirituality shows itself in each profession varies according to its focus. Psychologists and family psychologists focus on individual psychology that fits with families. In using the living web of socio-spirituality, psychologists have the unique focus of looking in detail at the pathological contribution to social injustice. Studying critical race theory and its psychological foundations could be a contribution to the further development of this model.

Social workers focus on the well-being of communities and the people who live there. Social injustice is the everyday experience of the social worker in the community. Many times, social workers work with community organizers to find ways to combat these injustices. A challenge to such social workers would be to interview community residents to find out what sustains them through these injustices. Using the living web as a background to their thinking could further develop spirituality as a counter to injustice.

Professional counselors may work in community agencies or private practice. In both the settings, it may be difficult to work on both sides of social justice and spirituality. Using the living web of socio-spirituality may offer a model that gives the clinician an integrative approach in counseling with clients. By identifying the strength of each profession, human life can improve through a heightened sense of spirituality.

Self, Systems, and Spirit Practice

Looking at the Living Web of Socio-Spirituality

This practice is designed for peer groups of students and/or supervisors. According to pre-assigned rotation, participants bring a clinical case for discussion and supervision. As an alternative, pre-practicum students can select a clinical case from a systemic family therapy textbook.

The facilitator distributes copies of Fig. 4.1: Living web of socio-spirituality to all participants. The session may begin with the discussion of this chapter. An alternate approach is for the facilitator to summarize the chapter contents. Group participants identify aspects of the living web of socio-spirituality in the clinical case. Then, the facilitator asks sub-groups or individual participants the following questions:

1. What aspects of the living web of socio-spirituality catches your attention?
2. How might you further develop that attention catching aspect?
3. How does that attention catching aspect apply to the clinical case?
4. How would you change the living web of socio-spirituality?

References

Akinyela, M. (2002). De-colonizing our lives: Divining a post-colonial therapy. *International Journal of Narrative Therapy & Community Work, 2*, 32–43. https://doi.org/10.1002/anzf.1041

Almeida, R., Hernandez-Wolfe, P., & Tubbs, C. (2011). Cultural equity: Bridging the complexity of social identities with therapeutic practices. *International Journal of Narrative Therapy & Community Work, 3*, 43–56.

Aponte, H. J. (2016). The person-of-the-therapist model on the use of self in therapy: The training philosophy. In H. J. Aponte & K. Kissil (Eds.), *The person of the therapist training model: Mastering the use of self* (pp. 1–13). Routledge.

Aponte, H. J., & Kissil, K. (Eds.). (2016). *The person of the therapist training model: Mastering the use of self*. Routledge.

Ashbourne, L. M., Fife, K., Ridley, M., & Gaylor, E. (2016). Supporting the development of novice therapists. In S. St. George & D. Wulff (Eds.), *Family therapy as socially transformative practice* (pp. 41–55). Springer International. https://doi.org/10.1007/978-3-319-29188-8

Carlson, T. S., McGeorge, C. R., & Toomey, R. B. (2014). Establishing the validity of the spirituality in clinical training scale: Measuring the level of integration of spirituality and religion in family therapy training. *Contemporary Family Therapy, 36*(2), 310–326.

Cook, R., & Alexander, I. (Eds.). (2008). *Interweavings: Conversations between narrative therapy and Christian faith*. CreateSpace Books.

Coyle, S. M. (2010). Spiritual narratives: Hope and healing through stories of faith. In Ellens, H. (Ed.) *The healing power of spirituality: Personal spirituality, 1*, 189–201.

Coyle, S. M. (2013). *Restoring your faith*. John Hunt Publishing.

Coyle, S. M. (2014). *Uncovering spiritual narratives: Using story in pastoral care and ministry*. Augsburg Fortress Press.

Dadras, I., & Daneshpour, M. (2018). Social justice implications for MFT: The need for cross-cultural responsiveness. In S. S. Poulsen & R. Allan (Eds.), *Cross-cultural responsiveness & systemic therapy* (pp. 1–20). Springer.

Denborough, D. (2008). *Collective narrative practice*. Dulwich Centre Publications.

Denborough, D. (2018). *Do you want to hear a story?: Adventures in collective narrative practice*. Dulwich Centre Publications.

Epston, D. (2010a). *Lecture*. Dulwich Centre.

Epston, D. (2010b). *Personal conversation*. Dulwich Centre.

Finger, T. (1983). What is narrative theology? *Christianity Today, 27*(15), 84. Retrieved from https://www.christianitytoday.com/ct/1983/104ctober-7/current-religious-thought-what-is-narrative-theology.html

Freedman, J. (2007). *Personal conversation*. Evanston Family Therapy Center.

Golemon, L. A. (2009). *Living our story: Narrative leadership and congregational culture*. Alban Institute.

Golemon, L. A. (2010a). *Finding our story: Narrative leadership and congregational change*. Rowman & Littlefield.

Golemon, L. A. (2010b). *Teaching our story: Narrative leadership and pastoral formation*. Rowman & Littlefield.

Hiltner, S. (1958). *Preface to pastoral theology*. Abingdon Press.

Hoyt, M. F., & Combs, G. (1998). On ethics and the spiritualities of the surface – A conversation with Michael White. In M. F. Hoyt (Ed.), *Constructive therapies* (Vol. 2, pp. 33–59). Guilford Press.

Kissil, K., Carneiro, R., & Aponte, H. J. (2018). Beyond duality: The relationship between the personal and the professional selves of the therapist in the person of the therapist training. *Journal of Family Psychotherapy, 29*(1), 71–86. https://doi.org/10.1080/08975353.2018.1416244

Lartey, E. Y. (2003). *In living color: An intercultural approach to pastoral care and counseling*. Jessica Kingsley Publishers.

Madigan, S. (2018). *Lecture, Narrative questions*. Vancouver School for Narrative Therapy.

McDowell, T. (2015). *Applying critical social theories to family therapy practice*. Springer.

McGeorge, C. R., Carlson, T. S., & Toomey, R. B. (2014). The intersection of spirituality, religion, sexual orientation, and gender identity in family therapy training: An exploration of students' beliefs and practices. *Contemporary Family Therapy, 36*(4), 497–506. https://doi.org/10.1007/s10591-014-9312-8

Mucherera, T. N. (2010). *Meet me at the palaver: Narrative pastoral counselling in postcolonial contexts*. Cascade.

Mutter, K. F., & Neves, C. M. (2010). A dialogical model for engagin spirituality in therapy. *Clinical Social Work Journal, 38*(2), 164–173.

Pearson, A. (2017). Working with religious and spiritual experience in family therapy: Manna for the journey. *Australian and New Zealand Journal of Family Therapy, 38*(1), 43–60. https://doi.org/10.1002/anzf.1202

Poling, J. N. (2011). *Rethinking faith: A constructive practical theology*. Fortress Press.

Poulsen, S. S., & Allan, R. (Eds.). (2018). *Cross-cultural responsiveness & systemic therapy: Personal & clinical narratives*. Springer.

St. George, S., & Wulff, D. (2016). Family therapy + social Justice + daily practice = transforming therapy. In S. St. George & D. Wulff (Eds.), *Family therapy as socially transformative practice* (pp. 1–8). Springer.

Waldegrave, C., Tamasese, K., Tuhaka, F., & Campbell, W. (2003). *Just therapy—A journey: A collection of papers from the just therapy team, New Zealand*. Dulwich Centre Publications.

Chapter 5
Spirituality in Individual, Tandem, and Group Supervision

Socio-spirituality lays the foundation for a spiritually integrated supervision. In this approach, supervisor and supervisee recognize the effect of self, system, and spirit in developing clients' stories. Social justice and spirituality in response to all diversities lifts the immanence of human experience. Spirituality also offers people the possibility of experiencing transcendence with God, One, or a big uplifting experience. As immanence and transcendence engage with each other, hope may emerge from dire situations. Spiritually aware supervision is necessary if students are to experience the full range of spirituality and engage with their clients in that reality. Supervision without that spiritual awareness cannot produce that transformation.

Challenges of Spirituality in Supervision

Focusing on the uniqueness of spirituality in supervision is a daunting task. A review of supervisory literature since the 1990s yields the general impression that addressing spirituality in supervision is desirable (Hull et al., 2016; Russell-Chapin & Chapin, 2011). Spirituality is often understood as a diversity that is vital in a client's life (Miller, 1999). This notion of spirituality also being a diversity in addition to more traditional areas such as race, gender, etc. expands our understanding of spirituality. It thickens spirituality as a lens through which all diversities can be viewed.[1]

At the same time, a review of MFT literature since the 1990s offers few references about the "how" of addressing spirituality in supervision. It sounds much like, "do what I say, not what I do." My suspicion is that many MFT supervisors do not

[1] "Thicken" is a term used in narrative practice that describes a way of richly describing a story or concept.

S. M. Coyle, *Spirituality in Systemic Family Therapy Supervision and Training*, Focused Issues in Family Therapy, https://doi.org/10.1007/978-3-030-92369-3_5

feel competent enough to provide such supervision. It may be that examining one's own spirituality could support a supervisor's confidence in addressing their work with trainees.

What is the answer to this dilemma? It seems to me that a beginning is to provide some learnable skills for supervisors. Informative and compelling books and articles have addressed systemic supervision. It seems likely that improving supervisors' competence in spiritually integrated supervision is a neglected basic skill. Improving a supervisor's relationship with their own spirituality will help make them more likely to focus on spirituality in supervision. The "how" involves both clinical skills and connecting with one's own spirituality.

Yet there is a dearth of MFT literature on spirituality in supervision. I believe that spirituality is often understood by systemic therapists as a rigid belief system that allows for little growth for clients who have a different worldview than traditional spirituality and religion. This viewpoint ignores an understanding of spirituality that encourages personal freedom and growth in service to the liberation of all people. Such an inclusive perspective on spirituality would fit well with MFT's view of the individual as connected to family and larger systems that encourage differences of opinion.

Receptiveness to Spirituality in Supervision

In a seminal study by Prest et al., 66.6% of MFT students expressed interest in learning ways to integrate spirituality into their clinical work, while 92.2% said they had not received any training in their programs on how to integrate spirituality into their clinical practice (1996). Another study focusing on AAMFT members found that 53% of participants believed that spirituality needs to be a part of MFT training. At the same time, 76% of these participants said that they had received no such training (Carlson et al., 2002). These studies are seminal studies that are often cited in systemic literature. Since this time, our society has experienced seismic paradigm shifts including 9/11, Black Lives Matter, Me Too, LGBTQ rights, COVID-19 global pandemic. Updating such studies would include generations who live in a different world than 1996 or 2002.

Gauging general receptivity to spiritually integrated supervision, Carlson et al. compared beliefs about the importance of including spirituality in MFT practice between AAMFT members and MFT faculty in an interesting study (2011). AAMFT members ranked the importance of having spirituality in their personal lives higher than did faculty members. At the same time, 81.7% of faculty members still found spirituality to be important in their lives, compared to 95% of clinical members (Carlson et al., 2011).

Interestingly, both the groups were less certain about directly addressing spirituality in clinical work and integrating spirituality in MFT training programs than in their personal lives (Carlson et al., 2011). It is unclear what this uncertainty indicates. My strong suspicion is that, in general, MFTs have not received significant training about spirituality in their programs. It is understandable that most therapists and academics are not comfortable practicing in an area in which they are not confident. The scant MFT literature that addresses spirituality in supervision suggests that developing an understanding and application of spirituality would be desirable (Russell-Chapin & Chapin, 2011).

Several major supervisory textbooks do not include chapters on spirituality in supervision or go into detail about the "how" of supervision that integrates spirituality (Jordan, 2016; Lee & Nelson, 2021; Todd & Storm, 2014; Storm & Todd, 2003; Vetere & Sheehan, 2017). A book on systemic supervision, edited by Vetere and Sheehan, approaches supervision from a postmodern perspective (2017). It does not address spirituality in supervision as a topic. Its approach, however, describes a non-hierarchical model of supervision that would be quite compatible with spiritual values. The importance of spirituality as a key theme in supervision and training has been stressed in peer-reviewed journal articles (Carlson & Erickson, 2001; Coffey, 2003; Miller, 1999; Miller et al., 2004; Prest et al., 1999; Stander et al., 1994). But supervision texts that are often used in the AAMFT Supervision Course do not specifically address spirituality in supervision.

The question that emerges is why no significant MFT literature describes how to integrate spirituality in supervision. The existing literature advocates for including spirituality in a training program. Authors describe two MFT courses in their institutions emphasizing spirituality (Patterson et al., 2000; Williams-Reade et al., 2018). No significant MFT literature, however, describes a spiritually integrated approach to supervision with thoughts on and methods for how to do that supervision. Supervision focusing on multiculturalism appears in a robust literature, yet the place of spirituality in multiculturalism is virtually ignored. There is no emphasis on the "how" of spirituality in supervision.

How is it that MFT as field is in this position? Several possibilities come to mind. Could it be that the MFT field believes that spirituality in supervision is not important? The literature in MFT belies that question. Could it be that MFT supervisors believe spirituality just automatically happens? MFT supervisors do not believe that is true in other supervision areas, as evidenced by the credentialing of the AAMFT Approved Supervisor. Could it be that MFT supervisors are unsure about how to integrate spirituality in supervision? This last question is what our discussion will pursue.

Current Approaches to Spirituality in Supervision

Current approaches to spirituality in supervision in MFT literature focus exclusively and explicitly on the implications of research studies on spirituality and supervision. Other approaches may examine the religious dimension of spirituality and religion, such as the effect of one's doctrinal beliefs from his or her religion on personal everyday life (Erickson & Carlson, 2014). The typical discussion, however, says that it is desirable to acknowledge spirituality, but without clear directives.

Scholars stress the importance of providing a receptive environment in which to address spiritual issues in supervision. Harris encourages supervisors to explore what spiritualities underlie MFT theories (1998). This approach in supervision as well as in general MFT training could be connected to encouraging students to thoroughly vet their own worldviews and how that worldview connects and does not connect with their favorite MFT theories.

Engaging in this type of phenomenological approach to spirituality could certainly lay a sound foundation for developing detailed skills in the practice of spirituality in students' clinical practice (Miller & Ivey, 2006). Systemic supervisors need to focus on the importance for students to be spiritually literate and spiritually sensitive if their supervisees are to engage in learning the skills around spiritually integrated practice. Haug stresses the need for supervisors to create a receptive environment where they encourage their students to discuss spiritual issues (1998). Only if supervisors convey to students the necessity of respecting their client's spirituality, can supervision address the whole gamut of the client's experience. Some of the concerns that may emerge for supervisees is the fear that spirituality and/or religion may be oppressive to their clients. Opening generative approaches to spirituality in clinical practice may address and allay students' fears.

First, we turn to some very practical approaches to spirituality in supervision that can be applied in a review of six spiritual assessment tools from Hodge (2005). The first assessment tool is the Initial Brief Spiritual Assessment. It has the following five questions: (1) I was wondering if you consider spirituality or religion to be a personal strength? (2) In what ways does your spirituality help you to cope with the difficulties you encounter? (3) Are there certain spiritual beliefs and practices that you find particularly helpful in dealing with problems? (4) I was also wondering if you attend a church or some other spiritual community? (5) Do resources exist in your faith community that might be helpful to you? (Hodge, 2005).

These five assessment questions are designed to use with clients in a counseling session and not in supervision. There are, however, some ways to modify these questions to use in supervision with a supervisee. Of course, supervision in its truest form is overseeing the way the supervisee works with the client, not imposing our clinical styles on the client. With that in mind, the following questions modified from Hodge (2005) can be directed to the supervisee: (1) I am wondering if your spirituality or approach to spirituality affects your work with your clients? In what ways might it be helpful? In what ways might it be a hindrance? (2) In what situations might you suggest to clients a spiritual resource or community of faith? Would you ever do this? The supervisor and supervisee could then engage in a discussion around these questions. Depending on the answers, the supervisor might assess the need to refer the student to focus on his or her self of therapist issues. The next step would be to consider five more complete spiritual assessments regarding the student's work with the client and your supervision of the student.

Such possibilities include a spiritual history as a verbal interview and spiritual life maps, spiritual genograms, spiritual ecomaps, and spiritual ecograms (Table 5.1).

To adapt a spiritual history to supervision would require the supervisee's permission. In individual supervision, it would be less difficult to manage the depth and

Table 5.1 Supervisory assessment—modified Hodge (2005)

Initial brief spiritual assessment	Supervisory spiritual assessment	Connection with living web of socio-spirituality
1. I was wondering if you consider spirituality or religion to be a personal strength?	1. I am wondering if your spirituality or approach to spirituality affects your work with your clients?	1. Supervisee/supervisor spiritual stories connect with client through awareness of immanence/transcendence
2. In what ways does your spirituality help you to cope with the difficulties you encounter?	2. In what ways might it be helpful?	2. LWSS understands spiritual stories focused on the social context of supervision to counter social injustice
3. Are there certain spiritual beliefs and practices that you find particularly helpful in dealing with problems?	3. In what ways might it be hindrance?	3. Freire's understanding of oppression uncovers ways knowledge needs to be shared in order to be liberating
4. I was also wondering if you attend a church or some other spiritual community?	4. In what situations might you suggest to clients a spiritual resource or community of faith?	4. Acknowledges the socio context that connects with spirituality and lives of supervisee and client
5. Do resources exist in your faith community that might be helpful to you?	5. Would you ever do this?	5. Supervisees' values can uncover their spiritual stories that lift up oppression
Citation:	Citation:	Citation:
Hodge, D. R. (2005). Spiritual assessment in marital and family therapy: A methodological framework for selecting from among six qualitative assessment tools. *Journal of Marital and Family Therapy, 31*(4), 341–356. https://doi.org/10.1111/j.1752-0606.2005.tb01575.x	Coyle, S. M. (2021). *Supervisory Assessment* (modified Hodge, 2005). IBSA	Coyle, S. M. (2021). *Supervisory Living Web of Socio-Spirituality*

detail than in tandem supervision.[2] Assessing a spiritual history with both supervisees would require a great deal of trust between peers and the supervisor. Spiritual histories are generally completed toward the beginning of the treatment. This living documentation gives the therapist an overview of the client's life. It seems that in

[2] Tandem supervision in marriage and family includes one supervisor with two supervisees.

tandem supervision, it would be more appropriate to move forward with some tentativeness.

Among the other graphic designs for assessing spirituality, the spiritual genogram is well referenced in MFT literature for working with clients (Frame, 2001; Hodge, 2001; McGoldrick et al., 2020; Şahin, 2017; Wiggins, 2009). Using a genogram gives the therapist an overall visual view of the different generations of a family and connections such as biological, medical, emotional, and spiritual. I believe it also lends itself well to assessing the ways in which the supervisee connects to their client's spirituality. MFT students are generally accustomed to sharing their genograms with one another in groups. Thus, doing this in tandem and group supervision seems to be a natural transition.

As the supervisee creates their spiritual genogram, the supervisor will then process the information with the individual supervisee and supervisees in tandem and group supervision. The spiritual genogram is not, however, a "standalone" as a supervisee's information. Basic questions can be used with several types of genograms in the field (Frame, 2001; Hodge, 2001; McGoldrick et al., 2020; Şahin, 2017; Wiggins, 2009). After the information is processed, the supervisor would then offer the following questions: (1) As you look at your spiritual genogram, what themes might help or hinder your work with your client's concerns? (2) Are there some themes that might have a significant effect on your client's spirituality?

Then, the option exists to focus on the isomorphic dynamics among persons in the supervisory group: (1) How do you envision your spiritual dynamics affecting your peers and supervisor? (2) Are there some spiritual themes with me as your supervisor and your peers that could adversely affect your learning? Asking such questions might be too intrusive, or on the other end of spectrum, very conducive to in-depth learning. The supervisor will need to proceed in a carefully constructed environment of safety and respect. Another option is for the supervisor to share his or her own spiritual genogram. Some supervisors would understand this option to be appropriate; others would see it as sharing too much personal information. Of course, all spiritual genograms can be most fully understood in the context of the supervisee's general genogram.

Understandings from the living web of socio-spirituality can be applied in addition to the aforementioned questions. The first step in creating a socio-spirituality genogram would be to focus on the themes of spiritual stories that the client and supervisee see as being foundational to who they are. Both the supervisee in working with the client and the supervisor in working with the supervisee would ask the question "What is a formative spiritual experience that you know is true for you?" (Coyle, 2013).

The next step would be to expand that story into understandings of family as well as one's community with a question such as "What family members share with you in that spiritual story?" Here one would identify the genealogical information that fits with this spiritual story.

As the interviewer moves forward, the intent is to expand the client/supervisee's spiritual stories into social justice. The person's life as depicted on the genogram is firmly situated in one's community and social location. A question could be "In what ways is your spiritual story supported or oppressed by your community and who you are?"

In moving the genogram forward, the living web of socio-spirituality then looks at how possibilities of immanence and transcendence in the client/supervisee's life. A question could be "In what ways do you practice immanence in everyday life?" Then, the question is followed up with "In what ways do you recognize experiences of transcendence?"

One would share a brief definition of immanence and transcendence to the client/supervisee. Immanence is the everyday day spiritual experiences that support you in your spirituality. Then, transcendence is the spiritual experience that lifts one up to an awareness that is not an everyday experience.

As these questions are implemented and reviewed, a completed genogram based on the living web of socio-spirituality might look like as given in Fig. 5.1.

Moving forward in the current view of spirituality in supervision, some research studies have outcomes that can be applied to spirituality in supervision. One example is Miller and Ivey's research on spirituality, gender, and supervisory style in supervision (2006). Miller created the Spiritual Issues in Supervision Scale specifically for this study. Each item focuses on an area that may be addressed in supervision. The following issues that emerge in supervision are as follows: (1) gender and identity, (2) acceptance, (3) family role, (4) morality, (5) diversity, (6) value of life, and (7) supervisory process. Examples include: "In the area of grief, loss, and death"; "With self of therapist issues, including your own family-of-origin issues"; "In the area of identity"; and "With issues concerning contraception or fertility" (Miller et al., 2004).

The focus of the study was to determine whether there was a correlation between supervisory style and the gender of supervisor/supervisee in determining the likelihood of supervisees discussing spirituality with their supervisors. The findings indicate that students are more apt to discuss spiritual issues in supervision with same-sex supervisors when there is also a compatible supervision style (Miller & Ivey, 2006). These findings suggest that it is important to have a comfortable supervisory relationship for students to feel free to discuss spirituality in supervision.

Miller and Ivey further our understanding of discussing spirituality in supervision by focusing on a relational dimension of supervision. Spirituality emerges out of relationships and interactions with people. Thus, the Spiritual Issues in Supervision Scale suggests that spirituality is a construct that can be addressed within supervision. Supervisors could use the Spiritual Issues in Supervision Scale (SISS) as an instrument to better understand how to engage a conversation with supervisors about what enables a discussion about spirituality to occur. It may be true, as the authors indicate, that addressing spirituality in scholarly areas in the field, more MFTs will feel comfortable practicing spirituality in supervision (Miller & Ivey, 2006).

We have discussed the importance of utilizing practical instruments for addressing spirituality in supervision such as spiritual histories and spiritual genograms. Moving forward from the implications of the SISS research study, an initial step in implementing a discussion of spirituality in supervision is for both supervisors and

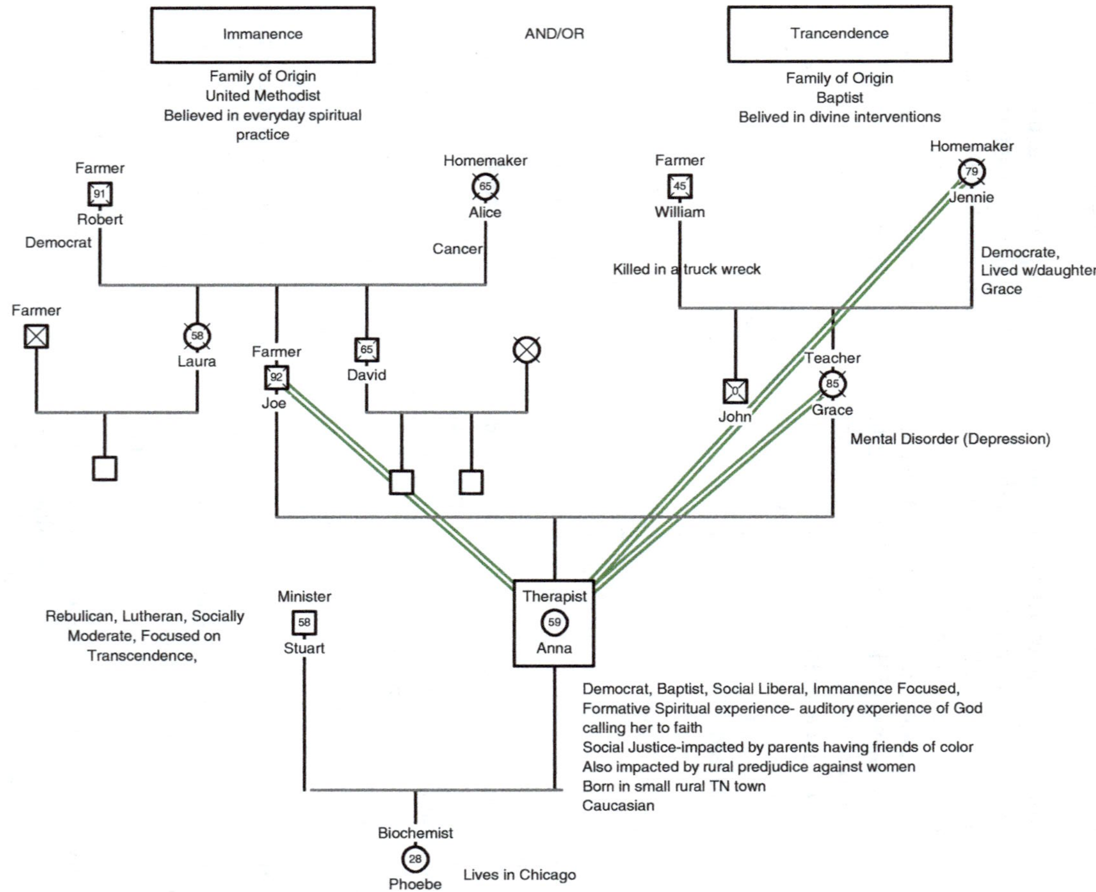

Fig. 5.1 Socio-spirituality genogram

supervisees to feel comfortable about that process. To further develop current supervisory practices, it could be helpful to convene a meeting with supervisors that focuses on a collaborative learning approach. Methods and techniques that can be used are curiosity, reflexive inquiry, deconstruction, outsider witness practices, and re-authoring approaches (Neden et al., 2011).

After discussing this process with supervisors, a modified discussion can occur with students. Another set of reflective questions, offered by Allen-Wilson, serve as a review of the spiritual process through reflective questions that focus on the following: (1) criteria for including spiritual questions in counseling session, (2) ways to discover conflicts in the intersectionalities of diverse concerns, (3) how the supervisees' spiritual history helps and hinders the clinical session, (4) ways that spiritual interventions helps and hinders the clinical process, (5) what might the supervisee do differently, and how can the supervisee monitor self of therapist issues regarding spirituality (2016). Such a process with isomorphic implications could lay solid groundwork for integrating spirituality with the program's supervisory experiences. Finally, it may be possible to share the discussions with both supervisors and supervisees in a community meeting. Such a community meeting would include supervisor and supervisees in a structured discussion with clear guidelines for conversation.

Spirituality in Collective Narrative Practice Group Supervision

I became acquainted with collective narrative practice when I trained at the Dulwich Centre in Adelaide, South Australia. This practice is a derivative of narrative therapy created by Cheryl White and David Denborough. The reader can delve into its richness through the writings of Denborough and by visiting the Dulwich website (Denborough, 2008, 2018). Collective narrative intends to create unity out of diversity and honor the multiple voices that experience both suffering and joy from dominant discourses. One of the most familiar collective narrative practices in narrative circles is The Tree of Life. This practice was created by David Denborough and Ncazelo Ncube-Milo in response to the genocide in Rwanda (Denborough, 2008). Since then, the Tree of Life has been adapted to various populations and contexts.

Here I maintain the structure and drawing of the Tree of Life. On a large piece of newsprint, usually a Post-it Super Sticky Easel Pad, I draw a large picture of a tree. The roots of the tree are shown as if viewing a cut away view of the earth with large roots. Moving up from the roots, the surface of the ground is depicted. Then, the tree is drawn with a very large trunk. Finally moving to the sky, the branches on the tree are show with leaves all over the tree. Some of the branches and leaves can be enlarged to make room for later descriptions. Finally, colorful pieces of fruit are drawn on the branches.

These questions being asked can be modified to focus on the group's experience of spirituality in group supervision. This can be a group of supervisors who would like to expand their personal connections to supervisory spirituality. Or it can be a group of supervisees who are eager to delve deeply into their personal connections with spirituality. The process takes a while to properly execute. So, it could be spread over a semester-long group supervision of students or a peer group of supervisors. It also lends itself to a retreat experience.

Participants need a poster-size sheet of paper and non-permanent markers in different colors so as not to deface tables. Everyone is directed to draw a large tree that includes the visible roots of the tree, the ground, a tree with a trunk, branches, leaves, and fruit.

The following are directions modified to address the effect of spirituality in supervision on the participants. The facilitator begins: "Today we are creating a Tree of Life on which we will show how we connect personally with spirituality in supervision. Some of us may experience this as an enriching experience; others as an unsafe experience, while still others may experience it as not needed in our supervisory learning experience. All these responses are acceptable. You received a written description of the process last week. Are there questions before we proceed?" The facilitator waits for people to respond and engage in a discussion. After a reasonable amount of time, the facilitator describes the following parts of the exercise.

The parts of the Tree of Life are explained in response to a question posed to the group about spirituality in supervision. The facilitator says, "Our question for this exercise is an important one as we ponder our learning about spirituality in supervision. How is our learning and experiencing spirituality in supervision affected by our origins, daily life, qualities, skills, hopes, dreams, and gifts from others?" Participants then create their Tree of Life according to the different parts of the tree.

The roots of the tree represent where you come from, family history, favorite songs about life, and a favorite place at home. We then move to the ground. The ground represents where you presently live and your daily activities. The trunk focuses on personal qualities and skills. Moving to the branches of the tree, these represent hopes, dreams, and wishes for the future. Then, we turn to the leaves of the tree, which represent people, pets, and things that are most important to you, either living or dead. Books and ideas can be represented, even a favorite toy from childhood. Finally, the fruit of the tree represents gifts that others have given you to nurture you on your journey (Denborough, 2008).

After each participant has drawn the tree, all the group members engage in a narrative round of telling, retelling, and retelling of the retelling of the story depicted on the tree. Each person shares their story by pointing out different parts of the tree. That individual sits down to listen to the retelling of his or her story. A group member volunteers to share what he or she sees in the story on the tree. Then, the facilitator asks the storyteller and creator of the tree to respond to how he or she experienced hearing the retelling of the story. Everyone in the group takes a turn. The trees are stuck in a group on the wall.

Every group member looks at the trees on the wall. The facilitator asks them: "Who do you think we are as trees together in the same forest? What are our qualities and challenges as we engage in a spiritual process in supervision? How do we gain strength during storms in our professional and personal lives together as a forest?"

The closing exercise can vary. Creating a ritual can be a powerful connector with group members as they continue a vulnerable journey of self and group discovery. My suggestion is that a group gather before this experience to create a ritual. Ideas can be gathered from the Denborough book as well as skimming "Friday Afternoons at Dulwich Centre" on their website. Loftis presents a ritual for a young client that takes the liturgical practices he learned in church and revises them to fit in the clinical setting. The web presentation, "Living in Stories: Embodiment in Therapy in Liturgical Practice," presents ways to apply liturgical practice to everyday life so that clients can overcome hurdles (2016). This type of collective narrative practice can be applied to clinical practice and even modified for group supervision.

I have led many groups in this exercise, from theological school faculty, graduate M.Div., and MFT students to MFT supervisors. Never are people neutral about the process. Feedback has overwhelmingly been not quite positive but grateful for the experience. It draws forth in people the immanence of spirituality in a way that connects humans to our earthly existence while offering transcendent hope in our futures. Inherently spiritual, it gives us all an "experience near" to quote Michael White on the process that connects to the earth and the heavens. The Tree of Life opens us all to the many diversities we hold and the richness of those multicultural experiences that both enrich and challenge.

Spiritual Integration Through Diversity in Supervision

So far, we have discussed myriad challenges in addressing spirituality in supervision. And to look back at the discussion in previous chapters, I would like to highlight some threads from scholarly perspectives on how spirituality fits with the "kitchen sink" diversities in the MFT CC 1.2.1 (MFT Core Competencies, 2004). Several authors contend that spirituality is indeed intimately connected with cultural dimensions of life (Holmberg et al., 2020; Marterella & Brock, 2008; Pearson, 2017).

Stander et al. authored an article on the importance of spirituality in the world of MFT as the field was beginning to give voice to spirituality (1994). Interestingly, the authors identified culture as a framework for religious issues. In the years since, others have also regarded spirituality and cultural issues as having a natural connection to MFT (Pearson, 2017). In looking at the MFT CC 1.2.1, religion and spirituality are the "invisible" diversity listed. It is possible that spirituality's non-tangible qualities help explain the lack of MFT literature. Perhaps the social sciences and the world of MFT look askance at an invisible diversity. But it is also a diversity that transforms the words of the therapy session into a living entity (Coyle, 2007). By understanding the heart and soul of what sustains all the multiplicities of humans, only then can MFTs embrace even more visible diversities such as race, age, and gender.

It is therefore dispiriting to believe that MFT can be content with not only a scarcity of literature on spirituality but also a belief in separating it from other dimensions of MFT. I thus lift the concept of socio-spirituality as an opportunity to weave societal diversities with spirituality. In this way, MFT can connect immanence and transcendence as a means of connecting human souls with the earthly and the heavenly.

I believe that going forward with this integration can theoretically serve not only the field of MFT but also the families for whom we care. Furthermore, we can develop spiritual competencies as discussed in an earlier chapter by supporting a socio-spiritual model of supervision. Thus, any multicultural competence in our field must also connect with being spiritually competent (Breunlin et al., 2014; Estrada, 2018). Few would question the appropriateness of addressing spirituality in a faith-based environment (Todd & Storm, 2014). And yet MFT training programs are situated primarily in secular university settings. So, we need to have spirituality, especially in supervision, that can draw from each student's unique spiritual resources.

Multicultural sensitivity is already well-established in the MFT field as an essential awareness and skill for students to acquire. At the same time, some MFT practitioners and scholars seem hesitant to introduce spirituality into training programs. I do believe that a great deal of this reluctance is related to simply not knowing how to do spiritual integration. Also, it is reasonable to expect that some of this hesitance may be related to fears that spirituality or anything remotely connected to religion may have some oppression connected to it. Perhaps, MFTs do not want spirituality to run amok. Certainly, many people have had negative experiences with religion. And welcoming spirituality in training programs may connect with those fears. Admittedly, destructive things have been done in the name of religion. That is not what we need to have in MFT training programs.

In training programs, then, a certain degree of caution is wise when integrating spirituality. Therefore, linking spirituality to a social justice and diversity ethos can balance spirituality with earthly concerns while offering the hope of transcendence to both clients and students. Spirituality is often understood as a diversity that is vital in a client's life (Miller, 1999). To that end, a model that integrates spirituality and diversity, introduced in earlier chapters, is presented here with a specialization of how it works in supervision.

Still the question lingers as to "why" MFT has not decisively responded to address spirituality in supervision given that the field has gone through multicultural supervision for the other diversities in the MFT CC 1.2.1.[3] We may never have the empirical answer until a serious research study is implemented. But in the interim, hundreds of MFTs graduate from training programs with no serious reflection in their supervision regarding spirituality. The time is now to propose a specific model for integrating spirituality in supervision. Then, practitioners and scholars can respond to that model, refining it and offering alternative approaches in supervision.

[3] Available at https://www.coamfte.org/Documents/COAMFTE/Accreditation%20Resources/MFT%20Core%20Competencies%20(December%202004).pdf.

Model of Socio-Spirituality in Supervision

Self, systems, and spirit lifts the need to address self of therapist concerns in a systemic context with a spiritual focus. We will first present the relational selves focus of the socio-spirituality model. Then, a case study will illustrate the actual supervisory process. It is here that supervision begins. The first area of discussion is the focus on relational selves. A series of deconstructive questions begins with the supervision. The format is flexible enough to accommodate different theoretical styles.

A model of socio-spirituality has at its heart respect for listening to the different voices that the supervisor and supervisee hold within themselves. It is enormously important for the supervisor to attend to the words as part of the supervisee's relational selves. Vygotsky, known for his contribution to narrative practice, says: "One words stands for a number of thoughts and feelings, and sometime substitutes for a long and profound discourse" (1987). Postmodern ethics also brings with it an invitational spirit that understands even "stumbles" as grist for the mill (Vedeler, 2017).

A socio-spirituality model of supervision recognizes that both spirituality and social justice are never neutral dimensions of supervision. Postmodern practice is often misinterpreted to mean a wishy-washy approach where anything goes. Nothing could be further from the truth. What is true is to recognize Vygotsky's zone of proximal development in which the supervisee stays close to the supervisor who provides a narrow band of options for the supervisee to copy. After some time of copying, the supervisee can then venture forth into new territory (Grøver, 2017).

Prior to focusing on relational selves in supervision, the supervisor needs to establish a connection with the supervisee as a person. An opening is: "What can you tell me about yourself that would enable me to fully appreciate you?" (White, 2007). This will be the opening of what might be one or several conversations (White, 2005). From this question, the supervisor will focus on a quality that the supervisee believes informs his worldview. The question to uncover this area might be, "I hear that you (enjoy singing, etc., some skill or personal quality). How might this skill/quality draw forth your inner self? Your relational selves with others?"

These questions and conversations lay the foundation for the web of socio-spirituality to be applied to supervision. As the supervisee's self-understanding unfolds into understandings of his or her multiple selves, the supervisor moves to have the supervisee determine which of the multiple selves connects in the strongest way to the client's story. A question that can develop this dimension of socio-spirituality is the following: "As you envision your client's story, which of your relational selves makes the strongest appearance?" The supervisee then answers this question with a discussion to follow.

As you move forward from this point, you and your supervisee begin to use a perspectival lens to move toward spirituality (Hiltner, 1958). In this living web of socio-spirituality, immanence and transcendence are grounding spiritual realities. At this point, we are thinking about the foundational beliefs of Freire, who determined that marginalized people need to look to the future as they take what knowledge they have at their disposal and move forward. Freire's quest for social justice overlaps with liberative theology as spirituality and social justice are woven together.

As we think of supervision, the next step is to determine how the supervisee's worldview and actions affect his or her clients in the therapy room. For all humans, a spiritual ethos moves them to ponder the world they inhabit and what to inhabit. This spirituality is not limited to a belief in God from the perspective of world religions, or even a Higher Power or Spirit. People who self-identify as agnostic or atheist have an inherent spirituality. It is common for all human beings to look to find meaning in something that is bigger than themselves. Some people may be involved in environmental causes, others in philosophical musings. It is the task of the supervisee to enable his or her clients to discover that spirit.

We might think that the expected path forward with a socio-spiritual model is to focus on what is observably human and earthly, or the "socio" part. This model, however, proposes a different path. It looks to a move toward transcendent experiences so that people may have hope in the face of current suffering, a tenet of liberative theologies. In socio-spiritual supervision, the supervisor is both de-centered and influential. So, the supervisor moves tentatively with the supervisee toward an unknown future of hope.

This movement in the supervision process looks something like this. The supervisor asks the following question: "You need to focus now on which relational self best connects with your client's story. What possibility of spirituality does that self see in your client?" A vibrant spirituality always infuses the believer or seeker with a sense of promise. What might happen in my life? A discussion follows as the outline of a future story of hope is envisioned. The supervisor needs to spend some time on this aspect of the supervisory process to ensure that the supervisee has securely attached to this possible hopeful vision for the client.

The supervisee will have a session or sessions with the client. In the interim, supervision sessions can take the format of whatever theoretical MFT approach both supervisor and supervisee think is desirable. At some point in the supervision process, the supervisor and supervisee will go forward and move to the human or immanent focus of the oppressing story that is holding the client hostage. Now, the supervisee working with the client must embody a hope for the client that can counter the oppressive story.

The supervisor can now formulate a question: "What story of hope does your client have now? How do you see yourself sustaining that hope in your client? What might be the obstacle? How might you speak to those obstacles?" A discussion follows that can span several supervisory sessions. Again, the supervisor and supervisee can engage in the preferred MFT model.

The supervisee and client now work toward creating a different story of the future. The supervisee's theoretical model can be CBT, solution-focused, or EFT, and so on. The overall container for the supervision of the supervisee remains the living web of socio-spirituality. The supervisee may likely have encountered a systemic obstacle to the client's satisfactory resolution of the problem story. For clients of color, racism has likely connected with the client's challenge of creating a hopeful future. Hope is understood here in a liberative sense as something that one has a fleeting taste of that encourages a sense that living in the present is possible with some periodic victories over the oppressive story.

The supervision will focus on the status of the supervisee's client. The supervisee may or may not see systemic oppression's effects on his or her client's life. At this point, the supervisor needs to decide how far his or her challenge to the supervisee on social justice goes forward. Adherence to this model does mean that at some point, both supervisor and supervisee must challenge the injustice with some action. Intellectually assenting to social justice is not enough. In this model, spirituality must have legs on this earth. Creating a social justice action is required. A decision for social justice needs to involve both supervisor and supervisee to have a truly transformative experience for them, and in an isomorphic manner, the client as well. Taking a social action will in turn change the relational selves of both supervisor and supervisee. We are where we began. The questions in supervision supporting social action will look something like this: "As you identify your client's problem story, how has or hasn't your client been able to envision a hopeful future?" "What would need to change in that story for them to engage that hopeful future?" "Are there systemic obstacles to this hope that your client would live to change?" "How might that happen?" "How will you sustain your client in that arduous journey?" "Are there social justice efforts you might engage outside the therapy room?"

You, as the supervisor, will need to connect with your supervisee's political, social, and spiritual viewpoints at this critical juncture in the supervision. It is likely that you and he or she will have different viewpoints—some conservative, some liberal. Your role as a supervisor is to sustain your supervisee at this point. If he or she makes significant social viewpoint changes, it will happen over time. My belief is that social viewpoints critically connect with spiritual perspectives. Both are sacred, and the sacred is an internal process (Table 5.2).

Table 5.2 Supervisory questions in a socio-spirituality model

Self—What can you tell me about yourself that would enable me to fully appreciate you? I hear that you (enjoy singing, etc., some skill, or personal quality). How might this skill/quality draw forth your inner self? Your relational selves with others?
Self/Socio-spirituality—As you envision your client's story, which of your relational selves makes the strongest appearance?
Systems/Spirituality—You need to focus now upon which relational self best connects with your client's story. What possibility of spirituality does that self see in your client?
What story of hope does your client have now?
How do you see yourself sustaining that hope in your client?
What might be the obstacle? How might you speak to those obstacles?
Spirituality/Social justice—As you identify your client's problem story, how has or has not your client been able to envision a hopeful future?
What would need to change in that story for them to engage that hopeful future?
Are there systemic obstacles to this hope that your client would live to change?
How might that happen?
How will you sustain your client in that arduous journey?
Are there social justice efforts you might engage outside the therapy room?

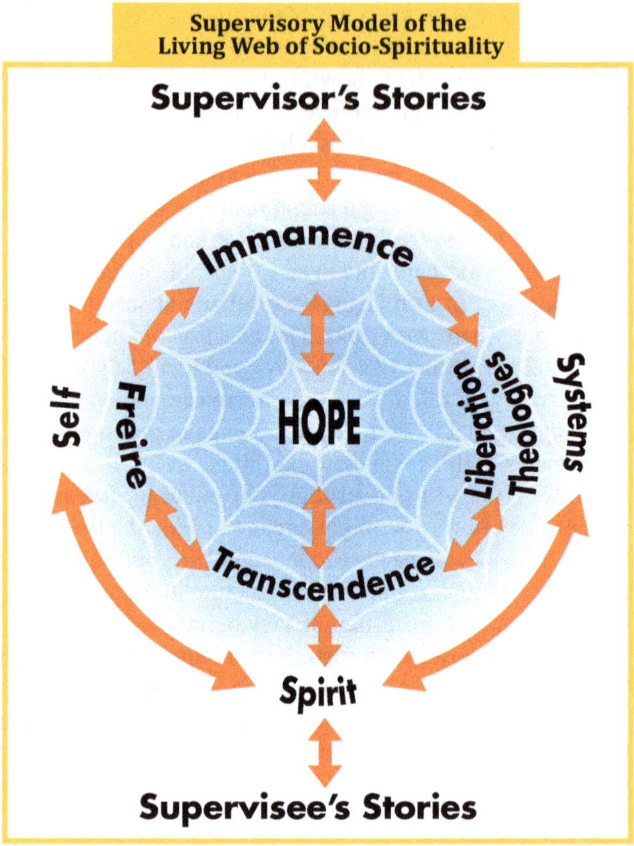

Fig. 5.2 Supervisory model of living web of socio-spirituality

The following case study demonstrates what the socio-spiritual model of supervision looks like in practice. The supervision of the case begins somewhere in the middle of the process, as was laid out. Supervision can begin anywhere. It also illustrates a case where supervisor and supervisee have quite different perspectives (Fig. 5.2).

Supervision Case Using a Socio-Spiritual Model

Mary is a middle-aged, Asian American AAMFT Approved Supervisor who self-identifies as agnostic. She is not sure that God exists, but she does not rule out the existence of a deity. What Mary is sure about is that the whole universe is somehow connected. Through that connection, she has sometimes had a transcendent experience that took her beyond her sense of self and provided a connection with others in her life. As a supervisor at a university COAMFTE training program, she tries to keep an openness of mind about God since she often supervises deeply religious students.

Jake is an entering student in practicum who is in his 20s. He is a Conservative Jew and participates in synagogue regularly. He appreciates the spirituality of his clients and tries to respect their perspectives. It is a bit of challenge for him. He grew up in a large northeastern city. Now he attends a university in the south. The religious and ethnic atmosphere here is quite different.

In practicum, Jake has started seeing an African American couple in their 30s, Scott and Kim, who both teach in the local public school system. They have no children. Recently, they experienced conflict over their future together. Scott wants to move to a large city where more job opportunities exist. Kim is happy where they live.

As Jake comes to supervision, he seems really confused one day as he discusses this case. Mary probes a bit. Jake shares that neither Scott nor Kim have any religious beliefs. He believes that some faith in their lives would help them just as much, or more than therapy. Jake says that they both were raised in liberal Protestant homes. Both Scott and Kim say they were harmed by their parents' liberal hypocrisy and do not want anything to do with religion. Jake brings the question of how to address spirituality to supervision.

Mary has never shared her agnostic positions with her supervisees. She does not want to do so now. Beginning with self-disclosure on her part is not an option. She has pondered using the socio-spirituality model in supervision. Now, with Jake presenting religion and spirituality as an issue, Anne wants to try the approach. So, she begins with the questions that focus more on spirituality after the relational selves dimension is typically explored. Modifying the following question: "What possibility of spirituality does that self see in your client?" she asks Jake, "What qualities in your clients do you believe have some spirituality in them?"

Jake ponders the question for a while. He tells Mary that he has only been thinking about religion as an option, not about a spirituality that non-theistic people can embrace. At his next therapy session with the couple, Jake shares that perhaps working with others and not focusing on themselves for a short time might help break the logjam. Scott and Kim seem surprised but begin to talk excitedly about their interest in environmental causes. They decide to focus on that issue.

At the next supervision session, Jake seems calmer about his distress about Scott and Kim now focusing on an environmental project. He tells Mary that this lifts a quality they both have for appreciating the contribution of nature. Jake continues to share his story with Mary, saying that he grew up in a deeply religious family. His parents could not see how anyone, Jewish, Catholic, Protestant, or Buddhist, could not espouse a formalized religion. Jake said he learned something about himself and plans to use that with other clients in the future.

Reflecting on the Supervisory Model of Socio-Spirituality

The supervisory model of socio-spirituality assumes that both supervisor and supervisee participate in supervision with different power stances despite what corrections each may try to bring to the situation. The supervisor has more power than the supervisee, even if the supervisor uses a postmodern approach to supervision. Also, most supervisees do want to learn from a supervisee, recognizing their supervisor's experience.

Stories in this model are the foundation of the supervision experience. By sharing stories, both supervisee and supervisor can get to know each other. Of course, sharing families of origin would be another way to know each other. That approach can be tricky, however, when truly intimate details of one's life tumble out. The result could be an impaired supervisory relationship. It seems that sharing stories may lessen such a danger.

Asking curious questions that focus on a socially responsible spirituality is an intervention that respects the supervisee's personal values and beliefs as was demonstrated in the supervisory relationship of Jake and Andrew. Utilizing such questions avoids too much interpretation on the part of the supervisor while challenging the supervisee's growth.

Lastly, this supervisory model of socio-spirituality offers flexibility as to the theoretical model both supervisee and supervisor practice. Admittedly, it is situated in a postmodern context. However, the model's structure allows for openness in applying the stories and questions to a specific MFT model. It can also be used for other mental health disciplines as the suggestions below indicate.

Supervisory Model of Socio-Spirituality Across Mental Health Disciplines

Psychologists, social workers, and mental health counselors/professional counselors all participate in supervising interns in some fashion. For some, supervision is embedded in the program, for others in private supervision and agency settings. And all these psychotherapy professionals have different theoretical orientations. In addition, their students may work in various settings that demand some tool to help students bridge the gap between the program and agency; also, between their academic learning and postgraduate supervision.

This model of socio-spirituality offers flexibility that all these mental health disciplines can utilize. By using this model, supervisor, supervisee, academic program, private practice, and the agency setting can benefit. The model also lends itself to each profession tweaking it to meet their specific needs.

Self, Systems, Spirit Practice

Seeking Socio-Spirituality in Supervision

This practice is designed for peer groups of supervisors. According to pre-assigned rotation, participants bring a clinical case of supervision for discussion. The facilitator distributes copies of Fig. 5.1: Supervisory model of the living web of socio-spirituality to all the participants.

The session may begin with the discussion of this chapter. An alternate approach is for the facilitator to summarize the chapter contents. Group participants identify aspects of the living web of socio-spirituality in the supervisory case. Then, the facilitator asks sub-groups or individual participants the following questions:

1. What aspects of the supervisory model of the living web of socio-spirituality catches your attention?
2. How might you further develop that attention-catching aspect?
3. How does that attention-catching aspect apply to the supervisory case?
4. How would you change the supervisory model of the living web of socio-spirituality?

References

Allen-Wilson, A. (2016). Integrating and addressing religion and spirituality in supervision and training. In K. V. Hardy & T. Bobes (Eds.), *Culturally sensitive supervision and training* (pp. 57–64). Routledge.

American Association for Marriage and Family Therapy. (2004). *Marriage and family therapy core competencies*. Author. Retrieved from https://www.coamfte.org/Documents/COAMFTE/Accreditation%20Resources/MFT%20Core%20Competencies%20(December%202004).pdf

Breunlin, D. C., Lebow, J. L., & Buckley, C. K. (2014). Using evidence in systemic supervision. In T. C. Todd & C. L. Storm (Eds.), *The complete systemic supervisor: Context, philosophy, and pragmatics* (pp. 274–294). Wiley-Blackwell.

Carlson, T. D., & Erickson, M. J. (2001). Honoring and privileging personal experience and knowledge: Ideas for a narrative therapy approach to the training and supervision of new therapists. *Contemporary Family Therapy, 23*(2), 199–220. https://doi.org/10.1023/A:1011150303280

Carlson, T. D., Kirkpatrick, D., Hecker, L., & Killmer, M. (2002). Religion, spirituality, and marriage and family therapy: A study of family therapists' beliefs about the appropriateness of addressing religious and spiritual issues in therapy. *American Journal of Family Therapy, 30*(2), 157–171. https://doi.org/10.1080/019261802753573867

Carlson, T. S., McGeorge, C. R., & Anderson, A. (2011). The importance of spirituality in couple and family therapy: A comparative study of therapists' and educators' beliefs. *Contemporary Family Therapy, 33*(1), 3–16. https://doi.org/10.1007/s10591-010-9136-0

Coffey, A. D. (2003). Spirituality: Lives and relationships in family-therapy concepts. *Spirituality and Family Therapy, 13*(1–2), 29–52. https://doi.org/10.1300/J085v13n01_03

Coyle, S. M. (2007). The bible, pastoral care, and conversational practices. In J. H. Ellens (Ed.), *Text and community. Essays in memory of Bruce M. Metzger* (Vol. 2, pp. 3–13). Sheffield Phoenix Press.

Coyle, S. M. (2013). *Re-storying your faith*. John Hunt Publishing.

Denborough, D. (2008). *Collective narrative practice*. Dulwich Centre Publications.
Denborough, D. (2018). *Do you want to hear a story?: Adventures in collective narrative practice*. Dulwich Centre. Retrieved from https://dulwichcentre.com.au/wp-content/uploads/2014/01/michael-white-workshop-notes.pdf
Dulwich Centre. (2016). *Living in stories: Embodiment in therapy through liturgical practice by Chad Loftis*. Author. Retrieved from https://dulwichcentre.com.au/living-stories-embodiment-therapy-liturgical-practice-chad-loftis/
Erickson, M. J., & Carlson, T. (2014). *Spirituality and family therapy*. Routledge.
Estrada, D. (2018). Training and supervision across disciplines to engage in cross-cultural competence and responsiveness: Counseling and family therapy. In S. Poulsen & R. Allen (Eds.), *Cross-cultural responsiveness & systemic therapy* (pp. 101–117). Springer. https://doi.org/10.1007/978-3-319-71395-3
Frame, M. W. (2001). The spiritual genogram in training and supervision. *The Family Journal, 9*(2), 109–115. https://doi.org/10.1177/1066480701092004
Grøver, T. (2017). The supervisor's power and moments of learning. In A. Vetere & J. Sheehan (Eds.), *Supervision of family therapy and systemic practice* (pp. 143–159). Springer.
Harris, S. M. (1998). Finding a forest among trees: Spirituality hiding in family therapy theories. *Journal of Family Studies, 4*(1), 77–86. https://doi.org/10.5172/jfs.4.1.77
Haug, I. E. (1998). Spirituality as a dimension of family therapists' clinical training. *Contemporary Family Therapy, 20*(4), 471–483. https://doi.org/10.1023/A:1021628132514
Hiltner, S. (1958). *Preface to pastoral theology*. Abingdon Press.
Hodge, D. R. (2001). Spiritual assessment: A review of major qualitative methods and a new framework for assessing spirituality. *Social Work, 46*(3), 203–214. https://doi.org/10.1093/sw/46.3.203
Hodge, D. R. (2005). Spiritual assessment in marital and family therapy: A methodological framework for selecting from among six qualitative assessment tools. *Journal of Marital and Family Therapy, 31*(4), 341–356. https://doi.org/10.1111/j.1752-0606.2005.tb01575.x
Holmberg, Å., Jensen, P., & Vetere, A. (2020). Spirituality–A forgotten dimension? Developing spiritual literacy in family therapy practice. *Journal of Family Therapy, 43*(1–2), 78–95. https://doi.org/10.1111/1467-6427.12298
Hull, C. E., Suarez, E. C., & Hartman, D. (2016). Developing spiritual competencies in counseling: A guide for supervisors. *Counseling and Values, 61*(1), 111–126. https://doi.org/10.1002/cvj.12029
Jordan, K. (Ed.). (2016). *Couple, marriage, and family therapy supervision*. Springer.
Lee, R. E., & Nelson, T. S. (2021). *The contemporary relational supervisor* (2nd edn). Routledge.
Marterella, M. K., & Brock, L. J. (2008). Religion and spirituality as a resource in marital and family therapy. *Journal of Family Psychotherapy, 19*(4), 330–344. https://doi.org/10.1080/08975350802475072
McGoldrick, M., Gerson, R., & Petry, S. (2020). *Genograms: Assessment and intervention* (4th ed.). Norton Professional Books.
Miller, W. R. (1999). Diversity training in spiritual and religious issues. In W. R. Miller (Ed.), *Integrating spirituality into treatment: Resources for practitioners* (pp. 253–263). American Psychological Association. https://doi.org/10.1037/10327-013
Miller, M. M., & Ivey, D. C. (2006). Spirituality, gender, and supervisory style in supervision. *Contemporary Family Therapy, 28*(3), 323–337. https://doi.org/10.1007/s10591-006-9012-0
Miller, M. M., Korinek, A., & Ivey, D. C. (2004). Spirituality in MFT training: Development of the spiritual issues in supervision scale. *Contemporary Family Therapy, 26*(1), 71–81. https://doi.org/10.1023/B:COFT.0000016913.62876.86
Neden, J., Barber, J., Bradbury, G., & Cheung, A. (2011). Bringing forth spirituality dialogues in family therapy education. *Journal of Family Therapy, 33*(2), 224–228. https://doi.org/10.1111/j.1467-6427.2011.00532.x

Patterson, J., Hayworth, M., Turner, C., & Raskin, M. (2000). Spiritual issues in family therapy: A graduate-level course. *Journal of Marital and Family Therapy, 26*(2), 199–210. https://doi.org/10.1111/j.1752-0606.2000.tb00289.x

Pearson, A. (2017). Working with religious and spiritual experience in family therapy: Manna for the journey. *Australian and New Zealand Journal of Family Therapy, 38*(1), 43–60. https://doi.org/10.1002/anzf.1202

Prest, L. A., Russel, R., & D'Souza, H. (1999). Spirituality and religion in training, practice, and personal development. *Journal of Family Therapy, 21*(1), 60–77. https://doi.org/10.1111/1467-6427.00104

Russell-Chapin, L., & Chapin, T. (2011). *Clinical supervision: Theory and practice*. Cengage Learning.

Şahin, Y. (2017). Using spiritual genograms in family therapies. *Spiritual Psychology and Counseling, 3*(1), 47–60. https://doi.org/10.12738/spc.2018.1.0030

Stander, V., Piercy, F. P., Mackinnon, D., & Helmeke, K. (1994). Spirituality, religion, and family therapy: Competing or complementary worlds? *The American Journal of Family Therapy, 22*(1), 27–41. https://doi.org/10.1080/01926189408251295

Storm, C. L., & Todd, T. C. (2003). *The reasonably complete systemic supervisor resource guide*. iUniverse.

Todd, T. C., & Storm, C. L. (2014). *The complete systemic supervisor: Context, philosophy, and pragmatics*. John Wiley & Sons.

Vedeler, A. H. (2017). Creating a dialogical culture for supervision. In A. Vetere & J. Sheehan (Eds.), *Supervision of family therapy and systemic practice* (pp. 121–141). Springer.

Vetere, A., & Sheehan, J. (Eds.). (2017). *Supervision of family therapy and systemic practice*. Springer.

Vygotsky, L. S. (1987). *The collected works of L. S. Vygotsky: The fundamentals of defectology* (Vol. 2). Springer Science & Business Media.

White, M. (2005). *Workshop notes*. Dulwich Centre. Retrieved from https://dulwichcentre.com.au/wp-content/uploads/2014/01/michael-white-workshop-notes.pdf

White, M. K. (2007). *Maps of narrative practice*. W.W. Norton & Company.

Wiggins, M. I. (2009). Therapist self-awareness of spirituality. In J. D. Aten & M. M. Leach (Eds.), *Spirituality and the therapeutic process: A comprehensive resource from intake to termination* (pp. 53–74). American Psychological Association. https://doi.org/10.1037/11853-003

Williams-Reade, J. M., Lobo, E., & Gutierrez, G. (2018). Integrating spirituality into MFT training: A reflexive curriculum and qualitative evaluation. *Journal of Marital and Family Therapy, 45*(2), 219–232. https://doi.org/10.1111/jmft.12314

Chapter 6
Spirituality in a Systemic Family Therapy Curriculum

Supervision in MFT training is a beginning point for a context in which supervisors and supervisees can find ways to integrate values and beliefs. The trainer and trainee family context offers an opportunity to better understand how individual members' values and beliefs interact to create a shared family narrative. Supervisory practice lends itself to a robust integration of spirituality into therapy.

Movement Toward MFT Training and Spirituality

Since the turn of the twenty-first century, interest in how to integrate spirituality into MFT training programs has steadily increased. This attention was likely propelled by growing interest in spirituality in family therapy that began in the 1990s, evidenced in articles and a decade-long review (Bonelli & Koenig, 2013; Stander et al., 1994; Anderson & Worthen, 1997). More theologically conservative universities have typically understood their focus to be faith. Some of these programs are Commission on Accreditation for Marriage and Family Therapy Education (COAMFTE) accredited in addition to being accredited seminary programs.

Prior to counseling training programs, many faith-based universities and seminaries espoused the use of Scripture and prayer by ministers as essential to faith-based counseling. The pastoral care and counseling movement in seminaries began in the 1950s as more schools sought to gain an identifiable status in theological faculties as a separate field of pastoral theology or practical theology. Pastoral counseling programs were known by various names, including pastoral theology, pastoral care and counseling, personality and theology, psychology of religion, and personality, culture, and religion. This movement eventually spawned groups such as the American Association of Pastoral Counselors (AAPC) for credentialed

S. M. Coyle, *Spirituality in Systemic Family Therapy Supervision and Training*, Focused Issues in Family Therapy, https://doi.org/10.1007/978-3-030-92369-3_6

pastoral counselors and the Association for Clinical Pastoral Education (ACPE) for certified chaplains. Former members of AAPC joined ACPE in the category of Psychotherapist.

These two organizations were initially limited to ordained clergy. In the 1950s and 1960s, specialized training gradually emerged at universities and colleges for marriage and family therapy. The religious track of AAPC was on a parallel trajectory, but for credentialing. A significant number of therapists made a conscious decision about a group with which to affiliate. Also, during this time, some divorced clergy were typically excluded from their denominations' pastoral counseling credentialing (Personal conversations, 1970–1989, n.d.). Some of those persons who were originally AAPC members joined the American Association for Marriage and Family Therapy (AAMFT).

In addition, the American Association of Christian Counselors was organized as an alternative to AAPC. Some differences characterized the two organizations. AACC identified state licensure as the requirement for membership. Members were asked to sign a statement affirming that they were committed Christians. Its members were secular licensed therapists who identified with more theologically conservative beliefs than did AAPC members.

In contrast, AAPC required members to complete a thorough clinical supervision process that emphasized spiritual integration with behavioral science. This group was initially composed of ordained clergy. The organization's requirement had the effect of limiting membership to women whose denominations ordained women, a low number at the time. Gradually, Catholic religious women protested. More denominations started to ordain women. The number of women in the organization increased as did the inclusion of laity. Theologically, AAPC became predominantly Christian, with some Jewish, Buddhist, Muslim, and Hindu members. Christian members included conservative, mainline, and liberal religious adherents.

Standardization of Best Practices

Systemic family therapy and other psychotherapies are disciplines requiring both creative and clinical skills. Training programs school trainees in self of therapist issues, theoretical models, and evidence-based practice. The art of becoming a therapist is a process aided by time and talent. Learning to implement skills in one's clinical expertise involves some degree of objectivity, as evidenced by evaluative supervisory assessments, objective structure clinical exercises (OSCEs), and now the opportunity for the Simulation Therapy exercise through AAMFT.[1]

Increasingly in our world, the standardization of business and professional practices is essential. Agreeing upon a set of practices in psychotherapy gives the

[1] Simulation Therapy is a mixed reality simulation program that provides interaction between actor(s) as avatars and a trainee through a roleplay based on a pre-created vignette. See https://www.aamft.org/enhance_knowledge/What_is_Simulation.aspx.

profession the ability to improve clinical outcomes. The result is that we are better able to care for clients.

Suicide prevention is an area that has greatly benefited from standardization of practice. One of my supervisees had a suicidal client. The trainee was quite distressed about how his client felt wanting to convey only warm feelings to him. Some of the skills the trainee employed with the client before the client's hospitalization made the client feel good but did not support the client's safety. At first, the supervisee just wanted affirmation from me. He was not able to hear the skills for suicide prevention that would have helped the situation.

A few weeks later, the student was able to listen with more objectivity about what he did that was helpful and what hindered his work with the suicidal client. Having a body of suicide prevention skills that promoted best practice was critical for the trainee's growth. With this example in mind, we move to various clinical competencies that have the potential to improve the trainee's clinical skills. Furthermore, these best practices can be applied to the art of counseling.

Foundations of MFT Core Competencies, COAMFTE Standards, and AMFTRB Domains for Curriculum MFT Competency and Accreditation Standards

In 2004, AAMFT gathered a group of interested stakeholders, including educators, trainers, regulators, researchers, policymakers, and the public to define the knowledge and skills needed for competence in MFT practice. The core competency that narrowly supports multicultural practice is CC 1.2.1 as follows: Recognize contextual and systemic dynamics (e.g., gender, age, socioeconomic status, culture/race/ethnicity, sexual orientation, spirituality, religion, larger systems, social context) (MFT Core Competencies, 2004).

This kitchen sink list of diversities situates this book's focus. Spirituality here connects to religion and the other components of gender, age, socioeconomic status, culture/race/ethnicity, sexual orientation, larger systems, and social context. Missing from the list is ableism. AAMFT recognizes that these diversities are a critical part of "contextual and systemic dynamics." The quandary is the method to address these dimensions.

The Commission on Accreditation for Marriage and Family Therapy (COAMFTE) in Version 12.5 Standards defines diverse communities as follows: "Diverse, Marginalized, and/or Underserved Communities refers to groups from non-majority populations currently discriminated against and underrepresented due to their race, age, gender, ethnicity, sexual orientation, gender identity, socioeconomic status, disability, health status, religious and spiritual practices, nation of origin or other social categories, immigration status, and/or language" (COAMFTE Version 12.5 Standards, 2021).

Both AAMFT and COAMFTE emphasize diversity as both a foundational concern and skill for competent and well-trained relational systemic therapists. These definitions addressing diversity are extensive. It is not likely that such terms and constructs will narrow soon. It is even more likely that an increasing number of terms will be created to provide focus for clinical practice. This presents challenges for instructors, supervisors, and practitioners who genuinely want to be faithful to a socially just model of family therapy. We all may feel somewhat defeated about how to keep up with the lightning speed of change in our society and how to develop family therapy that is more responsive to our changing life contexts. To that end, we build upon our previous discussions of spirituality and diversity to arrive at an approach that allows for responsiveness as well as rigor of practice.

Diversity is defined as a program's commitment to: (a) include the representation of multiple groups in the student body, supervisors, and faculty with regard to race, age, gender, ethnicity, sexual orientation, gender identity, socioeconomic status, disability, health status, religious and spiritual practices, nation of origin or other relevant social categories; and (b) ensure issues of diversity are central to all aspect of the training environment (COAMFTE Accreditation Standards Version 12.5, 2021, p. 36).

Version 12.5 requires family therapy programs to create a multiculturally informed curriculum, which it defines: "(a) an educational approach that represents a commitment to local and global diversity, and prepares students for living in a global world; (b) includes an understanding of how larger social processes lead to systemic inequality and disadvantage for diverse and marginalized communities; (c) endorses the ethical responsibility/role of MFTs in addressing and intervening in these systems when working with diverse and marginalized communities" (COAMFTE Standards Version 12.5, 2021, p. 39).

COAMFTE accredited programs can infuse spirituality through two standards: Standard I: Outcome-Based Education Framework & Environmental Support Programs; and Standard III: Curriculum. Furthermore, programs in Version 12.5 align the entire program with the COAMFTE Developmental Competency Components: (1) Knowledge of the MFT profession; (2) Practice of relational/systemic therapy as a qualified behavioral/mental health provider; (3) Commitment to ethical practice through ethical codes of the MFT profession and pertinent regulatory bodies; (4) Awareness, knowledge, and skill to responsibly serve diverse communities; (5) Development and application of research to further the knowledge and practice of the MFT profession (COAMFTE Standards Version 12.5, 2021, p.3).

Version 12.5 does not have a separate standard for multiculturalism. The understanding in Version 12.5 is that programs "must strive for diversity-promoting inclusion" throughout the academic and clinical components of the program (COAMFTE Accreditation Standards Version 12.5, 2021, p. 3). This gives programs an opportunity to infuse the curriculum with a focus on spirituality just as the other diversities are focused on throughout the program. Furthermore, the program can look for creative ways to integrate all diversities with one another.

As program directors engage Version 12.5 Standards, a new look at spirituality can serve the revised curriculums well. Spirituality now has the possibility of being the large lens through which other diversities are viewed, if the program desires. This means that an older view of spirituality that looked at the transcendent and did not connect with everyday human spirituality is now passé. Now spirituality can infuse every diversity. By comparison, the Association of Marital and Family Therapy Regulatory Board presents several integrative qualities of spirituality with other diversities.

Alongside these standards, the Association of Marital and Family Therapy Regulatory Boards (AMFTRB) has "practice domains" with that MFT graduates can study to pass the national exam. Under Domain 01 The Practice of Marriage and Family Therapy, task statement 01.04 requires that test takers "integrate multiple dimensions of diversity and social justice within a system treatment approach."

Other areas that require an understanding of spirituality in theory and practice are the following: Domain 02 Assessing, Hypothesizing, Diagnosing, task statement 02.06, task statement 02.11, task statement 02.11; Domain 03 Designing and Conducting Treatment, task statement 03.11; and Domain 05 Managing Crisis Situations, and task statement 05.09 (AMFTRB, 2017).

In summary, the AMFTRB domains focus on the therapist assessing "contextual understanding" that includes all the diversities delineated in MFT Core Competency 1.2.1, which includes spirituality as one of many. Therapists are expected to determine how the therapist formulates hypotheses that include a contextual understanding of the client's spirituality, assess the client's spirituality, choose therapeutic modalities that consider the client's spirituality, and consider the impact of the client's spirituality on his or her current crisis (AMFTRB, 2017).

The AMFTRB licensure exam contains a few questions that directly address spirituality. This licensure exam is the national exam that most state licensure boards use except for a few states such as California. It is highly unlikely that a test taker would fail the exam based on lack of knowledge about spirituality. The emphasis of the AMFTRB domains does, however, demonstrate the importance of a licensed MFT being both spiritually literate and spiritually sensitive in the implementation of clinical skills.

Need for Spirituality in MFT Training

Given the growing interest in spirituality in family therapy, there is a paucity of training programs that intentionally integrate spirituality. Two research studies indicate that over 60% of MFT therapists and students think it is important to receive training and supervision in how to integrate spirituality in therapy. At the same time, both the studies found that 70% of MFT therapists and MFT students said they did not receive training in how to do this kind of integration (Carlson & Erickson, 2002; Prest et al., 1999). In Prest et al., 75% of MFT students agreed that "every person has a spiritual dimension that should be considered in clinical practice" (1999, p. 66). In the same study, MFT students believe that it is important to receive supervision and training in spirituality, with 52.9% of them believing that this training should be part of the curriculum. However, 92.2% said they had not received such training in their program. Alongside these empirical studies, general MFT literature emphasizes the importance of considering spirituality in therapy (Haug, 1998; Moules, 2000; Roberts, 1999; Stander et al., 1994; Walsh & Pryce, 2003).

The challenge of this older research is that the students and faculty of today may have a very different perspective. These studies are seminal studies that are often cited in systemic literature. Since this time, our society has experienced seismic paradigm shifts including 9/11, Black Lives Matter, Me Too, LGBTQ rights, COVID-19 global pandemic. Research for follow-up studies to these seminal studies did not uncover studies within the last 5 years that follow up with previous research or initiate new studies. Two recent articles do explore the role of spirituality in training programs (Coyle, 2017; Williams-Reade et al., 2018). They do not however assess current attitudes among systemic students and practitioners about the role of spirituality in MFT. Follow-up to these original studies would contribute a great deal to the role of spirituality in family therapy.

As one considers integrating spirituality in training programs, it is important to weigh some ethical and practical matters. Despite the dearth of such training, it is certainly dangerous to assume that one can just magically "do" spirituality as they learn MFT theory and skills. A critical part of MFT training is to become self-aware of one's thoughts, emotions, and actions in therapy. MFT training programs supervise students in how to discern diagnostic impressions, complete a treatment, and transfer theoretical understanding to actual clinical practice.

Haug emphasizes the need for spiritual awareness and spirituality literacy (1998). In being aware of one's own spiritual beliefs, therapists must also ensure that those spiritual beliefs do not harm their clients. Spiritual literacy is also important for understanding the spirituality and religion of others. One of my students, an evangelical Christian, took a class in world religions. He said it was the most helpful class he took in our MFT program because it expanded his worldview.

Of course, one must be spiritually literate in addition to being spiritually aware. Spiritual literacy includes: (1) learning about various religious and spiritual traditions and practice; (2) examining which generative core beliefs of spirituality which can give meaning for the client; (3) creating a spiritual history; and (4) encouraging clients to discuss the role of spirituality in their lives along with its helpful and hurtful influence (Haug, 1998). The reader will see these practices, or modifications to them, in a review of the Master of Arts in Marriage and Family Therapy program at Christian Theological Seminary which is COAMFTE accredited.

Before creating a spiritually infused curriculum, it is critical to determine whether faculty are supportive. A spiritually infused curriculum will require faculty to develop skills for creating a methodology receptive to spirituality. It will also offer reflexive experiences to both faculty and students that develop their own spiritualities. An important research study gives us insight into this requirement. Grams et al. discovered that the majority of MFT faculty, along with MFT therapists and MFT students, think that spirituality is important in their personal lives as well as in MFT training (2007).

Furthermore, MFT faculty agreed more with general statements about spirituality and were less likely to agree with concepts they considered more intrusive, such as spiritual interventions in clinical practice. Over 50% of MFT faculty say that they include spirituality in their courses. Fifty-one percent of faculty agreed that a specific course on spirituality should be in the MFT curriculum (Grams et al., 2007). Two earlier studies indicated that 70% of MFT students said that they did not receive training on spirituality in their MFT programs (Carlson et al., 2002; Prest et al., 1999). These studies, however, included different participants and were separated by 5–8 years. Future research could include students and faculty at the same MFT training programs with questions that determine what each group understands spiritual integration to be.

Since MFT programs typically have little training on spiritual assessment, consideration should be given to responding to student requests by integrating that training into the curriculum. MFT programs can learn from the Joint Commission on Accreditation of Healthcare Organizations (JCAHO). Various spiritual assessments from JCAHO include the initial brief spiritual assessment, spiritual histories, spiritual lifemaps, spiritual genograms, spiritual ecomaps, and spiritual ecograms. Some clients may respond differently with the use of different tools. Thus, students who are familiar with different assessment approaches expand their ability to respond to their clients' spiritualities. The therapist's theoretical orientation may influence which of these qualitative assessments are used. A therapist using intergenerational approaches will likely employ spiritual genograms and spiritual ecograms. If the therapist is more concerned with present-day issues, spiritual ecomaps, spiritual lifemaps, and spiritual histories may be more helpful (Hodge, 2005).

A few quantitative spiritual assessments offer other options. The Spiritual Well-Being Scale assesses the client's well-being on two psychological dimensions: the quality of one's existential relationship with God and the quality of one's relationships with other people.[2] Its use is limited to theistic clients (Ellison & Smith, 1991; Paloutzian & Ellison, 1982). Another quantitative instrument is the 21-item Religious Orientation Scale, which assesses the degree to which religion is a significant part of a client's life for people who profess a traditional religion (Allport & Ross, 1967). A few follow-up studies re-evaluated the instrument (Donahue, 1985; Gorsuch & McPherson, 1989). An additional recent instrument is the Intrinsic Spirituality Scale, which assesses spiritual motivation for both theistic and non-theistic clients (Hodge, 2005).

Carlson and Erickson have suggested that therapists' hesitancy in integrating spirituality in family therapy may be due to the lack of training (2002). The general dislike of intrusive measures on the part of therapists is a factor in deciding whether to use quantitative assessments (Grams et al., 2007). These spiritual assessment tools may be quite helpful in a training program due to their structured format. Quantitative assessments can provide a degree of objectivity. Further research on

[2] The Spiritual Well-Being Scale was created in 1982 by Paloutzian and Ellison. It is referenced in various articles.

perceptions of such instruments is required to determine how such quantitative and qualitative assessments support therapists' and clients' understandings of what is needed to make the curricular integration of spirituality in an MFT program doable.

Focusing on self, systems, and spirit, this discussion looks at the value of humanness to access both immanence and transcendence in spirituality. To this end, spiritual assessments can be introduced to trainees. Such instruments, however, are not a substitute for the spirituality that the therapist and client recognize in each other. This human connection transcends barriers of diversity and is accessible by theistic and non-theistic therapists and clients alike. Thus, an approach integrated in the self of the therapist is applicable to different MFT models such as solution-focused, emotionally focused therapy, cognitive behavioral, and dialectical behavioral therapies is desirable. Such an approach lays a foundation for spiritual literacy and spiritual sensitivity.

In terms of addressing the integration of spirituality, some programs have created focused courses on spirituality (Coyle, 2017; Patterson et al., 2000; Williams-Reade et al., 2018). The focus in these courses is largely reflexive in their methodology and addresses both AAMFT Core Competencies and COAMFTE standards. In addition to specific courses, private universities and seminaries affiliated with denominations infuse their curriculum with beliefs and values that are consistent with their theological/spiritual orientation.

Offering specific courses on spirituality and MFT clinical practice is a critical step toward giving trainees the tools they need to successfully integrate spirituality in family therapy. At the same time, it is not enough. It is too easy to assume that just because you have completed one course on spirituality in clinical practice, you know everything that is needed. COAMFTE standards require that programs have a strong emphasis on multicultural education that is fully integrated into the entire curriculum. Spirituality is included in the MFT Core Competency 1.2.1. This core competency includes all the various diversities. COAMFTE leaves it to the institution to determine how to infuse the program with multiculturalism. COAMFTE Site Visits do respect each institution's orientation to spirituality/religion. Typically, the Site Visit Team is composed of faculty who teach at religious institutions if the school having the Site Visit has a religious connection.

Ambivalence toward integrating spirituality in the curriculum seems to be prevalent across COAMFTE accredited programs. Research universities understandably need to ensure that communities of interest do not perceive the program as favoring a particular religion. Students and faculty represent major religions such as Judaism, Christianity, Islam, Hinduism, and Buddhism as well as "spiritual but not religious" and agnostic/atheist preferences. It seems understandable from the COAMFTE position that an accrediting body sees the inclusion of spirituality, just like politics, to be the purview of the institution. The academic institution needs to find creative ways to integrate spirituality in the curriculum without presenting it in a partisan manner.

Addressing spirituality in MFT programs must be more far-reaching than one course in the curriculum. The answer is to include it as one of the diversity concerns identified in MFT CC 1.2.1 with no more emphasis or less emphasis (MFT Core Competencies, 2004). Of course, private religious universities and seminaries have the option of making spirituality a central component of the curriculum. Some authors agree with the presupposition that for MFTs to take spirituality seriously there must be a re-ordering of both priorities and methodology. In *Family Process*, Wendel argues that both rigorous methodology and interdisciplinary work must occur (2003). He cites Hiltner's correlational approach in integrating theology/spirituality with psychological concepts (Hiltner, 1958, 1972). This perspectival approach can be used with narrative practice (Coyle, 2014).

A perspectival approach has the advantage of connecting various viewpoints without eliminating any. While one looks through the lens of one perspective, the other lenses are available at any time. This is a part of the living web of socio-spirituality. Correlation is also part of this book's approach in the way in which spirituality and social justice talk to each other and inform the outcome of the conversation. Wendel sees this cross-disciplinary process as necessitating rigorous training (2003), which of course requires additional training in religion and clinical practice. Few MFTs meet those qualifications.

The strict definition of a correlational approach is to have two independent bodies of information that converse with each other. Both the bodies of knowledge maintain their independence. In contrast, integration is strictly defined as a combining of the two bodies of knowledge. The living web of socio-spirituality utilizes some dialogical and integrative approaches to spirituality and social justice. A socio-spiritual approach will be referred to as integrative, which is the term that MFT literature typically uses. Wendel critiques MFT literature as having little evidence of a robust methodology (2003). The living web of socio-spiritualty is an integrative approach between a systemic family therapy perspective and a theological/spiritual perspective that seeks to utilize the best of both.

Elements of diversity are part of the living web of socio-spirituality. This socio-spirituality construct sees social justice as a response to marginalization of persons. Therapists and supervisors can use this construct as they encounter clinical issues of power, privilege, and oppression (Gutierrez & Natrajan-Tyagi, 2018). These issues can affect clients in their unique ways as well as informing their spirituality. Both diversity and spirituality engage with each other. Spirituality is a diversity recognized in the MFT Core Competencies (MFT Core Competencies, 2004). Spirituality is an aspect of culture (Carlson et al., 2011). "Most importantly, spirituality is often important and is an aspect of diversity that is neglected in MFT training" (Williams-Reade et al., 2018, p. 12).

Spiritual Competencies

Creating specific spiritual competencies can bolster the role of spirituality in a COAMFTE accredited program. The Spiritual Competencies are drawn from the living web of socio-spirituality. In a competency format, programs can integrate these spiritual competencies into the program to enhance spiritual literacy and spiritual sensitivity for students. Spiritual literacy covers knowledge of spirituality and the ways it connects to diversities through immanence and transcendence. Spiritual sensitivity covers the attitudes and skills that connect through immanence and transcendence to bring hope to clients' lives.

The COAMFTE Developmental Competency Components refer to the primary areas of professional learning and skill development that are central to the effective and ethical practice of a future Marriage and Family Therapy professional, including knowledge of the profession; practice of therapy; human diversity and social structures; professional identify, ethics, and law; and research and evidence-based practice. This framework is intended to encompass historical, current, and future elements of MFT professional identity and practice and to organize student learning outcomes that are expected of a graduate of a COAMFTE accredited program (COAMFTE Accreditation Standards Version 12.5, 2021, p. 3). It seems reasonable that the Spiritual Competencies fall under this category. Thus, the Spiritual Competencies would be an approach that COAMFTE accredited programs could use to emphasize spirituality and meet standards at the same time. Also, the competencies are not limited to use in COAMFTE programs. They represent a freestanding evaluation structure that can be applied to non-academic settings as well as other mental health disciplines.

The Spiritual Competencies focus on the following competency components: knowledge of the profession, practice of therapy, human diversity and social structure, and professional identity. The spiritual literacy emphasis will cover knowledge of the profession, practice of therapy, and diversity and social structure. Spiritual sensitivity covers practice of therapy, human diversity and social structure, and professional identity.

All these components will be covered in Standard I Outcome Based Education Framework and Environmental Support as well as Standard III Curriculum of Version 12.5 Standards. Table 6.1 delineates the Spiritual Competencies and the ways in which they are infused throughout a COAMFTE curriculum. The Spiritual Competencies, however, are not limited to a COAMFTE program. They can easily be implemented in a psychology, social work, or professional counseling program.

Overview of a Spiritually Integrated MFT Program

Self, systems, and spirit are components of the spiritually integrated curriculum at Christian Theological Seminary, which recognizes self of therapist concerns, systemic practice, social justice, and theological/spiritual reflection. The curriculum has evolved over the years, based on a theologically inclusive worldview. The Seminary is an ecumenical seminary affiliated with the Christian Church (Disciples of Christ) and attracts students from a variety of religious and non-religious backgrounds. The institution advocates for welcoming and affirming values. The MAMFT program has attracted students who are Pentecostal, non-denominational, Baptist, Lutheran, Disciples, belong to independent Christian churches, are United Methodist, Lutheran, Catholic, Jewish, Presbyterian, spiritual but not religious, and who self-identify as agnostic/atheistic.

Table 6.1 Spiritual competencies

Spiritual literacy
Spiritual competencies in knowledge of profession
1. Develop knowledge of the spiritual/religious literature that gives a foundation to understanding the role of spirituality/religion in clients' lives.
2. Develop knowledge of ways in which a specific diversity connects with a specific spirituality.
Spiritual competencies in practice of therapy
1. Understand knowledge of different religions and non-theistic spiritualities that lends itself to clinical practice.
2. Understand the difference between healthy spirituality/religion and destructive spirituality/religion.
Spiritual competencies in human diversity and social structure
1. Understand the intersectionalities of various diversities and how they may connect with spirituality.
2. Learn how to administer some spiritual inventories and the possible connection to social structure.
Spiritual competencies in professional identity
1. Understand how spirituality/religion differs from emotions and feelings.
2. Discover the difference between professional functioning between a chaplain, minister, and MFT in addressing the client's spirituality.
Spiritual sensitivity
Spiritual competencies in knowledge of profession
1. Develop a personal theoretical approach to addressing a client's spiritual/religious concerns.
2. Understand ways to enable clients to bring their spirituality up to date to correlate with their changing worldview.
Spiritual competencies in practice of therapy
1. Demonstrate skill in helping families respond to spiritual crises.
2. Develop spiritually integrated interventions that connect with one's own spiritual worldview.
3. Demonstrate skills integrating spiritual and social justice practices in addressing diversities.
Spiritual competencies in human diversity and social structure
1. Engage in antiracism training to increase one's sensitivity to clients' race, ethnicity, and class.
2. Seek out supervision that focuses on diversity and social structure.
Spiritual competencies in professional identity
1. Deepen one's own spirituality through personal therapy, spiritual formation, and spiritual practices.
2. Explore one's family of origin in the area of spirituality and diversity.

Note: Spiritual Competencies can be used under the following COAMFTE Version 12.5: *COAMFTE Develop. Comp. Components–knowledge of the profession; practice of therapy; human diversity and social structure; and professional identity*

The program's goal is for every graduate to be both spiritually literate and spiritually sensitive. The spiritually literate goal requires each student to take several courses that ground them in religious traditions, a wide diversity of multiculturalism, family and larger systems, and spiritually integrated courses.

To be spiritually sensitive, students are required to engage in reflexive learning that plumbs their understanding of their own self-awareness and how that awareness makes relationships with self, peers, faculty, supervisors, administrators, and clients into transformative experiences. Students are required to be in personal and/or couple therapy while they are in practicum. Several supervision groups require a thorough examination of self of therapist concerns as they integrate their self-examination with client work in practicum.

Finally, in lieu of a thesis, students are required to complete a capstone presentation. This includes a case presentation of a couple family using video clips. Clinical documentation, including a clinical assessment, case conceptualization, and treatment plan, supports this presentation. Finally, a spiritually integrated paper of 15–20 pages features self of therapist, clinical presentation, and theological/spiritual integration with clinical practice.

Building on this overview of the MFT program at Christian Theological Seminary, other programs can create their spiritually integrated curriculum by identifying special components of their curriculum that address the uniqueness of their institution. The basic components of such program are the following: (1) foundation course in religion/spirituality; (2) MFT course that integrates the basics of self, systems, and spirit; (3) self of therapist experience in which students identify family of origin dynamics and how these connects with their worldview; and (4) clinical experience that emphasizes spirituality.

Let us begin with addressing with the first component of the curriculum. Understanding the foundation of religion and spirituality along with their similarities and differences is a critical aspect of fully integrating spirituality in clinical practice. Major universities and many small colleges have a religion department. MFT students could take one religion course of their choosing that fits in their worldview. If such courses are not available in the university, the program could contract with a religion scholar or minister, rabbi, imam, or priest to lead a didactic course.

Second, a program could create an integrative course that blends clinical theology and practice, social agency, and spirituality. The first step in this process would be to identify the ethos of the institution and program that would be integrated in such a course. The course could be the creation of one faculty member or taught by a team.

Third, an experiential didactic or practicum experience that requires the MFT students to identify their worldview and eventually, their spirituality, is essential. Some possibilities for this practicum experience would be to focus on clinical cases and then identify where self of therapist enters in the treatment. This experiential practice directed toward self of therapist concerns could also be part of a course.

Last, the curriculum could include a practicum experience that could integrate spirituality in the actual clinical practice. For example, live supervision could include a simple question such as "Where does spirituality emerge in the case?" to the observation team. Another possibility would be to require that each individual/tandem supervisor ask the same question of supervisees.

Contemporary systemic family therapy training does not always occur in academic settings. Some group practices now incorporate and form large clinical training centers that provide post-masters training as the resident works toward full licensure. The same process can apply in those contexts.

Courses in the Curriculum Focusing on Spiritual and Social Justice Integration

The religion courses required in the CTS curriculum have evolved since my arrival in 2004. Initially, four religion courses were required. Now, we required three. With variance in requirements as determined by the faculty, the following courses are required: (1) Introduction to Theology; (2) New Testament or Hebrew Scripture; and (3) a religion elective. Exceptions are sometimes made with the required Bible course, depending on the student's religious perspective. Some MFT students have expressed appreciation for taking a world religions class as an elective.

All students take P617 Integration of Self, Systems, and Spirit. This course is the preparatory course for the capstone presentation. The next chapter provides a detailed explanation of this course.

Courses That Offer Multicultural and Larger Systems Awareness

The course Sexuality, Gender, and Culture integrates diversity aspects of this book's understanding of socio-spirituality.[3] The course description is as follows: *This course is required and utilizes a reflexive methodology that contributes to the students' self-awareness of various diversities.*

P 646 Families and Larger Systems is not a required course, and yet many students enroll to fulfill the Social Justice Electives option. The course description and objectives are as follows: *Family systems analysis of dynamics and ways of entering and functioning in larger systems such as churches and institutions.*

1. *Students will learn an integrated approach in using select family systems theories to assess, intervene, and function in large systems.*
2. *Students will learn to apply a basic understanding of select family systems theories—Bowen as explicated by Friedman, narrative therapy, and collaborative therapy—to larger systems.*
3. *Students will participate in experiential training in Bowenian approaches (Friedman and community genograms), narrative approaches (The Public Conversations Project and collective narrative practices), and collaborative approaches (appreciative inquiry), which can be used in the context of larger systems.*
4. *Students will explore the dynamics of larger systems such as churches, mental health/social service systems, medical systems, school systems, and business systems.*
5. *Students will integrate theological reflection in their learning of family systems theory and larger system contexts.*

---

[3] Jacqueline Braeger, Ph.D., LMFT created and teaches this course.

Reflexive Learning Through Self-Awareness and Clinical Practice

A critical component of our curriculum is the requirement that all students have their own therapy throughout their practicum course. Initially, students do individual therapy, while partnered students have the option of couples therapy. This requirement for personal therapy links to our supervision approach. If significant self of therapist issues emerge in individual supervision, the student's supervisor will instruct the supervisee to take this issue to his or her own therapy.

Following completion of this personal therapy requirement, students participate in a series of professional formation cohort groups. Students do not receive supervision credit for these groups. They complement the larger curriculum of the Seminary, with its emphasis on cohort groups that are non-credit. These groups have evolved over the course of a decade.

I was struck by several presentations at the 2009 Annual Conference of the Society for Pastoral Theology entitled "Engaging Differences." One presentation that was eventually published focused on race and ethnicity (Lee, 2009). Another presentation focused on sexuality and sexual orientation (Marshall, 2009). These topics were challenging to students. Up to this point, faculty and supervisors had not found an effective way to address sexual orientation and race/culture in personal, academic, and clinical dimensions.

In addition to these topics on race and sexuality, I began to wonder about what other topics caught the attention of our students in practicum and engaged them in sometimes heated conversation. The answer was immediate: spirituality! So, I chose three areas of "differences" that brought with them difficult conversations for students.

Our first foray was to present these differences in our weekly community meeting, a combined meeting with both the marriage and family therapy program and the mental health counseling program. We met periodically to discuss the following topics: (1) engaging differences: culture and race; (2) engaging differences: gender and sexuality; and (3) engaging differences: spirituality.

During these discussions, we had another hour-and-a-half peer group that was quite like an interpersonal relations group from the Clinical Pastoral Education model. It typically focused on each student's personal issues and could be at times confrontational. Gradually, this interpersonal peer group shifted to a self of the therapist group influenced by the POTT model.

Students thought the topics were quite timely, yet discussion time was truncated. They requested more time to process these topics. Given student feedback and the interest, faculty and supervisors of both the programs met to determine what changes might be helpful. The first decision was to have the "engaging differences" groups meet at the same time and to eliminate the interpersonal peer/self-of-therapist group. The next step was to blend a self of the therapist group with the engaging differences group. Genograms were used in all groups for each student to present as well as to connect that genogram to a case focusing on the "difference" during each semester. We then had the challenge of naming the groups. I suggested the following names: Professional Formation Cohort Group; Culture, Professional Formation Cohort Group; Gender and Sexuality, and Professional Formation Cohort Group; and Spirituality. The group agreed to these names. We have continued in this manner ever since.

Spirituality in Live Supervision Groups and Individual Supervision

As our work continued with spirituality, I began to see how we were gradually infusing spirituality throughout the program. Student feedback confirmed that they believed that they were gradually understanding more of what it was to "integrate spirituality." Then, suddenly one day, I realized that we did not infuse spirituality at all in our MFT live supervision. I began to work on these deficiencies. The result was the incorporation of spirituality in one semester of the MFT Live Supervision Group. Now, one semester of live supervision focuses on spirituality. Students have indicated that this approach helps them truly practice spirituality in their clinical practice. A detailed description of this live supervision process will be described in detail in a later chapter.

One of our ongoing challenges is how our individual MFT supervisors integrate spirituality in their individual supervision of students. We come from a variety of backgrounds. Some of our supervisors have never received formal training in a spiritually infused supervision or completed religion/theology coursework. Others have graduated from our own MFT program with its emphasis on spirituality. Still other supervisors have completed master's and doctoral degrees in theology. I plan to address this gap in our program with our supervisors soon.

Spirituality in the Capstone Presentation

The capstone presentation is structured so that students can demonstrate spiritual literacy and spiritual sensitivity. Prior to registering for the capstone presentation, students must complete P617 Integration of Self, Systems, and Spirit. During the semester when they present their capstone, students enroll in the Self, Systems, and Spirit Supervision Group in Practicum, which is led by me or another theologically trained faculty member. In addition to the MFT faculty member, students select another faculty member who teaches only theology classes as their non-counseling faculty mentor. To round out the evaluators, the student's individual supervisor is on the team.

The students select a couples or family case to present with video clips at the presentation, which uses PowerPoint. Then, the student completes a clinical assessment, case conceptualization, and treatment plan for the couple or family. All students who will present a capstone are members of this supervision group during the semester. The group begins with the faculty member presenting a review of P617 and then a summary of different approaches to spiritual integration. Then each student gives a mock capstone presentation to their peers, the MFT faculty mentor, and the non-counseling faculty member. Feedback from that presentation is then channeled into the writing of the 15–20 pages, emphasizing the integration of self of therapist concerns, clinical case issues, the MFT theoretical approach, and theological/spiritual reflection.

Suggestions for Integrating Spirituality in an MFT Curriculum

The case study of an MFT curriculum presented here has some limitations. Such an intensive infusion of spirituality into a secular university or college program would not be possible. Faith-based colleges, universities, and seminaries have much more latitude to accomplish the task. Some basic possibilities do exist for non-faith-based institutions, however. Several components would strengthen a program's emphasis on a social justice responsive spirituality. First is the inclusion of a religion course. Second is including a course that focuses on spiritual integration, and third is a reflexive learning course that emphasizes self of the therapist concerns. Finally, there is a multicultural course that emphasizes spirituality.

Creating a Spiritually Integrative Curriculum Across Mental Health Disciplines

This chapter's suggestions for a spiritually integrated curriculum in an MFT program can easily apply to various mental health disciplines. No revision of the curriculum process will be needed for a masters or doctoral program. For psychologists, social workers, and mental health counselors, the curriculum will just have the clinical theory that the individual program teaches.

Some modification will be needed for psychiatric rotation. I suggest that an overall comprehensive course be offered in medical school. Faculty from the religion department of the university can be invited to offer a module about spirituality as psychiatrists learn how to address religious and spiritual components of patients' care.

Self, Systems, Spirit Practice

Creating a Spiritually Integrated Curriculum

One of the biggest challenges in creating a spiritually integrated curriculum in a training program is achieving "buy-in" with faculty and students. The following suggestions will lay the groundwork for a successful curriculum change.

1. Share curriculum requirements with faculty and students prior to starting curriculum discussions.
2. Create a survey for faculty and students to complete to determine what the desired goals are.
3. Organize a brainstorming session for the faculty and another for students.
4. Take feedback from the students to the faculty at a separate meeting.
5. Create a curriculum team of faculty and student representatives.
6. Interview MFT program leadership at schools that have a spiritually integrated curriculum.
7. Create a trial curriculum.
8. Create a survey for faculty and students to get feedback on the trial curriculum.
9. Integrate feedback into the final draft for administrative approval.

References

ACPE. (2020). *Spiritually integrated psychotherapy (SIP) program*. Author. Retrieved September 20, 2021, from https://acpe.edu/programs/spiritual-integrated-psychotherapy

Allport, G. W., & Ross, J. M. (1967). Personal religious orientation and prejudice. *Journal of Personality and Social Psychology, 5*(4), 432–443. https://doi.org/10.1037/h0021212

American Association for Marriage and Family Therapy. (2004). *Marriage and family therapy core competencies*. Author. Retrieved from https://www.coamfte.org/Documents/COAMFTE/Accreditation%20Resources/MFT%20Core%20Competencies%20(December%202004).pdf

Anderson, D. A., & Worthen, D. (1997). Exploring a fourth dimension: Spirituality as a resource for the couple therapist. *Journal of Marital and Family Therapy, 23*(1), 3–12. https://doi.org/10.1111/j.1752-0606.1997.tb00227.x

Association of Marriage and Family Therapy Regulatory Boards (AMFTRB). (2017). *Examination in marital and family therapy*. Author. Retrieved September 20, 2021, from https://amftrb.org/exam-info/

Bonelli, R. M., & Koenig, H. G. (2013). Mental disorders, religion and spirituality 1990 to 2010: A systematic evidence-based review. *Journal of Religion and Health, 52*(2), 657–673. https://doi.org/10.1007/s10943-013-9691-4

Carlson, T. D., & Erickson, M. J. (2002). A conversation about spirituality in marriage and family therapy: Exploring the possibilities. *Journal of Family Psychotherapy, 13*(1–2), 1–11. https://doi.org/10.1300/J085v13n01_01

Carlson, T. D., Kirkpatrick, D., Hecker, L., & Killmer, M. (2002). Religion, spirituality, and marriage and family therapy: A study of family therapists' beliefs about the appropriateness of addressing religious and spiritual issues in therapy. *American Journal of Family Therapy, 30*(2), 157–171. https://doi.org/10.1080/019261802753573867

Carlson, T. S., McGeorge, C. R., & Anderson, A. (2011). The importance of spirituality in couple and family therapy: A comparative study of therapists' and educators' beliefs. *Contemporary Family Therapy, 33*(1), 3–16. https://doi.org/10.1007/s10591-010-9136-0

Commission on Accreditation for Marriage and Family Therapy Education. (2021). *COAMFTE Accreditation standards: Graduate & post-graduate marriage and family therapy training programs Version 12.5*. Author. Retrieved from https://www.coamfte.org/documents/COAMFTE/Accreditation%20Resources/2018%20COAMFTE%20Accreditation%20Standards%20Version%2012%20May.pdf

Coyle, S. M. (2014). *Uncovering spiritual narratives: Using story in pastoral care and ministry*. Augsburg Fortress Publishers.

Coyle, S. M. (2017). Integrating spirituality in marriage and family therapy training. *Australian and New Zealand Journal of Family Therapy, 38*(1), 142–155. https://doi.org/10.1002/anzf.1195

Coyle, S. M. (n.d.). Personal conversations between S. M. Coyle and various divorced clergy in the U.S., 1970s–1989s.

Donahue, M. J. (1985). Intrinsic and extrinsic religiousness: Review and meta-analysis. *Journal of Personality and Social Psychology, 48*(2), 400–419. https://doi.org/10.1037/0022-3514.48.2.400

Ellison, C. W., & Smith, J. (1991). Toward an integrative measure of health and well-being. *Journal of Psychology and Theology, 19*(1), 35–45. https://doi.org/10.1177/009164719101900104

Gorsuch, R. L., & McPherson, S. E. (1989). Intrinsic/extrinsic measurement: I/E-revised and single-item scales. *Journal for the Scientific Study of Religion, 28*(3), 348–354.

Grams, W. A., Carlson, T. S., & McGeorge, C. R. (2007). Integrating spirituality into family therapy training: An exploration of faculty members' beliefs. *Contemporary Family Therapy, 29*(3), 147–161. https://doi.org/10.1007/s10591-007-9042-2

Gutierrez, N. S., & Natrajan-Tyagi, R. (2018). Client-centered advocacy in education and clinical training from the supervisees' perspective. In S. Poulsen & R. Allen (Eds.), *Cross-cultural responsiveness & systemic therapy* (pp. 79–100). Springer.

Haug, I. E. (1998). Including a spiritual dimension in family therapy: Ethical considerations. *Contemporary Family Therapy, 20*(2), 181–194. https://doi.org/10.1023/A:1025077425777

Hiltner, S. (1958). *Preface to pastoral theology*. Abingdon Press.

Hiltner, S. (1972). *Theological dynamics*. Abingdon Press.

Hodge, D. R. (2005). Spiritual assessment in marital and family therapy: A methodological framework for selecting from among six qualitative assessment tools. *Journal of Marital and Family Therapy, 31*(4), 341–356. https://doi.org/10.1111/j.1752-0606.2005.tb01575.x

Lee, K. S. (2009). Engaging difference in pastoral theology: Race and ethnicity. *Journal of Pastoral Theology, 19*(2), 1–20. https://doi.org/10.1179/jpt.2009.19.2.002

Marshall, J. L. (2009). Differences, dialogues, and discourses: From sexuality to queer theory in learning and teaching. *Journal of Pastoral Theology, 19*(2), 29–47. https://doi.org/10.1179/jpt.2009.19.2.003

Moules, N. J. (2000). Postmodernism and the sacred: Reclaiming connection in our greater-than-human worlds. *Journal of Marital and Family Therapy, 26*(2), 229–240. https://doi.org/10.1111/j.1752-0606.2000.tb00292.x

Paloutzian, R. F., & Ellison, C. W. (1982). Loneliness, spiritual wellbeing and the quality of life. In L. A. Peplau & D. Perlman (Eds.), *Loneliness: A sourcebook of current theory, research and therapy* (pp. 224–236). John Wiley & Sons.

Patterson, J., Hayworth, M., Turner, C., & Raskin, M. (2000). Spiritual issues in family therapy: A graduate-level course. *Journal of Marital and Family Therapy, 26*, 199–210. https://doi.org/10.1111/j.1752-0606.2000.tb00289.x

Prest, L. A., Russel, R., & D'Souza, H. (1999). Spirituality and religion in training, practice and personal development. *Journal of Family Therapy, 21*(1), 60–77. https://doi.org/10.1111/1467-6427.00104

Roberts, N. L. (1999). *Spiritual diversity in couple and family therapy training student perspectives*. https://hdl.handle.net/10365/26728

Stander, V., Piercy, F. P., Mackinnon, D., & Helmke, K. (1994). Spirituality, religion, and family therapy: Competing or complementary worlds? *The American Journal of Family Therapy, 22*, 27–41. https://doi.org/10.1080/01926189408251295

Walsh, F., & Pryce, J. (2003). The spiritual dimension of family life. In F. Walsh (Ed.), *Normal family processes: Growing diversity and complexity* (3rd ed., pp. 337–372). Guilford.

Wendel, R. (2003). Lived religion and family therapy: What does spirituality have to do with it? *Family Process, 42*(1), 165. https://doi.org/10.1111/j.1545-5300.2003.00165.x

Williams-Reade, J. M., Lobo, E., & Gutierrez, G. (2018). Integrating spirituality into family therapy training: An exploration of faculty members' beliefs. *Contemporary Family Therapy, 29*(3), 147–161. https://doi.org/10.1111/jmft.12314

Chapter 7
Creating a Spiritually Integrated Course in an MFT Program

Creating a spiritually focused course in the family therapy curriculum is the primary means of integrating spirituality into an MFT program, according to scholars. To date, two articles have described different courses (Patterson et al., 2000). Reviewing these courses leads to a detailed description of "Integration of Self, Systems, and Spirit" at Christian Theological Seminary and the ways it serves as a foundation for the entire spiritually infused curriculum.

Historical Background of Spirituality Courses

"Spiritual Issues in Family Therapy," a one-credit course at the University of San Diego, a private Catholic university, is designed to address the systemic effects of an individual's or family's spiritual issues. The goals of the course are: "(1) training in opening a dialogue with individuals and families about religious issues and discerning when referral may be necessary; (2) expanding an awareness about wisdom traditions through use of comparative religions material; and (3) identifying from current practice many of the religious issues that may arise in the clinical setting" (Patterson et al., 2000, p. 203). The course is taught in an interactive discussion format. Students interact in the process of defining spirituality and religion throughout the course. No exams are given. Instead, three papers are assigned that pertain to different aspects of spirituality. The final assignment is a paper that requires students to relate a spiritual issue to the context of family therapy. Students who are not seeing clients select a film and imagine meeting with the family (Patterson et al., 2000).

The second course, taught at Loma Linda University—a private Seventh-day Adventist institution—is a methodologically reflexive spirituality practicum course. Students' self-awareness is incorporated into therapeutic practice. The goal of this course is to provide a training model to develop spiritual integration activities in

S. M. Coyle, *Spirituality in Systemic Family Therapy Supervision and Training*, Focused Issues in Family Therapy, https://doi.org/10.1007/978-3-030-92369-3_7

MFT. This course is part of a practicum sequence that consists of the following: (1) Gender and Social Context and Practicum; (2) Self of Therapist and Practicum; and (3) Spirituality and Practicum. Students' learning outcomes correlate with AAMFT core competencies and COAMFTE Standard 2 Version 12.[1] The course structure includes an introductory class discussion, personal spiritual assessment and presentation, readings and discussion, case presentation and feedback, and finally, case presentations and summary (Williams-Reade et al., 2018).

Both the courses utilize readings, group feedback, personal reflection, and a reflexive learning approach. The spirituality integrative course at CTS, "Integration of Self, Systems, and Spirit," employs all these dimensions. It differs in that it connects with a final capstone presentation to provide more in-depth knowledge. In addition, it creates connections with other components of the MFT curriculum to bolster the role of spirituality throughout the curriculum. The course was initiated in the spring of 2016 and has been taught five times. The teaching methodology has varied from face-to-face instruction, a hybrid version integrating face-to-face and online LMS, and a hybrid version integrating Zoom and online LMS. Through the years, the course has been revised somewhat based on student feedback. Readers can review the most recent syllabus in the appendices.[2]

Bridge to Integration of Spirituality Course

Students who attend our institution come from a variety of religious backgrounds: Pentecostal, Evangelical, mainline Protestant, non-denominational, Catholic, Buddhist, Jewish, spiritual but not religious, and a few agnostics/atheists. Christian Theological Seminary is an ecumenical seminary affiliated with the Christian Church (Disciples of Christ).

Reviewing these requirements for accreditation, MFT competence, and test completion, several themes emerge that will be illustrated in the following course description and curriculum design. (1) Spirituality is viewed as an important dimension of each person's life. (2) Students need to learn how to address spirituality in clinical practice. (3) Spirituality is understood as having a body of literature associated with it. (4) Spirituality/religion is placed in the same categories as other diversities, multiculturalism, and social justice concerns.

These themes are simple, and yet the MFT literature previously cited indicates that training programs do not train students well enough in this area. Attention to the following components of an MFT curriculum will give faculty and program directors some ideas for their own settings.

[1] Some COAMFTE accredited programs will adopt Version 12.5 beginning in January 2022.

[2] Integration of Self, Systems, and Spirit Syllabus is Appendix B.

Background Leading to Self, Systems, and Spirit Course

I am a faculty member at Christian Theological Seminary, where I also direct the COAMFTE accredited MAMFT program that was initially accredited in 1994. My employment at the Seminary began in 2004. The program was primarily theoretically informed by object relations when I arrived. With staff changes, the program evolved to a theoretically systemic program. Its general ethos has a postmodern approach.

At the same time, the program offers supervision and training from CBT to EFT and solution-focused to narrative and collaborative approaches. Students are expected to discern what their worldview is and what theoretical approaches best fit with that viewpoint. They can also elect to choose an integrated approach. Underlying all the theoretical perspectives is an emphasis on theological/spiritual reflection and how to integrate it with MFT practice.

In 2010 and with faculty support, I initiated a change from a thesis requirement at graduation to a capstone presentation. The rationale was based on the professional trajectory of our students, most of whom do not pursue postgraduate studies. They prepare to join community agencies, and some eventually set up private practices where they perform clinical work with individuals, couples, and families.

Working with students on their theses, I realized that several students had problems integrating theological/spiritual reflection into their requirement. At that time, the only theological/spiritual input students had was to complete four religion courses—one in theology, one in Hebrew Scripture, one in New Testament, and one general religion elective. For MFT students, that elective course was usually in Christianity and Culture, which focuses on social justice and larger social structures through a Christian lens. Students received no didactic preparation for integration of theology/spirituality to prepare them for writing the thesis. Their thesis mentor provided input to help students integrate theology/spirituality. Mentors for the theses were theologically and clinically trained faculty who taught in the two counseling programs in marriage and family therapy and clinical mental health counseling.

In informal feedback, students said that they were not receiving enough preparation in spiritual integration to meet the expectations for writing the thesis. At the same time, the faculty wondered about the purpose of a thesis given the students' professional trajectory. So, I began creating a capstone project. This change was passed by faculty through the institution's process for making curricular changes. A faculty member submits a requested program change to the Academic Council. The request is either approved or not approved. Approved proposals for change then go to the faculty to be approved or not approved.

Part of students' preparation for the capstone presentation is to take a supervision group in practicum called "Self, Systems, and Spirit." It meets weekly for 50 minutes, 12 times in the fall and spring semesters, and 10 times, or for 10 weeks, in the summer semester. During the supervision group, the student presents their preliminary capstone project. After a few semesters, students told me in informal feedback that while they found the "Self, Systems, and Spirit" group helpful, a full semester course would be most helpful. In contrast, the projected integration of spirituality class would meet 3 hours for 14 weeks. In response to student feedback, I created the course "Integration of Self, Systems, and Spirit." (See Appendix B for the "Integration of Self, Systems, and Spirit" syllabus.)

Methodology of "Integration of Self, Systems, and Spirit"

The course has three-tiered foci of self, systems, and spirit. Self is identified as the inner sense of identity that all humans have. Traditional self of therapist issues are concerns here. Systems is identified as recurrent patterns that create both family and larger systems including MFT theories, diversity concerns, and their connections with families. Spirit is identified that immanent/transcendent sense of spirituality that must be critically reflected on from a theological and/or spiritual perspective. The integration of self, systems, and spirit is the course's focus. The overall structure was created in response to students who completed a SurveyMonkey questionnaire that asked them to identify their learning needs and goals for the course. The course is evaluated through student outcomes that are correlated with the AAMFT Core Competencies and the COAMFTE Accreditation Standards Version 12. The next course will be aligned with the COAMFTE Accreditation Standards Version 12.5.

A reflexive approach is utilized in the course. Students are challenged to identify their personal worldviews and how that worldview is reflected in their theoretical and clinical practice. Examination of self is accomplished using several approaches. Each class begins with an experiential exercise that is designed to support students to assimilate issues about self, systems, and self in their personal and relational identities. An example is to ask students to focus on a spiritual story and how this has impacted their lives. Students then meet in dyads to share this experience.

Reflecting teams meet during the class either face-to-face or on teleconferencing platforms. In these teams, students practice reflexive behaviors that can be applied to their work in the therapy room with clients. Such experiences adhere to mutually agreed upon guidelines among group members to encourage openness and safety.

Students reflect in these groups on their own connection with self, systems, and spirit as well as with one another so that both the personal and professional identities of the student are transformed. Rounding out the explicitly reflexive aspects of the course is a spiritual conversation with the professor. Prior to this 30-minute conference, each student completes a survey with questions designed to assess his or her worldview as a foundational step for how to assimilate self, systems, and spirit. The professor then works with each student to contextualize the course for them based on their worldview. To support this reflexive approach, students read and complete re-storying exercises by this author to introduce students to their spiritual stories that are lying under the surface. In addition to these personally transformative assignments, some written assignments contribute to the course.

In summary, this course integrates theological/spiritual reflection with systemic theories and professional formation. Students begin the course by focusing on their professional and personal development through self of the therapist emphases. As students identify self of therapist concerns, they begin to identify their worldview. Then, that worldview relates to relational systemic concepts that evolve into methodological considerations of integrating self, systems, and spirit. Finally, students are introduced to ways in which learnings from this course contribute to their relational systemic competence.

Course Objectives

The course objectives of "Integration of Self, Systems, and Spirit" are the following: 1) Explore understandings of spirituality, religion, and theology and the ways in which they are similar and different, 2) Explore personal and professional self-of-therapist concerns through experiential and reading assignments 3) Explore relational systemic concepts and ways in which they connect with MFT models of therapy 4) Explore methodologies of integrating self, systems, and spirit (5) Apply learning from the class to relational systemic clinical practice and 6) Integrate learnings in a mock MFT capstone paper.

Didactic Reading and Writing Assignments

Readings for the course include an introduction to theology text, an introduction to systems thinking, several articles about self of the therapist, and some readings by this author. In addition, students are required to select a theology book that matches their worldview and spiritual perspectives. Finally, they read more in-depth about the MFT theory of their choice. Class discussions include spiritual interventions to try with clients from the instructor's experiences as well as textbooks (Helmeke & Sori, 2006).

Moving from the reading, the course is offered in several formats: face-to-face, hybrid, and online. The face-to-face course has the highest degree of interactive lectures. The writing assignments in some versions of the course encompass several themes. In the *statement of self paper*, students are required to reflect upon who they are and their stage of personal and professional development. Students are also required to write *reflection papers* on selected readings. These papers cover three areas of focus: self of therapist, systems, and spirituality. Students select one reading of their choice under each focus area. I have discovered that students are more engaged in a writing project if it is an area in which they are interested.

Earlier versions of the course focused on choosing either a *methodology of integration paper* or a mock capstone paper. In the methodology of integration paper, students will be required to submit a paper demonstrating his/her own methodology of integration. This methodology paper will be in response to a couple or family case they are seeing in practicum. (Students do not need to be in practicum. They can respond to a case vignette from their introductory MFT text or work with a practicum intern on one of the intern's cases.) They then integrate their favorite theologian/theological approach/spirituality approach in this paper. Finally, they select an MFT theoretical model or common factors model and their choice of theological perspective/theologian to integrate with his/her statement of self paper, which comprises the methodology of integration paper.

Current versions of the course offer the possibility of a *mock capstone paper*, which is evaluated using a capstone rubric evaluation.[3] The evaluation rubric was the primary difference between the methodology of integration paper and the mock capstone paper.

The final assignment is a fun and challenging way to offer a reflexive approach to learn how to integrate. My graduate studies and years in ministry and teaching have led me to believe that integrating theology/spirituality with systemic thinking is partly linear thinking, partly non-linear thinking, but primarily creative thinking. Drawing from my former life as a music major, this *creative arts project* gives me an opportunity to be creative along with students. I give students a simple exercise, included in the appendices, to activate their left brain. Some use it and some do not. The goal of this creative arts project is to illustrate the challenges in methodological integration of self, systems, and spirit. For example, it could be a light-hearted skit, a presentation of appropriate art, composed music, and/or a combination of these. Students then present these projects in class.

Suggestions for Faith-Based MFT Programs

Readings

Faith-based MFT programs need to determine their spiritual/theological ethos, and the primary readings in the course should follow along those lines. Of course, students who differ from that orientation should be given the option to substitute readings with the instructor's approval. All students should read mostly the same books. MFT faculty can consult with the religion department to get a list of suggested readings. Then, students should be given the opportunity to read one spirituality/theology book that goes with their own spiritual worldview.

[3] This rubric was adapted with permission from one of the Diane Gehart rubrics from the MFT Competencies System that our program purchased years ago.

Reflection Papers

Readings should be selected from self of therapist, systemic, and spiritual readings. Students can select from a variety of readings.

Self of Therapist Paper

The student reflects upon his or her family of origin and the role that spirituality has played in the family. A spiritual genogram can be used as a supporting document.

Reflecting Teams

Students should be divided into reflecting teams that reflect a diversity of age, race, and gender. The groups will meet during the class period to discuss questions. Also, they will participate in experiential exercises.

Final Methodological Paper

Students need to be assigned a final paper where they present a clinical case and integrate spiritual themes with clinical concerns. It is important to use a systemic framework for the integration. The student needs to include his or her own spiritual perspective and how it helps and hinders work with the client. The paper should be referenced with primary sources from spiritual and clinical authors.

Suggestions for a Secular MFT Program

The main differences for a secular college or university will be in readings as well as discussion. The readings would have a component of world religions and existential material. An outstanding book by Bidwell (2019), *When One Religion Isn't Enough: The Lives of Spiritually Fluid People*, would be a solid basic book for all students. All students will select a book that aligns with their spiritual orientation.

Another uniqueness is to determine which faculty will teach the course. The department can decide whether a faculty member with interest in religion and/or spirituality can teach the course. Either choice would work. Or the course can be team taught by a family therapy faculty member and a university faculty member or community member with an interest in religion and/or spirituality.

A major consideration for a secular university is to determine what written assignments are most appropriate. A school having a capstone paper could use much of the methodology from the CTS program. In contrast, a school having a thesis would want to determine if a spiritually integrated section in the thesis would be desirable.

Creating a Spiritually Integrated Course Across Mental Health Disciplines

Psychology, social work, and professional counseling in graduate programs would have similar objectives as family therapy in creating a spiritually integrative course. The methodology of such a course would need to be consistent with the department's overall purpose for training clinicians. Is spirituality desirable as a major emphasis alongside such emphases as theoretical approaches? On the other hand, is spirituality considered under the umbrella of multiple diversity concerns? Will such a course be required or an elective? After such questions are answered, it would be helpful to have a mini-retreat for faculty to determine how to go forward.

A psychiatry department would need to consider how such a course would or would not fit in the medical school curriculum. Putting a dedicated course to spiritual integration would certainly require vetting on many levels. One important consideration would be to match such an emphasis on spirituality to the Joint Commission standards that hospitals follow in the clinical documentation about the patient's spiritual orientation.

Self, Systems, Spirit Practice

Discovering Creativity in Teaching Spirituality

Creating a spiritually integrated course for a clinical training program should be just that—creative. So, how do faculty engage in a creative process with competing administrative, publishing, and teaching deadlines? Set aside time for a mini-workshop of 2 or so hours. The following are suggestions that will take a morning or afternoon, whether virtually or face-to-face.

Mini Workshop

Pre-meeting

- Gather one to three resources that nurture your own spirituality however you define it. Review those resources. What catches your attention?
- What are some questions to consider in small groups?

Dreaming

Show a series of abstract pictures such as clouds, swirls of color, nature photo, etc. Have music playing in the background.

- What gives you energy to dream dreams?
- How big are your dreams about your clinical training program?
- Describe a visual image of a dream about a spiritually integrated course?
- Group discussion

Hurdling

- Now, in your mind's eye, see yourself running toward a track and field hurdle. What do you have to get over the hurdle?
- Do you envision hurdles to overcome in achieving that dream?
- Group discussion

Journeying

- Describe what dreams and hurdles you will take with you on the journey to create a course with a spiritual emphasis
- Group discussion
- How might your spiritual resources you gathered prior to this future journey sustain you?
- Group discussion

  Brainstorm where, as faculty, will you go from here?

References

Bidwell, D. R. (2019). *When one religion isn't enough: The lives of spiritually fluid people*. Beacon Press.

Helmeke, K. B., & Sori, C. F. (2006). *The therapist's notebook for integrating spirituality in counseling: Homework, handouts, and activities for use in psychotherapy* (Vol. 1). Hawthorn Press.

Patterson, J., Hayworth, M., Turner, C., & Raskin, M. (2000). Spiritual issues in family therapy: A graduate-level course. *Journal of Marital and Family Therapy, 26*(2), 199–210. https://doi.org/10.1111/j.1752-0606.2000.tb00289.x

Williams-Reade, J. M., Lobo, E., & Gutierrez, G. (2018). Integrating spirituality into MFT training: A reflexive curriculum and qualitative evaluation. *Journal of Marital and Family Therapy, 45*(2), 219–232. https://doi.org/10.1111/jmft.12314

Chapter 8
Preliminary Research in the Integration of Spirituality and Systemic Family Therapy

Spirituality may be taught in systemic family therapy programs in academic courses. Supervision in programs often addresses self of therapist issues, theoretical approaches, and clinical skills. Periodically, spiritual issues emerge which are addressed in training. Scant reference to addressing spirituality in systemic supervision exists.

Spiritual training for supervisors is therefore crucial in developing competent clinicians. Due to the lack of existing content in training programs, an open question is how best to train therapists for spiritual work. Below I demonstrate that spiritually focused self of therapist explorations, combined with guided interventions in live supervision, instill the skills necessary for addressing clients' spiritual concerns. Thus, spirituality training for trainees may improve both students' satisfaction with their programs and their own perception of their competence with spiritual interventions.

Introduction

The spiritual training project at the core of this pilot study was conducted at Christian Theological Seminary and formulated as an addition to existing curricula. Unlike many counseling programs, Christian Theological Seminary already integrates spirituality in its therapy training program. As such, it will be useful to briefly review the state of the Master of Arts in Marriage and Family Therapy (MAMFT) program at Christian Theological Seminary.

An integration course on spirituality, a spiritually infused academic curriculum, a professional formation group on spirituality, and a final capstone paper requiring spiritual integration were gradually added to the program over the years. This training was provided by both theologically trained and non-theologically trained

S. M. Coyle, *Spirituality in Systemic Family Therapy Supervision and Training*, Focused Issues in Family Therapy, https://doi.org/10.1007/978-3-030-92369-3_8

supervisors. Supervisors address spirituality in individual and tandem supervision. All supervisors in the program are open to addressing competence in students in addressing their clients' spiritual concerns in a clinical setting. Students are encouraged to respond to clients' various spiritualities, including conservative and liberal Protestants, Catholics, Jews, Buddhists, Muslim, agnostic, atheistic, and spiritual but not religious.

Despite the spiritually aware curricula at CTS reviewing the evaluations from this corps of faculty and supervisors, the integration of spiritual/theological reflection was strong with some students and not strong with other students. The self of the therapist and clinical/theoretical integration seemed more consistent with the students than the spiritual integration. That therapists in training at a seminary would not consistently report high levels of proficiency in spiritually sensitive counseling underscores the degree to which it can be difficult to adequately train therapists in this competency. The core faculty and supervisors began to wonder how we might better equip our students in their ability to both conceptualize and implement spirituality in their clinical practice.

Students' clinical skills were also more solid on theoretical approaches in their work with clients. At times, their integration of spirituality in clinical skills was strong, while at other times, not so much. In reviewing the curriculum, spiritual integration had been infused in different aspects of the program except for live supervision. In live supervision, theoretical approaches and self of therapist were often foci for the group to the exclusion of spirituality. However, the need for students to respond more fully to their clients' spirituality became clear.

Having reviewed the institutional context and motivation for the pilot study, I now turn to describing the existing spiritually focused changes to the CTS live supervision curriculum put in place directly prior to the pilot project. These changes motivated and served as the basis for the pilot project interventions, which are discussed later.

Background: MFT Live Supervision Group on Spirituality

Implementation of Re-storying Exercise in Live Supervision

Curricular change in clinical practicum began in spring 2019 with the inclusion of spirituality in live supervision groups. This change took the form of a self of therapist exercise that emphasized the student's spirituality. Students were apprised prior to the beginning of the supervision group that the focus of the group would be on the spirituality that emerged in the live supervision session. Each group was composed of practicum and pre-practicum students. The pre-practicum students were enrolled in the P522 Introduction to MFT Practice.

Practicum students were responsible for bringing an individual, couple, or family to live supervision and were part of the observation team, as were pre-practicum

Table 8.1 Re-storying spirituality exercise

Telling of the Story (interviewee): Think about a formative spiritual experience and share it with us. (A formative spiritual experience is defined as a spiritual experience that you know is true for you and serves as a source of strength. It takes you beyond self and relationships to something that is bigger than you.)
Questions: How does this story support you?
Re-telling of the Story (other members): What part of the story resonates for you? Re-telling of the Re-telling of the Story (interviewee): How does this re-telling of your story resonate for you? (Coyle, 2019).

students. The pre-practicum students were instructed to share what they observed and not to make interpretations. The supervisor of each group facilitated the process by encouraging the contributions of both practicum and pre-practicum students.

The program's integration of self, systems, and spirit is a curricular focus. Additionally, a foundational dimension of that focus is the self of therapist in the program. To explore the spirituality dimension of self of therapist, each student in the live supervision groups participated in a "Re-storying Your Faith" exercise that is a part of the Staff of Spirit collective narrative process (Coyle, 2014). Given the importance of this exercise to the spiritual training project, I will now describe this re-storying process, which was adapted to the live supervision groups.

The supervision groups are composed of both pre-practicum students and interns. In live supervision, interns are the therapists in the CTS Counseling Center. They bring their clients to live supervision for in-depth supervision. Pre-practicum students who are taking either Introduction to MFT Theory or Introduction to MFT Practice are part of the live supervision observation team. After a few weeks of experience in the observation team, pre-practicum students may join interns as members of a reflecting team.

In this re-storying exercise, interns sit in a circle with pre-practicum students sitting in a circle around them. The supervisors ask questions, following the format and content shown in Table 8.1. People tell their formative spiritual experience as the sharing moves around the circle.[1] The supervisor asks each student to tell a story of a formative spiritual experience with the following definition: "A formative spiritual experience is defined as a spiritual experience that you know is true for you and serves as a source of strength. It takes you beyond self and relationships to something that is bigger than you" (Coyle, 2013).

[1] These questions can be used both in a live supervision session, other supervision experiences, or an experiential self of therapist exercise.

Live Supervision Process

The interns in the MFT Live Supervision Group were students in the "Narrative and Collaborative Approaches to Therapy" class.[2] Each student was required to bring individuals, couples, or families to the live supervision group. In the first counseling session, the intern was to employ a collaborative approach using a reflecting team. The reflecting team guidelines came from Gehart's third edition of *Mastering Competencies in Family Therapy: A Practical Approach to Theories and Clinical Case Documentation* (Gehart, 2018).

The collaborative reflecting team guidelines were as follows: Students instructed clients that they could listen or not listen to the comments of the reflecting team. The client was to focus on comments that "strike a chord." The reflecting team was to comment only on what was seen or heard. They took a "curious" position to enable the client to generate new perspectives. Multiple perspectives were encouraged. Reflecting team members did not make interpretations but shared what they observed. The team and the family were in the same room but did not talk with each other.

In the second counseling session, which focused on narrative therapy, interns created a definitional ceremony with outsider witnesses. The following guidelines were followed according to Michael White:

> These are four categories of response that can be considered by reflecting team members as they prepare themselves for an outsider-witness retelling. These can also be of assistance to therapists as they get ready to interview outsider witnesses when this group is not composed of professional counselors who are familiar with the tradition of acknowledgment that characterizes definitional ceremony. Categories of response are not exclusive but provide an example of how the contribution of outsider witnesses might be structured within the terms of this tradition of acknowledgment. Categories of response are: 1) identify the expression, 2) describe the image, 3) embodying responses, and 4) acknowledging transport (White, 2005).

No preliminary research analysis of this live supervision process was conducted. However, the following qualitative interview gives a flavor of the spiritual process engaged in the live supervision group.

Sharing formative spiritual experiences was quite moving and influential for several students. Through this sharing of story and response by colleagues, students had an opportunity to look at previous experiences in a different light that gave them a deeper understanding of how they connected with themselves and others. An interview with such a student may give the reader deeper insight into the process itself.

---

[2]The spring 2019 supervision group described here consisted of students in "Narrative and Collaborative Approaches to Therapy," which I taught. I also supervised the one supervision group described here.

A Student's Story

Sam is an MAMFT student in his 40s. After the students and I gathered around to receive the stories, Sam was the first to volunteer. As he began, he was hesitant. He said that he did not think of himself as spiritual but did believe in God. The supervisor encouraged Sam as she repeated the following definition of a formative spiritual experience: "A formative spiritual experience is defined as a spiritual experience that you know is true for you and serves as a source of strength. It takes you beyond self and relationships to something that is bigger than you" (Coyle, 2013).

Sam said he would try. As he began, he described his growing up years and attitudes around spirituality and religion. He indicated that his mother was raised Catholic. Her experiences led her to decide that she would not give direction to her children regarding religion. So, Sam's mother and father did not encourage or discourage him and his siblings when it came to religion. There was no directive except to just be a "good person."

Through Sam's childhood and teen years, he often felt like an outcast. In his family, he was the only one with light coloring, freckles, and blonde hair. This was also true in his peer group. He told a story that was a "formative spiritual experience." During middle school, he remembered that his buddies often received many valentines during Valentine's Day parties at school. Sam was unhappy and had low self-esteem.

One day, Sam looked up and said, "God, if you're up there, I have no self-confidence. I want girls to like me. They don't now. I'm not popular. I'll never be able to have sex. Please help me."

With a laugh Sam says, "It certainly wasn't the spiritual request. But it was what I needed. It was made from desperation. I had a human need and needed to be validated." By some serendipity, Sam began getting valentines at school. His confidence grew. He became quite popular in high school and dated many girls.

After asking Sam about the impact of the experience on his life today, he said that it gave him hope and a belief in gratitude. Now he always tries to be grateful for what comes his way. Sam succeeded in the media business before deciding to become an MFT therapist. His wife is a beautiful, accomplished professional. Together they have a son and daughter who are equally accomplished. In a final assessment, Sam believes in God and identifies as spiritual but not religious. He sometimes attends a mainline Protestant denomination. His connection with gratitude that emerged from that middle school experience has led to an understanding of the "communion of the saints." While he is not explicitly religious, Sam does understand that his family and loved ones who have died and those loved ones on this earth connect for him in a supportive sense of connection (Sam, Personal interview, October 1, 2020).

The informal report from students in the live supervision groups prompted continuing discussion in supervisor de-briefing. We supervisors reflected on the

"Re-storying Spirituality Exercise." It seemed to us that a helpful way forward was to engage in a modest pilot study. So, we proceeded.[3]

Preliminary Research Study on Therapists' Own Spiritual Narratives in Spring 2020

Supervisors who implemented the adapted "Re-storying Exercise" (Coyle, 2019) debriefed about their experience in MFT Live Supervision in spring 2019 decided to create a formal pilot project integrating that exercise. The purpose of the study was to determine the following: How does a therapist's own awareness of his/her own spiritual narratives enable the therapist to re-author the client's own spiritual narratives? This approach contrasts with current MFT approaches to spirituality in therapy that focus primarily on the client's spirituality as well as spirituality inventories that assess the client's spiritual constructs (Coyle et al., 2020). The research component of the project aimed at qualitatively evaluating the outcomes of the spiritually focused training interventions.

This research proposal was submitted to the IRB at Christian Theological Seminary that focused on an integrative approach blending spirituality/theological reflection with self of the therapist and clinical practice. The purpose of this project was not to conduct a full-scale quantitative study. A small sample would not produce results that would be consistent with a robust MFT research study. Further, a literature review did not discover any type of research that focused on the process of spiritual interventions in systemic family therapy.

Thus, the intent of the project was to explore areas of spirituality that had not yet been explored in the field. The pilot study would need to start quite literally from scratch. This qualitative study could focus on phenomenological experiences of students as they look at ways who they are affect what they do in clinical practice. The methodology was influenced primarily by the spiritual/theological method that is now the foundation of the living web of socio-spirituality.

Thus, the intent of the 2020 study and then the 2021 study was to explore interdisciplinary fields that do not have the same standards as a straightforward systemic family therapy project. It is grounded in spiritual/theological methodology. This preliminary research study was conducted during one semester of live supervision. Pre- and post-tests were given to nine students. One of these students was enrolled in practicum and was actively seeing clients during live supervision. The remaining students were pre-practicum and continued as observers. The pre- and post-tests took the form of spirituality and self of therapist assessment statements. Students responded on a 5-point scale where 1 was "strongly disagree," 2 was "somewhat disagree," 3 was "neither agree nor disagree," 4 was "somewhat agree," and 5 was "strongly agree."

[3] MFT Live Supervision supervisors were Suzanne Coyle, Christina Davis, and Kimberly King.

Table 8.2 Spirituality and self of therapist

Q1:	I am able to identify my own spiritual narratives.
Q2:	I am able to identify the spiritual values and/or stories I hold dear.
Q3:	I have intentionally reflected on my spiritual narratives as they connect with my conducting therapy.
Q4:	I am able to identify how my spiritual values connect with those of my clients.
Q5:	I am able to identify how my spiritual questions connect with the clinical questions of a case.
Q6:	I am able to identify the ways in which the spiritual values and/or stories of my clients resonate with me.
Q7:	Awareness of my own spiritual narratives affects my ability to thicken my clients' spiritual narratives in therapy.

The pre-test was administered at the beginning of the semester to all students. Following the pre-test, students participated in a re-storying of spiritual narrative exercise. Practicum students were then asked a specific set of questions prior to and following meeting with their clients at several points throughout semester as the pre-practicum students observed the process and the life sessions with clients. The post-test was administered at the end of the semester to all students.

Following the post-test, responses for each of the seven questions were tabulated and grouped together into three categories: "disagree," which combined the strongly disagree and somewhat disagree responses; "agree," which combined the strongly agree and somewhat agree responses; and "neutral," which included neither agree nor disagree responses.

Based on the decrease in "disagree" responses and increase in "agree" responses from the pre-test to the post-test, it was determined that the re-storying exercise had a positive effect on responses for the questions in Table 8.2 (Coyle et al., 2020).

Pilot Project on Spiritual Interventions in Spring 2021

Anecdotally, the students expressed interest in self of the therapist issues and spirituality those two semesters. They indicated in informal conversation that they experienced personal and professional growth because of the pilot project. At the same time, they still conveyed to me that they did not know how to address spirituality in a therapy session.

I began to reflect upon my own assumptions about self of the therapist and its potential connection with spirituality. My reflection on the two semesters' experiences of addressing self of therapist issues affirmed my understanding that spirituality is a part of our relational selves. Struggling with self of therapist issues can have an influence upon one's spirituality. A gap still existed, however, between the student's personal self and the way in which students were able or not able to address their clients' spirituality. Some of my most clinically adept students expressed a sense of inadequacy in responding to spiritual concerns in a therapy session.

The interns' awareness of their own personal spiritual stories did indicate promise in using this reflexive experience to help student deepen their own spirituality. However, it did not directly influence the interns' clinical interactions with their clients.

At this point, I decided that a live supervision group focused on actual spiritual interventions might be helpful for students to engage more fully in their clients' spiritual process. The IRB at Christian Theological Seminary approved the project Spiritually Focused Interventions' Effect on the Therapist's Sense of Competency in Addressing Clients' Spiritual Concerns The result was a pilot research project I supervised that required students to intervene with spiritual questions in therapy sessions. Details of the project are described below.

Purpose of the Study

This pilot research study considers the following question: Can training in spiritually focused interventions positively affect a therapist's personal sense of competence in addressing clients' spiritual concerns?

The purpose of this pilot study is to train beginning therapists in an MFT training program to make spiritual interventions with their clients that will create an environment where clients can thicken their spiritual narratives. The desired outcome is that therapist will be better able to make spiritual interventions with their clients. It is hoped that the interns will have an increased sense of competence in addressing their clients' spirituality in therapy sessions. Sense of competence here is understood as the therapist's improved confidence in their clinical skills to support their clients' life challenges.

Currently, MFT literature acknowledges the absence of MFT training for students to develop clinical skills that utilize spiritual foci as a therapeutic tool. Extant literature also indicates that the majority of MFTs believe that spirituality is an important aspect of their clinical practice. Yet, they also say that they do not have the skills to intervene clinically around spirituality. Furthermore, MFT students indicate that they want their training programs to train them on spirituality. This research study will lay foundations for MFT students to be both spiritually literate and spiritually sensitive (Carlson et al., 2002).

Description of the Project

Five students who were members of their matriculating cohort group were invited to participate in the research study as part of MFT Live Supervision in spring 2021. The students then had the option to participate or not participate as part of their MFT Live Supervision for the following semester. As the principal investigator, I informed them of the research study by e-mail, indicating that students who participated would receive alternative relational hours for their preparation and session

Table 8.3 Pre/post research questions for pilot research project

Please answer on a scale from 1 to 5.
1 = strongly disagree
2 = somewhat disagree
3 = neither agree nor disagree
4 = somewhat agree
5 = strongly agree
1. I am able to utilize spiritual interventions in clinical sessions.
2. I am able to identify what are the openings in clinical session for spiritual interventions.
3. I have reflected on my personal spiritual narratives and how they affect clinical work with my clients.
4. I am able to expand my clients' spiritual narratives to facilitate their personal growth.
5. I am able to identify my clinical challenges that connect with spiritual concerns.
6. I am able to articulate my challenges about spirituality in clinical practice with my supervisor.

participation as well as credit for the required 6 hours of didactic training. Alternative relational hours include participation in observation teams in live supervision.

Students who elected to participate in the research study accrued the following practicum hours: for each MFT Live Session where live clients came to participate, each student received 2 hours of clinical supervision and 2 hours of relational hours. In addition, each student received 1 alternative relational hour for session preparation and 1 alternative relational hour for de-briefing with their supervisor. For each session, each student was eligible for 2 additional hours of alternative relational and 2 supervision hours if they participated in an end-of-semester group at the end of MFT Live Supervision with the supervisor. All the five interns opted to participate in the group. Three pre-practicum students who participated in the observation team opted to participate in the research project. These students received 2 alternative relational hours for each live supervision session for participation in the observation team.

Prior to the beginning of MFT Live Supervision, I provided, as the group supervisor, the first three chapters of this book to read. During the supervision group, I showed a video of me in a role-play demonstrating spiritual interventions.

Students completed the following questions prior to each session. They also responded to the questions after the completion of each session (Table 8.3).

Procedures

Pre-session of Live Supervision

I asked the intern for a brief description of the client(s). Then, the following question was asked, "What is one concern you have about the case to focus on tonight?" I asked the intern the following question: "What spiritual values and/or story you hold dear, connects you to this client?" Interns and pre-practicum students then asked questions about the whole case.

After discussion of the questions, all team members turned off their video and muted the audio to enable them to observe the Zoom session. The therapist for the clients chose three people to function as the reflecting team. The reflecting team followed Gehart's guidelines in Mastering Competencies *Mastering Competencies* (2018). Various theoretical approaches could be utilized by the intern.

During the Session

The session was recorded for my review later. I marked the interventions I thought met the criteria for the spiritual questions on which the students were trained. Interns also indicated places in the session where the intern made a spiritual intervention or where they thought the student could have.

This live supervision was conducted during the exceptions the program made for the COVID-19 pandemic in spring 2021. All students in the supervision group logged into a HIPAA compliant Zoom platform. The intern who brought the clients to the session conducted the session with the audio and video turned on in Zoom. Other members of the supervision group turned off their video while viewing and listening to the session.

Table 8.4 Questions for socio-spirituality interventions through self, systems, and spirit

Self
Can you tell me something about yourself that would let me understand more about what is spiritually special to you?
What qualities about yourself let you open yourself up to new possibilities?
How do these qualities connect you to others?
Define relational selves. How does your sense of what is spiritual allow you to fully connect with others?
Which of your relational selves sustains/gives you support as you explore your spirituality?
Systems
What possibilities/hopes and dreams do you envision in your connections with others/communities?
What story of hope do you gather from others and your communities?
How do you see yourself sustaining hope in a world filled with hopelessness?
What/who might stand in the way of this hope?
How might you speak to these obstacles?
Spirit
How have you been able to envision a hopeful future through the spirit of the everyday and the spirit of what is not seen? How not?
How might you change your spiritual stories so you can engage a hopeful future?
Are there some human systems that stand in the way of your thickened spirituality?
How might you use the everyday (immanence) and the unseen (transcendence) to sustain yourself on this arduous journey to hope?
Are there social justice efforts you might embrace outside this room/virtual session to connect you to what is spiritual and just?

The students were trained to utilize a set of questions created by the researcher as a support for spiritual interventions (Table 8.4).

Post-session

Interns and some pre-practicum students formed the observation team. The supervisor then asked the intern where he/she thinks they made a spiritual intervention. Then, the intern is asked where he/she might have made an intervention. Then, I asked the observation team the same question. Further discussion among team members then took place.

Results

Following the post-test, responses for each of the six questions were tabulated and grouped together into three categories: "disagree," which combined the strongly disagree and somewhat disagree responses; "agree," which combined the strongly agree and somewhat agree responses; and "neutral," which include neither agree nor disagree responses (McMillen, 2021) (Table 8.5).

None of the pre/post-test question response distributions were individually formally significantly different at the 95% confidence level according to a one-sided Wilcoxon test. Nevertheless, some of the question response distributions were suggestive of being different pre- versus post-test (within the 90% confidence interval). Aggregating all the question responses into a single pre-test distribution and single post-test distribution, however, results in a significant improvement in self-reported competence in spiritually focused therapy according to a one-sided Wilcoxon test (p-value of 0.005).

Table 8.5 Results

Differences in responses by question. p-values indicate the significance of a one-sided Wilcoxon test under the null hypothesis that the pretest response distribution median did not increase compared to the posttest distribution median. "Number of Disagree Response Changes" means the number of Strongly Disagree or Disagree responses that increased at least one level. "Number of Agree Response Changes" is defined analogously.

Question	Number of disagree response changes	Number of agree response changes	Number of unchanged responses	p-Value
1	1	4	3	0.07
2	1	4	3	0.11
3	2	0	2	0.09
4	3	3	2	0.20
5	3	1	4	0.23
6	1	3	4	0.09

Several possibilities exist for future research. (1) Examine the meaning of competence for MFT trainees and revise the pre- and post-test questions accordingly. (2) Re-work the pre- and post-test questions. It is unclear to what degree the students' responses indicate how their perception of their competence with spirituality interventions really translates into how well they actually do with their clients. For example, some students indicated a decrease in their sense of their ability to implement the spiritual interventions after the training and clinical experience regarding spirituality. Did the new learning cause the students to set a higher bar for themselves? (3) Increase the sample size so that quantitative analysis on a question-by-question level is more certain. (4) Create a longitudinal study in which beginning students take the same questions before they have had any classes about spiritual integration. (5) Solicit several MFT programs that would like to be part of a larger study.

Debriefing Session and Post-test Questions

I conducted a debriefing session with the interns after the live supervision session intervention on Zoom, which included all students who answered the post-test questions. In addition, I debriefed interns who conducted the clinical session after each clinical session.

Debriefing Select Interns' Live Supervision Experience Through Video Material

The debriefing of select students about their experience in the pilot project is described below.

Intern A

Intern A, a biracial male, brought a white male client with an autism diagnosis to supervision. The student had seen Client A for several months. Intern A commented that he was amazed that the reflecting team's comments correlated with much of what he and the client had discussed. He used one of the spiritual intervention questions with the client. The client then shared the importance of prayer in his life and how he had prayed most recently for this father when he was quite ill. The student was surprised that prayer was as important to his client as the client expressed (Student A Debriefing, February 5, 2020).

In a conversation, Intern A said, "Faith didn't come up for the client during our sessions. But, using this question, it did come up." Intern A then said that he would consider how to address prayer in future sessions. I then asked Intern A, "How does your own spirituality connect with your client's spirituality?" He identified the following aspects: (1) they both share a systemic understanding about other religions and faiths in some way connecting, and (2) they both can express doubt as part of their faith. Finally, the student said that it was good to have an opportunity to do conceptualization around spirituality with a supervisor. This was not an experience he had had so far in the program.

The supervisor and group members reviewed the session. A comment that led to spirituality was the client's comment, "You pray, and hope things go better." The intern responded with an affirmation of his client's connection with prayer. He followed that comment with "waiting is the name of the game" to which the client nodded. And then, he followed with asking the client if he got "any peace out of prayer," to which the client said "yes."

Intern A then asked the client "What are your values in your spirituality?" to which the client responded, "It's peace for me and a relationship with God and others." The client concluded that the journaling he had been doing was helpful and connected well with the prayer.

The students and the supervisor highlighted these junctures as places where Intern A did helpfully use spiritual interventions. They all agreed that the intern really connected with the client when he discussed spirituality. At the same time, everyone agreed that those interventions could have been helpfully expanded (Group Debriefing, April 12, 2021).

Intern B

Intern B is an African American female who brought an African American client to the live supervision session. In my debrief session with the student, she began with the Scripture verse that says that Paul planted the seed, Apollo watered, and God gave the growth. Apollo plants the seed, another waters, and then the increase comes. As Intern B viewed the video of the session, the student compared that growth of a seed with hope that expanded through the counseling session. The initial question from the set of spiritual intervention questions referenced in Table 8.2 prompted the student's assessment of hope as a possibility in the relationship between the client and her mother (Student B Debriefing, April 8, 2021).

The client's contentious relationship with her mother had been a piece of the therapy process. The hope intervention came when the client shared an experience with her mother that was not contentious but peaceful. It was here where the student made the intervention about hope. Intern B commented to me in the debriefing session, "Just that newness to their relationship was peace where hope could be built."

Intern B then shared that her understanding of liberation theology supports the dimension of hope in clients' lives. She said, "There needs to be a safe place where hope can grow in intimate moments of a relationship." While Student B acknowledged the role of a spiritual intervention around hope in the session, she also acknowledged that there were other relationships in the client's life that could be expanded. I asked her, "Where might you have made more spiritual interventions?" Intern B replied that the client mentioned in the session that she was appreciative of her husband's efforts to support her. "Yes, I could have encouraged the client to expand her appreciation of her husband." The supervisors asked the intern, "Is there a spiritual story or set of values that you hold dear that connects you with this client?" The student responded that it was how she sees grace and mercy. She said that she is motivated by these values as she engages with clients. A follow-up from the supervisor queried, "Is there any particular issue about spirituality?" to which the student responded simply, "hope."

As the video was reviewed, the intern asked her client, "Can others show compassion for you?" Lowering her head, the client responded, "No. I did have a conversation with my mother." The client talked rapidly and expressed her sense of many people not understanding her. Intern B's client then expressed her efforts to push against that in her life. Intern B affirmed her.

I later asked the question of Intern B, "What did you do that were spiritual interventions?" The student responded that she focused on hope and connected that with the client's mother.

The observation team then responded to the notion of hope. "Hope lifted up the client" and "I thought hope was already there before the intervention."

I then asked, "How do you build on things to identify the human in every person?" One student responded with a question, "How do I understand my own worth as a human?" Intern B responded that compassion must be a part of that answer. The supervisor closed the review session with a question, "How do we prepare a path for client to be receptive to spirituality?" The student responded, "I suspect it would have touched on hope" (Group Debriefing, April 12, 2021).

Debriefing Spirituality Through Video Material with Group Members

I reviewed the marked interventions in the recorded session. Then, those marked interventions were compared with those from the intern and the observation team. The following is a summary of the post-session review of videos by the whole supervision group of interns and pre-practicum students.

After the semester supervision group concluded, I debriefed the whole group about their experience. I queried the group, "What was your thinking about spirituality and making spiritual interventions with clients before the supervision experience?" Several students said that they had always been hesitant to use spiritual interventions or talk about spirituality because it seemed that they might offend someone. Some students also said that they had not discussed how to do this in classes, so they thought it was best to leave it out. One student said she was "uncomfortable" with "those kinds of things."

One student, however, indicated that she had always thought it was important to discuss with clients. She went on to say that she had tried to address spirituality without much guidance. Another student said that such spiritual interventions needed to be done "skillfully."

I finally asked the group, "What is your thinking about spirituality and making spiritual interventions after focusing on this process for a semester?" The group was quite enthusiastic in their responses. "I feel more confident now. I think I'll try it some." "I want to develop my own way of doing spirituality. But this focus has been helpful." "I learned some new ways to think about spirituality." "This is an important area that we need to learn about" (Group Interview, April 19, 2021).

Finally, I queried an intern about her experience.

Intern C

Intern C is an African American female who works with Client C, a white female who is a waitress. Client C came out of an abusive relationship. She recently had a baby. Intern C describes Client C as someone who is "ready to do the work." The supervisor then asked the student if there was a particular concern she wanted to focus on in the counseling session. Other questions focused on the spiritual stories or values the student has and how those values connected to her client. The student said the client being ready to work resonated with her. She saw herself as wanting to do that in practicum. Like the client, she wanted to find her best self (Student C Debriefing, March 19, 2021).

For a while, Client C did not want to speak to her mother and felt abandoned. After the birth of her child, however, she has started to reconnect with her mother. At one point in the video, Client A says she often feels overwhelmed and that things sometimes feel like a "waste of time." To counter this narrative, the student asks, "What qualities can you identify about yourself?" The client says that she is adaptable. She also says that she is becoming more able to separate herself from other people.

Client C responds to the student that she is "working on allowing grace." The client softly begins to cry. Intern C then says "You have a spiritual sense of self. What does that mean for you—spirituality?" with the client responding, "fate or destiny."

As the video is reviewed, the supervisor asks the intern, "Where did you make a spiritual intervention?" The intern cited the session juncture where the client cried as being spiritual with her follow-up. She then said that overall, she would expand some of the answers.

Implications

Researching spirituality and the spiritual interventions that are possible is a new adventure. The pilot project described in this chapter is only a beginning. An informal conversation with the interns and pre-practicum students who participated in this study revealed that they had a greater sense of confidence after the spiritually focused training that occurred in the live supervision group. The positive effect the pilot project had on the trainees is also quantitatively confirmed when considering the aggregated results across the questions in the pre- and post-tests.

The process engaged in this study focused on the actual interventions. It did not look at overall spiritual themes. Below is an intern's case study with an analysis utilizing the living web of socio-spirituality presented previously in this book. This analysis will give the reader a sense of possibilities using this model.

Intern D Case Study

AM and AF are a couple who see Intern D in couples therapy. AM is a high school teacher; AF a stay-at-home mom who homeschools their four children. They have been married for 20 years. The family self identifies as evangelical Christians. The past 8 months has been characterized by behavioral problems with their 15-year-old male child. They came to counseling to get the tools to help the family function more fully. The wife takes an anti-depressant. The husband often seems cold and distant. He is a cancer survivor. As a result of his cure, he "appreciates the little things in life" and sees his faith as central to his life.

The couple says that they select a Bible verse for each academic year to guide the family's everyday life. The past year's verse was Romans 12:2: "Do not conform to the pattern of this world but be transformed by the renewing of your mind. Then you will be able to test and approve what God's will is—his good, pleasing and perfect will." In addition to this verse, the family always emphasizes serving and hospitality as Christian values in their home.

In one session, Intern D asked the couple about the role of prayer in their lives. The couple responded that they put everything in prayer to God: kids' conflicts, big worries, their marriage. They further responded to the student that they regularly use the Bible verse to give their lives hope.

The reflecting team that listened to the couple during live supervision wondered how the sharing of emotions as a family connected or did not connect with the verse. One realization from the wife was that when she was calm, she was better able to share that calmness with the kids. Furthermore, AF cried, saying, "I want to turn things to God so that something will come from it." The couple also acknowledged that peace and hope is what they yearn for as a family. The family also expects godliness and perfection (Student D Interview, July 16, 2021).

Spiritual Critique

The intern and reflecting team were able to look at different junctures where spiritual interventions were helpful as well as appropriate. The students all believed that the answer to godliness and perfection was grace. The supervisor countered with the question, “How do they accept grace? What are the steps?” Several times, the couple mentioned the need for hope, not grace. So, the spiritual critique that comes now is to look at ways the socio-spirituality model can offer a method for clinically encouraging clients’ spirituality.

The first step is to look for a theme for this family that exists in their everyday lives as well as their spiritual lives. This family members are disconnected from one another. They are also overwhelmed. “Everything is just too much.” They yearn for peace. They are also focusing inwardly on themselves. Their worlds are the homes and the church.

How might this family expand their worlds? They can enter the socio-spirituality world. Instead of just existing in a spiritual world, the family can move toward social justice. Typically, one understands social justice to apply only to progressive, liberal people. However, evangelical, and conservative people believe it is important to house and feed those who have basic needs. This social need connects directly with the family theme of hospitality that clients identified.

This family could work at a soup kitchen and take the kids. It would involve hospitality in a social realm. Furthermore, this connects with Freire’s socio-spirituality model, which focuses on people who do not have much (Freire, 2018).

Adaptation to Secular Environments

The spiritual interventions in clinical practice presented in this chapter are situated in an ecumenical seminary with students from seekers, evangelical, liberal, Jewish, Muslim, and Buddhist backgrounds. The living web of socio-spirituality is a tool, however, that can be adapted to various spiritual orientations including those persons who identify as agnostic and atheist. I contend that all humans have spiritual capacity, which is defined as a “value or concern bigger than oneself and relations” (Coyle, 2013). Secular universities and institutions have the capacity to modify the intervention questions to fit their contexts in the best way.

Spiritual Interventions Across Mental Health Disciplines

Live supervision is a unique form of supervision that conceptually and practically belongs to family therapy. Other mental health disciplines such as psychology, mental health/professional counseling, and social work all work with students in individual and group contexts. Psychiatry supervises through case report.

Despite these differences with family therapy, I suggest that the questions that are offered as possible spiritual interventions can certainly be used by supervisor in working with supervisees. They do have a postmodern flavor. At the same time, they lend themselves to different theoretical modalities. Spiritual interventions could be used well in medical family therapy in a hospital setting. In both private and hospital settings, psychiatrists could use some of the questions posed in this chapter, as social workers and professional counselors also could.

Self, Systems, Spirit Practice

Possibilities for Further Research

Invite a group of private practice clinicians, agency clinicians, faculty, supervisor to explore possibilities for researching spirituality in systemic family practice.

Several discussions can be held:

1. What determines trainees' sense of competence in clinical practice?
2. In what way does spirituality determine that sense of competency?
3. What is a challenging aspect of integrating spirituality in clinical practice?

References

Carlson, T. D., Kirkpatrick, D., Hecker, L., & Killmer, M. (2002). Religion, spirituality, and marriage and family therapy: A study of family therapists' beliefs about the appropriateness of addressing religious and spiritual issues in therapy. *American Journal of Family Therapy, 30*(2), 157–171. https://doi.org/10.1080/019261802753573867

Christian Theological Seminary. (2020, October 1). Personal Interview with Sam.

Coyle, S. M. (2013). *Re-storying your faith.* John Hunt Publishing.

Coyle, S. M. (2014). *Uncovering spiritual narratives: Using story in pastoral care and ministry.* Augsburg Fortress Publishers.

Coyle, S. M. (2019). *Re-storying exercise.* unpublished document.

Coyle, S., Davis, C., King, K., & McMillen, E. (2020). *Using the therapist's own spiritual narratives as a lens in relational systemic live supervision to facilitate thickening of clients' spiritual narratives.* Unpublished manuscript.

Freire, P. (2018). *Pedagogy of the oppressed.* Bloomsbury.

Gehart, D. R. (2018). *Mastering competencies in family therapy: A practical approach to theory and clinical case documentation.* Cengage Learning.

Group Debriefing. (2021). Zoom.

Group Interview. (2021). Zoom.

McMillen, E. (2021, July 28). Personal email communication to Suzanne Coyle.

Student A Debriefing. (2020). Zoom.

Student B Debriefing. (2021). Zoom.
Student C Debriefing. (2021). Zoom.
Student D Interview. (2021). Zoom.
White, M. (2005). *Workshop notes*. Dulwich Centre. Retrieved from https://dulwichcentre.com.au/wp-content/uploads/2014/01/michael-white-workshop-notes.pdf

Chapter 9
Expanding Spirituality to Community-Based Service Contexts

Community-based service settings are more often connected with social work than family therapy. However, both the professions share a systemic orientation. This systemic perspective can be used as promisingly by MFTs as by social workers. Furthermore, the additional clinical training of MFTs, in contrast to social workers, gives MFTs an advantage in working with community centers that too often MFTs do not access. Collective narrative practice is a methodology that values the distinctive timbre of many voices in a collective context. Thus, MFTs can practice their systemic clinical training through this methodology to use social justice with spiritual implications.

Context for Socio-Spirituality in MFT Training

MFT training and supervision in the living web of socio-spirituality provides context for integrating diversity and social justice with spirituality. This type of integration can be intimately linked to a spiritually infused model of social action that enriches all the systemic dimensions of individual, family, and larger systems. As MFT students delve into systemic theories and practice their clinical skills, they generally remain within the academic class environment and active practicum setting. Student learning revolves around an exploration of self that informs their supervised clinical practice.

We MFTs do not talk enough about larger systems and the interconnectedness of all systems with the family dynamic. Students would have more in-depth learning about larger social structures if they were able to interact with those systems beyond the classroom and therapy room. Admittedly, many of our students are placed in community mental health agencies where they see clients in counseling. They participate in treatment team meetings to discuss cases. In those groups, larger system dynamics are part of the conversation. However, for treatment team gatherings, larger system dynamics are not the primary focus.

The multicultural emphasis in our MFT programs does focus on diversity concerns that are presented in the MFT CC 1.2.1 (MFT Core Competencies, 2004). Students discuss these concerns in classes emphasizing multiculturalism, participate in experiential groups, and connect multiculturalism to self of therapist

S. M. Coyle, *Spirituality in Systemic Family Therapy Supervision and Training*, Focused Issues in Family Therapy, https://doi.org/10.1007/978-3-030-92369-3_9

concerns in supervision and their own therapy, if desired. Few programs are likely to place students directly in larger community systems due to the priority on internships where students counsel individuals, couples, and families. At the same time, students may lose important experiences if they do not have some placements in community agencies that focus on support groups and larger community involvement.

Such group experiences may have transformative potential for students as well as agency clients. Interacting with larger systems on a regular basis provides a real-life experience. For example, trainees may not fully understand the difference between working with a client who works in a large medical center and a client who works in a private medical practice. The client may present a similar work-related problem in a counseling session. The response of the therapist to the client, however, should differ depending upon the systemic nuances between a large medical center and a private practice. Interns who have had professional experiences in large systems could have a deeper understanding of the two contexts.

Students in MFT programs would benefit from engaging with a clinical practice setting that connects diversity concerns with social justice and spirituality. Such a model would offer students a learning environment where social action could be practiced, and spiritual conversations could occur. Yet, such an approach, where theoretical and practical conversations can take place in a living community agency, is difficult to find. It is rare to find theoretical models that recognize both individual and community experiences at the same time and as being interrelated. I discovered collective narrative practice to be such a model.

During my training at the Dulwich Centre in Adelaide, South Australia, I became familiar with collective narrative practice.[1] This approach to narrative practice looks to sustain individuals, groups, and communities who experience hardship. It is also accessible for everyday people who have not had extensive professional mental health training. Narrative therapy ideas are put into an everyday narrative practice. At the same time, the effects of collective narrative practice are to lift the voices of many who are oppressed and want to experience unity with others who experience hardship. It also encourages people who are marginalized and oppressed to contribute to the lives of others experiencing hardship (Denborough, 2008).

Collective narrative practice does not have an inherently spiritual focus in a limited sense of the word. I do believe, however, that its effects on people are quite spiritual. Transcendence in collective narrative practice depends on the individual and the community's learning, individually and together, about their depth of being. Collective narrative practice also moves toward an explicit desire to make social change and to be an agent for social justice. Thus, I contend that it is a powerful support to the living web of socio-spirituality as explicated in this book.

The rest of this chapter's discussion will focus on the following: (1) a more comprehensive discussion of collective narrative practice; (2) the means of connecting spirituality with collective narrative practice; (3) a case study of a collective

[1] See https://dulwichcentre.com.au/.

narrative project through the Desmond Tutu Center for Peace, Justice, and Global Reconciliation; and (4) a description of how MFT training programs can implement a collective narrative practice in the community.

Collective Narrative Practice and Social Sustenance

Collective narrative practice is best understood by its four basic principles: (1) to listen for double-storied experiences, not only the hardships but also how people have responded; (2) to find a way to richly acknowledge the effects of oppression; (3) to link the marginalized person's life and experience to some collective or larger group; and (4) to enable the marginalized person to make contributions to others' lives (Denborough, 2008).

An individual can tell a story about his or her hardship within a group of other individuals who experience hardship or are socially marginalized. In collective narrative practice, the concept of ritual and definitional ceremony is significant. White translated the concept of definitional ceremony to involve "outsider witnesses" to the reflecting teamwork developed by Andersen. It is a different process than Andersen's reflecting team. In the definitional ceremony, individuals or families are interviewed about whatever problems they have faced. "Outsider witnesses," who can be persons facing the same problem or professionals, act as an audience to this interview. The outsider witnesses then speak to what they have heard from the family while the family is in the audience position. The roles are then reversed so that family members reflect on what was spoken by the outsider witnesses (Denborough, 2008). Ritual here is a process by which the storyteller and the audience both hear and respond to the same experience. After processing the experience in a different way, participants may be able to repeat the experience in unique settings.

White developed four categories of responses by outsider witnesses: (1) Identifying the expression: What expressions you heard caught your attention? (2) Describing the image: What images did those expressions evoke? (3) Embodying responses: What is it about your own life/work that accounts for why these expressions catch your attention? and (4) Acknowledging transport: How have you been moved by being an audience? Where has it taken you that you would not otherwise be? (White, 2005).

After this portion of the definitional ceremony, collective narrative practice is interested in enabling a sense of unity for the person's past and future and with others in the collective group. Multiple possibilities exist for realizing definitional ceremonies, such as letter writing or a ritual enacted in the present, face-to-face with others. Some examples of rituals include storytelling, meetings, murals, protest marches, and composed songs. For centuries, religious communities have identified rituals that bring back memories of sacred importance. Whether explicitly secular or religious, a ritual can perform such a function in the lives of participants, as narrative practice describes it. Creating one's own narrative practice around spirituality can be an experience such as learning from Chad Loftis (2016). An anthology of new collective narrative practices in addition to Loftis' innovative approach to therapy through liturgy can be found in Denborough's new publication (2018).

The cultural anthropologist Barbara Myerhoff describes some definitional ceremonies that are about much more than merely redefining identities and are instead forms of social action (1986). At times, one can imagine social action to be a narrow protest. Collective narrative practice as a form of social action can take stories of hardship and marginalization and turn them into community stories that give members encouragement. It may be that such activity can result in a social movement. An example of a sustained social movement is the modern feminist movement, which did not have protests or political action at its inception. Now it has expanded to include womanist, Latina, Asian, and other ethnic identities that connect with the liberative theologies we have discussed. Denborough talks about White's narrative maxim, "the person is not the problem, the problem is the problem" and expands it to "the person is not the problem, the problem is the problem and … the solution is not only the person" (Denborough, 2008). Problems that exist in families thus have a social origin. By using collective narrative practice, MFTs can focus on both the individual and the family as well as the societal connection when it comes to meeting familial challenges.

Collective narrative practice richly describes how people react to experiences of social injustice. It finds ways to document the skills, knowledge, and values used in those responses. Rituals and ceremonies may sustain what has occurred through repeating the stories in one's memory. At times, a therapist can listen to these stories of memory in a way that encourages clients to use them as a source of resilience. We then find ways for marginalized persons to contribute to the lives of others who are affected by social injustice. Finally, we find ways to look to local culture for everyday experiences that can give hope to people's futures (Denborough, 2008).

In summary, collective narrative practice has the potential to spark social movements. It connects the personal with the community while not collapsing one into the other. It also reaches deeply into the hearts of people where their spirits live (Denborough, 2015). A striking example of a social movement that connects social justice and spirituality is the Civil Rights Movement as led by Dr. Martin Luther King Jr. It was a movement sustained by non-violence and love alongside feelings of anger and hurt.

I took a group of M.Div. students from Christian Theological Seminary to commemorate the 50th anniversary of Bloody Sunday.[2] We traveled through Atlanta, Montgomery, Selma, and Birmingham, ending in Memphis at the National Civil Rights Museum. I stopped in one room that focused on the Freedom Riders' contribution to civil rights. On the wall was a framed document typed by Dr. King. The document outlined directions to the Freedom Riders when they boarded the bus. It said that despite the treatment they might receive from bus drivers, they were to remain respectful and practice love. Love. How powerful, the essence of spiritual

[2] Bloody Sunday refers to Sunday, March 7, 1965, in Selma, Alabama. Peaceful civil rights protesters were bludgeoned by some law enforcement officials.

power. Storytelling in this movement served to share powerful experiences with people who were not there and across generations.

Spirituality can powerfully connect human hardship and social movements so that the human diversities that characterize our immanent existence can be transformed. Through both immanent and transcendent experiences, spirituality can come forward through collective narrative practice as we open ourselves to experiences larger than ourselves and relationships that sustain us and others. We are then able to both increase our vulnerability as well as our resilience to hardship.

Yet, it is not only collective narrative practice that offers an environment for personal and social transformation. MFT programs can utilize the rights of our families to tell their stories. At the Tenth International Narrative Therapy and Community Work Conference in Brazil in 2014, the Dulwich Centre launched a "charter of storytelling rights." Penned by David Denborough, this charter "defends people's rights to name their own experiences, to define their own problems, and to honour (sic) how their skills, abilities, relationship, history and culture can contribute to reclaiming their lives" (Dulwich Centre, February 27, 2014). Here it is the charter:

Article 1 Everyone has the right to define their experiences and problems in their own words and terms.

Article 2 Everyone has the right for their life to be understood in the context of what they have been through and in the context of their relationships with others.

Article 3 Everyone has the right to invite others who are important to them to be involved in the process of reclaiming their life from the effects of trauma.

Article 4 Everyone has the right to be free from having problems caused by trauma and injustice located inside them, internally, as if there is some deficit in them. The person is not the problem, the problem is the problem.

Article 5 Everyone has the right for their responses to trauma to be acknowledged. No one is a passive recipient of trauma. People always respond. People always protest injustice.

Article 6 Everyone has the right to have their skills and knowledges of survival respected, honoured (sic) and acknowledged.

Article 7 Everyone has the right to know and experience that what they have learnt through hardship can contribute to others in similar situations (Dulwich Centre, Charter of Storytelling Rights, 2014).

Using the principles of the Charter of Storytelling Rights provides a solid foundation for any community project that an MFT program might initiate on behalf of justice for marginalized people. Several connections between this charter and collective narrative practice will be made clear in the following description of the Tutu Center project. Just under the surface of a collective practice are the lights of spirituality. We move now to an explication of ways in which spirituality and social justice can weave together prospects for a hopeful future.

Spirituality in Collective Narrative Practice

Spirituality is not a primary focus of collective narrative practice. Collective practice primarily focuses on the hardships of marginalized people. In this sense, such projects encourage multiple voices to express their experience with oppression as it affects human diversities such as sexism, racism, agism, ableism, gender identification, sexual orientation, and socioeconomic distress. Spirituality and religion are indeed diversities themselves that can influence collective narrative practice in multiple ways.

Discrimination on account of religious adherence is, of course, a diversity that needs to be guarded so that people have freedom of choice. However, I would offer that spirituality is more of an inner process that is much less subject to discrimination than the other diversities listed in MFT CC 1.2.1 (MFT Core Competencies, 2004).

Spirituality begins as an interior reflection encompassing all the relationships and personal connections that we experience. However, spirituality goes beyond that immanence and expands to the transcendent—that which is larger than self, others, and the earthly.

As we look at the description of collective narrative practice, an ethos emerges that beckons us to reflect upon spirituality. Oppressed people yearn for relief. They are normally able to identify who and what the proximate oppressors are. They are not always able to identify the systems of oppression that take place through large institutions, however. As their recognition of oppressions grows, they are able to develop a fleeting vision of what kind of future they want. As they reflect upon their vision of the future, they are also able to fully experience the pain of the present.

It is at this point that collective narrative practice encourages people who are experiencing the same oppression. The many lift their voices. In the polyphony of voices, witnesses may hear the voices as one choir. However, individual voices are part of that great chorus. If one listens closely, one can hear a high voice, a low voice—voices that produce different sounds. Each person in the group who has undergone the same oppressive experience experiences it in a different way.

Here, collective narrative practice endeavors to keep each individual voice in consort with others: to have unity through diversity, the Freirean ethos (Freire, 2018). With each individual voice comes some loneliness and isolation. Listening to others who are singing from the same page of pain, people still experience emptiness. At this point, individuals need to decide what they will do. A typical response is to either isolate oneself or seek comfort from others. The collective practice offers the option of presenting others who can share anger, offer comfort, and connect with a common experience. Or the person can elect not to connect with others. My experience is that deciding to be alone is less common.

Still, even while connecting with others in the collective experience, loneliness and hopelessness can emerge. It is here that spirituality appears. Collective narrative practice does not name spirituality. But spirituality becomes the unnamed sustenance that individuals can reach for. Here we have individuals engaging with others through a collective. But they still have needs and still feel emptiness. The emptiness is characteristic of the search for a spiritual dimension.

Where then does spirituality fit in collective narrative practice? Let us go back to the living web of socio-spirituality. We have there the balance of immanence and transcendence, along with the liberation theologies that push marginalized people toward hope. It is in the possibility of hope where people can envision a future.

As marginalized people face the grim reality of oppression, I believe that many people want to choose freedom and hope. Even with emotional and intellectual resources and a community of supporters, however, the reservoir runs dry. At that moment and in others, spirituality shows up to sustain people. So, how does that occur?

The facilitator in community groups or even members of the group can offer some spiritual light. Having a list of questions available prior to the beginning of the group can give the group and facilitators a degree of confidence. It can even inspire hopefulness.

So, let us define hope. Hope is a living construct that speaks to clinical, social justice, and spiritual concerns. We can describe in operational terms what hope looks like. Any clinician or spiritual leader can recognize the signs. A hopeful person can be identified by expressing realism about the oppressions of the present while committing to changing the present. As he or she looks at the present, attention is paid to the tiny specks of light that beckon to the future. The person talks about that brief aspect of light with others. He or she engages them in conversation about the future. That person decides to take a tentative action of change in moving toward the future. He or she may invite others to join the action. In any case, it is acted upon. This is hope in action.

And yet hope in action does not move forward in a straightforward way. Stops and steps backward occur. During these times, the hopeful person does not keep hopelessness captured inside. He or she shares that hopelessness with others quite ironically as an expression of hope. For hope without hopelessness is really a hope totally disconnected from our world.

As the person is stalled in hopelessness, he or she again looks around to discern the presence of hope. At this point, spirituality can be accessed. One lesson from Hebrew Scripture is the story of the Hebrew wandering in the wilderness for 40 years. They cursed, they lost their vision, but they persevered. So is hope the story of perseverance. The hopeful person looks to past experiences when God or a sense of transcendence lighted his or her way, enabling them to go forward. At this point, let us highlight liberation theologies for wisdom in the hope of spirituality that is not just clinical, not just social justice, but active spirituality. Liberation theologies differ from other theologies in their confidence in future hope that is alive in everyday life. They believe that spirituality for everyday people is not contained in creeds or ritual beliefs. Inherent in its spirit is the notion that others, as well as the person, must engage in social actions that can free people from hopelessness. The spiritual dimension of liberation theology is the hope that a future dream can be achieved.

Tutu Center for Peace, Reconciliation, and Global Justice Project

The Desmond Tutu Center for Peace, Reconciliation, and Global Justice (DTC) was a 5-year joint partnership from 2013 to 2018 between Butler University and Christian Theological Seminary. It was launched to promote the legacy of Archbishop Tutu, the Nobel Peace Prize Laureate, in Indianapolis, Indiana, with Allan Boesak serving as the inaugural chair of the Desmond Tutu Center from 2013 to 2017. A native of South Africa, Boesak's early activism and service led to international recognition as an influential leader in the fight against apartheid. During the 1980s and 1990s, he worked alongside Desmond Tutu and Nelson Mandela to lead efforts against apartheid and to promote reconciliation.

At the core of DTC programming was the objective to initiate and encourage vigorous scholarly engagement on global justice through research and exchange with individuals, institutions, and networks. The Tutu fellows program supported the training of researchers at Butler University and Christian Theological Seminary, many of whom are uniquely poised to be leaders on global justice issues. The DTC provided funds for projects that aligned with the center's mission. I was chosen as a Tutu Fellow for 2014–2015. The following is a description of the funded project.

Local Engagement of MFT Students in Global Justice: "Hearing Our Voices—Marginalized People Affected by Poverty Speak Out"

Introduction

Persons who are marginalized by poverty and trauma often experience that there is no place for them in the dominant culture. North American culture values economic and vocational success as necessary steps to reaping benefits from the American dream. Persons who do not have these markers of success are often viewed as non-contributors to society. This section presents a project for the Desmond Tutu Center for Peace, Reconciliation, and Global Justice that uses storytelling to affect social justice.

Furthermore, labels such as "lazy" are often attributed to these individuals. These labels contribute to an identity narrative that marginalized persons often internalize. In turn, such internalization negatively contributes to their experience of themselves in a success-oriented culture.

At this point, a vicious cycle begins. In accessing resources such as food stamps and welfare funds, and even vocational rehabilitation, marginalized persons may come to believe that they are unable to move out of a cycle of poverty (Payne, 2005). As their economic and vocational resources dwindle, it may be that their lack of success as defined by the dominant culture becomes intertwined with their personal identities.

Several different models of strengthening personal identity in the face of socioeconomic challenges exist. Many of these approaches utilize awareness of the oppressive system in which the person lives as well as the available resources to provide exits from the oppressive system. Furthermore, there are therapeutic interventions to support the individual in processing areas of trauma, with the goal of resolving personal conflicts.

Other approaches to address socially inflicted pain on individuals may include family therapy. Working with whole families is a common approach that seeks to understand the identity narrative of an identified patient as it pertains to the whole family. This approach certainly provides appropriate therapeutic results.

At the same time, family therapy has been critiqued for not looking beyond the family system to the broader societal system. When this occurs, personal concerns such as socioeconomic disadvantage are not adequately addressed. Another challenge in this regard is the omission of broader social concerns.

Narrative therapy has long been concerned with the politics of personal concerns. The saying, "every personal concern has its origin in a social issue," is its mantra. Thus, narrative therapy has an innate interest in political issues and righting social wrongs. At the same time, narrative therapy emphasizes that every person is the expert of his or her story. This flattens the hierarchy of the therapist as expert.

The political foundation of narrative focuses on the multicultural nature of working with people. All people have cultural backgrounds that need to be respected by the therapist. In turn, the therapist has a cultural background that influences his or her perspective on the client's problem and world. That is why narrative advocates for the therapist adhering to an ethic that is "de-centered and influential" (White, 2005). In this context, de-centered refers to the therapist not being the focus of the therapy but rather the client. In turn, the client's stories and sensibilities guide the therapeutic process while the therapist seeks to have a beneficial effect on the client.

A strength of the narrative approach lies in its understanding that the client's future is to be determined by what he or she desires. This future is to be determined by a preferred story that the client shares with the narrative therapist. In turn, the therapist supports the client to envision multiple stories can thicken the client's future life story. Underlying these multiple stories are various accounts of cultural identities that color both the client's world as well as the cultural discourses in society that shape formative discourses against which the client must create his or her identity.

Personal discourses for individuals can be strengthened by connecting them with undiscovered discourses through collective narrative practice, a relatively new methodology in narrative practice. A brief discussion of collective narrative at this point will be helpful to bridge the path to other approaches to cultural awareness and the project of this Tutu Fellowship.

Collective Narrative Foundations

One can see the cultural richness in collective narrative therapy. As the foundation for the Tutu project, my contention is that it provided a rich extension of previous approaches to cultural thickness in peoples' stories. A discussion of those approaches will now follow before an elucidation of the actual project.

Collective narrative practice is based on the following ten themes: 1) As we listen to people's stories, we understand that these stories not only represent personal experience but also result from broader social issues, 2) Despite the degree of hardship, individuals and communities are always responding to their situations. They are not static, 3) Experts from outside should not bring our own initiatives to the situation. Rather, we need to unearth the skills, values, hopes, and dreams that are implicit in people's responses to hardship. 4) Once we involve people's initiatives, we seek to find other communities for whom those initiatives will resonate. 5) By doing this, people who are experiencing hardship can make significant contributions to other's lives through sharing their stories. 6) Intergenerational sharing can alleviate many causes of suffering and hardship. 7) People's responses to hardship and trauma are forms of local social action. People can expand on the description of the experience. In this way, experiences become linked to reclaiming their lives from trauma. 8) "Local folk culture" can strengthen local healing knowledges that emerge from mediums such the written word, spoken word, song, film, dance, poetry, and celebration. 9) Through this process, we work for "the invention of unity in diversity" (Freire, 1994, p. 157). This is the way we acknowledge the rich diversity of people's skills, knowledges, values, and hope. 10) We then look for a broad view and long timeline where many generations can be engaged (Denborough, 2008).

Foundational Approaches to Cultural Awareness

For decades, family therapy has recognized the need to address the socioeconomic contexts of populations that do not fit into the culturally dominant white middle-class ethos. Historically, Salvador Minuchin has addressed the uniqueness of minority persons. Beginning with his work in New York with young Black men, he recognized the uniqueness of the Black community amid the normativity of white family life. From New York, his work at the Philadelphia Child Guidance Clinic saw the development of structural family therapy that expanded understanding of the Black family to include the extended kinship system as its basis.

From this important start in family therapy, ecosystemic structural family therapy is now a lively conversant as the ecological environment of larger systems and the ways in which it impacts families is examined. Current work in family therapy is seen in Nancy Boyd-Franklin's systemic work with African American families. In addition, the development of Multisystemic Family Therapy in working with adolescents has improved treatment while recognizing the impact of multiple systems on families.

Recent approaches to addressing the need for social justice come in the model of social empathy (Ham, 2014). Social empathy understands empathy, contextual understanding, and social responsibility to be a path toward social justice. It addresses affective response/mirroring in conversations with people as well as recognizing cognitive processing and the need for conscious decision-making as part of necessary ethical awareness. From this juncture, contextual understanding can occur as the impact of systemic conditions and the historical background are brought to light. This contextual understanding then makes it possible for social responsibility to be exercised, since empathy and contextual understanding have laid the foundation resulting in social empathy.

Social empathy can find a growing place through narrative responses to social injustice. When persons and communities experience poverty and trauma, they need both comfort and courage to face further challenges. Social empathy, as described above, is one such approach. A related approach is cultural equity, which is understood as a bridging the complexity of social identities with therapeutic practice. It focuses more on the narrative idea of identity than social empathy does. The complexities identified in the social matrix are power, privilege, and oppression (Almeida et al., 2011). The authors contend that cultural equity is more appropriate for conversations in our society around social dilemmas in our country.

Building a conversation around cultural equity would allow engagement in new ways with the notion that minority status means experiencing an inordinate amount of poverty and trauma, and much more than the white middle class, which is protected by white privilege. At the same time, the middle class includes many pockets of socioeconomic injustice, such as medical and educational indebtedness. Professional training around multiculturalism in recent decades does not seem to have improved the lot of minority communities. In fact, understanding multicultural training as a separate endeavor can have the effect of turning minorities into an Other. Other here refers to the objectification of persons based on people's misunderstanding of them. Integrating multiculturalism into all of family therapy is a laudable objective with many challenges.

In focusing on the Other, many different perspectives have emerged, often with good intentions, that have disintegrated into further isolating minorities by encouraging privileged whites and helpers to learn what to do "to help." When it comes to looking at ways that responses to trauma can be seen as a source of strength for people, little is discussed. Almeida et al. propose that instead of "Other," a new term, "Otherizing," can be used to encourage the development of new paradigms in addressing social injustice. Without new paradigms, people may objectivize minorities and in doing so, encourage racial and ethnic prejudice (Almeida et al., 2011).

Looking at an extension of a cultural equity paradigm, it becomes critical to move from the context of exclusively focusing on the ethnic and cultural to exploring more fully the idea of identity and the ways in which identity is impacted by culture. To avoid "Otherizing" a client, it is necessary to work toward collective change. In this context, social transformation begins with dialogue, inquiry, group reflection, and action. These are characteristics of collective narrative practice, which we shall see as this discussion proceeds.

Cultural equity in therapy is defined as "the systemic analysis of systems of domination and subordination across and within cultures, by addressing the interplay of power, privilege and oppression in family and community life" (Almeida et al., 2011, p. 46). Power is a given in life and has both positive and negative aspects as it is exercised intentionally and unintentionally. It can harm or help. Privilege refers to identity markers such as preferred ethnicity, gender, class, and sexual orientation that give certain individuals and groups unearned advantages (Almeida et al., 2011). Oppression refers to the unjust exercise of authority and power over resources by one group over another. It has five faces: exploitation, marginalization, powerlessness, cultural imperialism, and violence.

In contrast, a cultural equity perspective defines healing as second-order changes whereby individuals and families confront experiences of socialization by challenging the effects of privilege, power, and oppression in their own lives and the lives of others. Finally, the authors offer the following building blocks for therapy:

1) Build critical consciousness to challenge policies and practices of privilege that deliver and sustain harm and inequality to historically marginalized groups.
2) Embrace teamwork involving therapists, advocates, mentors, and clients and a dislodging from the therapeutic tradition of a single therapist working with a single client or family.
3) Create circles of healing and liberations, including clients, allies, activists, and therapists from multiple locations.
4) Legitimize (sic) resident activists to the therapeutic practice.
5) Build coalitions that embody social exchanges that deliver at the macro and micro-system levels.
6) Invite allies from dominant groups to partner with therapeutic endeavors.
7) Build bridges between therapeutic practice and social action strategies.
8) Institute rituals that empower clients and their choice communities to create and perform their own rituals that open and bind paths toward liberation.
9) Encourage clients to enroll in wellness programs to heal from current and historic injuries (Almeida et al., 2011).

Selection Process for Tutu Project

Students in the Tutu Project were selected from a COAMFTE accredited Master of Marriage and Family Therapy program at Christian Theological Seminary in Indianapolis where I am program director. One program is an MAMFT-only program while the other is a dual with a Master of Divinity Mand MAMFT. Five students were selected as Tutu student fellows: Deidre, a Haitian American M.Div./MAMFT student; Sherri, a Caucasian MAMFT student; James, an African American MAMFT student; Greg, an African American M.Div./MAMFT student; and Isabella, a Mexican M.Div./MAMFT student. Selection criteria included the following: interest in social justice concerns, willingness to attend regular collective narrative practice, and participation in leading collective narrative group.

The context for conducting the storytelling groups was the Edna Martin Christian Community Center, a United Way Agency, in the Martindale Brightwood community in Indianapolis. The center was chosen for two reasons. The Martindale Brightwood is a community impacted by socioeconomic challenges that also has cohesion. Second, the Edna Martin Center is an active community center that offers needed services to all community residents regardless of race, religion, etc. and is greatly trusted by its residents. In addition, the project planned to work with a homeless population that met in a downtown congregation. Both the student fellows and the community center were ratified by the Tutu Center for Peace, Justice, and Reconciliation.

Procedures

The project consisted of two phases: training and implementation. Initially, the students met with the principal investigator to discuss their hopes and dreams for the project. Students' comments included: "I really am interested in working with the homeless. My heart goes out to them." "Narrative work really connects for me. And to do it in the community setting is quite exciting."

The students met for 2-h didactic and discussion sessions based on selected readings on narrative therapy and collective narrative practice for a total eight sessions. The books read were *Narrative Therapy, Collective Narrative Practice: Responding to Individuals, Groups and Communities Who Have Experienced Trauma* and *Uncovering Spiritual Narratives: Using Story in Pastoral Care and Ministry* by Suzanne Coyle as well as a website www.spiritualnarratives.com (Coyle, (n.d.); Coyle, 2014; Denborough, 2008; Madigan, 2011).

Coyle's "Staff of Spirit" was selected as a methodology for the project with modifications to fit the shortened time frame (Coyle, 2014). An earlier method of narrative practice that can be used with individuals can be found in Coyle's *Re-storying Your Faith* (2013). Usually, the Staff of Spirit methodology takes a 6 hour retreat to complete, or 6 weeks of 90 minute sessions. In consultation with Edna Martin Center staff, we determined that this would be a pilot project with the Center to determine future possibilities for the model. Four women from a support group at the Center were chosen, based on availability and interest in the project. The facilitator of that support group and I also attended. Deidre and Jason participated as student facilitators.

The following is a description of the abbreviated methodology as practiced by the Tutu student fellows: The Staff of Spirit practice is rooted in Christian practice. Aspects of the practice can be adapted to other religions or spiritualities of agnostic, atheistic, or spiritual but not religious people. For the Tutu project, the following movements and questions were adapted for a spirituality that could apply to various beliefs and values.

Spiritual practice #1: Telling Your Story of Spirituality. A formative spiritual experience is defined as a spiritual experience that you know is true for you and serves as a source of strength. Taking turns, each participant tells the story of a formative spiritual experience. What other significant people have a relationship with you through these spiritual qualities? Describe your formative spiritual experience to the group. What spiritual qualities does that story call forth in you? What spiritual qualities draw you closer to God?

Spiritual practice #2: Retelling and Responding. How has this spiritual story sustained you? How does this story call for the stories from Scripture? What effects do these stories have on you now? What does the story call forth in you?

Spiritual practice #3: Spiritualities of the Everyday. The facilitator says, "You have shared a formative story of spirituality that has some sacred meaning. As we enter the world each day, we encounter many events and stories that may seem to have no connection with our spiritual story. Think of a challenge of just the past week and reflect on the following questions." What qualities does it call forth from you? How did it move you to concerns that were bigger than you?

Spiritual Practice #4: Witnessing to Spiritual Stories. What stories on the Staff of Spirit most sustain you as you face challenges? What are those challenges? What qualities do you need for this challenge? (Coyle, 2014)

After the Staff of Spirit was selected, it was determined that the student fellows would participate in their own Staff of Spirit facilitated by the principal investigator. This would enable them to personally experience the effect of the practice and join as a working group of colleagues. It was deemed that the Staff of Spirit was appropriate as a methodology for the project since it was compatible with the values of the Edna Martin Center yet flexible enough for persons with some varying beliefs.

"Hearing Our Voices" Process at Community Center

Two of the five students who were trained in the collective narrative project joined me and a staff member at the Edna Martin Christian Center prior to the collective experience with four women from the surrounding community. The Edna Martin Christian Center is a United Way community agency. Jason, an MAMFT African American student, and Deidre, a Haitian American M.Div./MAMFT student, served as storytelling facilitators. The storytelling process was scheduled at the Center as a community offering. The women in attendance were regular participants in support group events at the Center. "Hearing Our Voices: People Marginalized by Poverty Speak Out" was promoted online in the center's schedule of events as well as by word of mouth in the community and with flyers. It was advertised as a spiritual support group.

The students and I decided to modify the spiritual practices of the Staff of Spirit to adjust to the allotted hour-and-a-half slot. We focused on telling their stories and on the questions in Spiritual Practice #1. Also, we did not use the Staff of Spirit as a storytelling instrument. The Edna Martin Christian Center support group facilitator, Justine, attended the group with me. Four women from Justine's support group attended. Laverne, a 35-year-old divorced African American woman; Janice, a 45-year-old married African American woman; Grace, a 48-year-old divorced African American woman; and Tina, a 41-year-old married African American woman. All the women had children and were currently employed.

After describing the process, we focused on Laverne's story and the effect of the storytelling on her. I began the process with the following statement: "Thank you all for joining us today to engage in some storytelling about your lives. Thank you, Justine, for gathering these women today. Let me tell you about the process. Each of you will think of a formative spiritual experience that you know is true for you and sustains you in difficult times. You will share that story. My understanding from Justine is that all of you have struggled with poverty. So, it may be that your stories will connect with that. After each person shares her story, other members will share how they heard your story. Then, you will respond with how hearing them retell your story affected you. Are there questions?"

The women asked me questions for clarification. Then, after answering those questions, I turned to the women: "Deidre will begin with the questions. Who would like to share her story first?" Laverne indicated her willingness and shared the following story.

> *I didn't know what story to share. I've had so many struggles with picking myself up from the floor time after time. But the thing that just popped up is a spiritual surprise that overwhelmed. I had been on drugs, primarily cocaine, and lost my job as a receptionist. Then, I plummeted to the bottom. No money, living out of my car. My kids were nine and six. My husband had deserted us. I had no one to turn to but my mother. I begged her to take my kids in. After telling me what a loser I was, she said she would.*
>
> *That began a long time of stealing to get money for drugs. I tried to get a job. But when they saw how bad I looked, it was always no, no, no. (She starts to cry.) Then, it happened. I was sleeping in my car. As I opened my eyes, I had this warm feeling come over me. And suddenly, I just knew that Jesus was with me. All the time. Jesus will be with me. (She continues to cry.)*
>
> *It didn't happen overnight, but I gradually began to think about my kids and how I needed to get off drugs. I went to the Salvation Army Drug Treatment Center. They took me in. And every day, I thought of that experience.*
>
> *Finally, I got clean. The center helped me interview for jobs. It was slow. Poverty kept pulling me down. But, finally, I found a job. Then, my kids and I found an apartment. I just kept thinking that Jesus will be with me. (Laverne stops her story and wipes her tears.)*

After Laverne finished her story, Deidre asked Laverne questions, which prompted the following answers:

What spiritual qualities does that story call forth in you? Laverne said, *I think that I persevere like the Bible says to do. I don't go to church much. But I do believe that God looks out for me in some way. I also always hope for something good. After that experience, I hope for good. … Hope for good.*

What other significant people have a relationship with you through these spiritual qualities? *My kids. They know I'll always look out for them. I try. I try hard.*

What spiritual qualities draw you closer to God? *The harder I fall; the more God lifts me up. Need to look to future—always look to the future.*

After Laverne answered these questions, the other women commented on her story. The following are some of their responses: "A lot of strength. That sister has a lot of strength." "Reminds me of my bad times—always poor. Couldn't get up." "Her faith is always looking to what can be better." Then Deidre gave Laverne an opportunity to respond to her peers' retelling of her story. *It feels good. (Starts to cry.) Good. (Pause) Being poor didn't get me down. But it's hard. Hard.*

The process continued with the other women. Then, the storytelling ended.

Reflection on "Hearing Our Voices"

The storytelling was an open-ended process. In Laverne's story, the oppression of poverty she experienced was interwoven with hope. Her everyday experiences of having a hard time just getting up and moving forward sometimes overshadowed her ability to be hopeful. That future vision was sometimes blocked. But she kept going. Her spiritual experience of somehow knowing that Jesus was for her sustained her even in dark times. She lived in her car and had no one to rely on. But she kept saying, "Jesus, Jesus."

Her story was retold in many ways. Hopelessness, perseverance, Jesus, hope, all were possibilities that supported her and gave her a vision of a new future. Laverne would be able to connect with others. She also was able to see her oppression and the need for social justice to be sustained by her spirituality—by hope.

Some of the questions posed to Laverne did focus on spirituality directly. Other questions and conversation did not focus directly on spirituality. The question may arise: What makes a question spiritual? Certainly, an explicit question is easy to discern. However, a question may be implicit and still have spiritual implications.

Spirituality as implemented at the Edna Martin Center took the form of question. A question points toward undiscovered earthliness and as well as future divineness of transcendence. A spiritual question is a question that truly points to the many underlying stories of hope that a person does not yet recognize but yearns to know.

Follow-Up to the Social Justice Project

The student fellows and I led a worship experience on the students' personal stories as evoked by the Staff of Spirit collective narrative methodology. Highlighting the service was a parapet hanging from the lectern that depicted images that students created focusing on their experience as they participated in the Staff of Spirit. The service "Hope from the Margins" can be viewed at the Desmond Tutu Peace Lab at Butler University website (n.d.).

I presented a lecture, "Local Engagement of MFT Students in Social Justice" at the International Family Therapy World Congress in Kona, Hawaii, March 31 to April 2, 2015. Following that event, I presented the same collective project at the Society for Pastoral Theology Annual Conference in June 2015.

Implications for Other Programs' Social Justice Community Projects

As I have illustrated at the Edna Martin Center, a program can take the structure of the Staff of Spirit and apply it to other settings. In this example, participants did not use the Staff of Spirit, which has a Christian focus. The questions as they are presented here can be used without a logo. If a program desires, different logos can be created for the different spiritualities of the students. Using a visual aid such as a logo can extend the collective narrative questions so that they have a deeper effect for persons who are visual. Let us review some possibilities for logos.

In focusing on the major religions, a Star of David could be the logo for Judaism. One could incorporate the main Jewish beliefs in the star as follows: God exists. There is only one God. Worship only one God. God is transcendent. God does not have a body.

In Islam, one would use the symbol of the Star and Crescent. The following beliefs could be incorporated into the Star and Crescent: Belief in the existence and oneness of God (Allah); belief in the existence of angels; belief in the existence of the books of which God is the author; the Quran (revealed to Muhammad), the Gospel (revealed to Jesus), the Torah (revealed to Moses), and Psalms (revealed to David).

In Buddhism and the Buddhist tradition, there are eight symbols: a white parasol, a conch shell, a treasure vase, a victory banner, a dharma wheel, a pair of golden fish, an endless knot, and a lotus flower. One could use any of these symbols. The lotus flower is appealing in that it grows in the mud and then opens itself to the light, a fitting spiritual notion of moving toward the future. Buddhists believe that nothing is fixed or permanent and that change is always possible. Life is both endless and subject to impermanence, suffering, and uncertainty. These beliefs could be incorporated in one of the symbols. For Hindus, Aum, a letter, is seen as a fundamental component of the physical and metaphysical tenets of Hinduism: the means and the goal of life, the world and the Truth behind it, the material and the Sacred, all form and the Formless. Hindus believe that salvation is the goal of life nested in a circular, rather than linear, concept of time.

A universal symbol, the COEXIST symbol, could be used to represent all the religions of the world and a desire for spiritual balance. Another possibility for humanists or agnostic/atheistic individuals could be a symbolic circle that would indicate the notion of unity and unending time.

Programs can determine if they would like to use a symbol. Regardless of the decision, the questions and different spiritual practices that are offered in sequence lend themselves to raising questions that thicken people's stories. Certainly, as in the original design of the Staff of Spirit, one can have storytelling groups in a retreat setting, sessions over a period of time, and a single session.

In addition to the Staff of Spirit, the program can explore Denborough's two excellent books on collective narrative practice to get some ideas (Denborough, 2008; Denborough, 2018). The Tree of Life is a collective narrative practice that can be adapted to various settings (Denborough, 2008).

The first step for programs to consider is determining the community agency with which they have the strongest connection. What are the demographics of the community agency? What social issues do they address? What are the social justice interests of students in the program? How does the home institution view this kind of project? Finding answers to these questions is essential.

A next step would be to provide training for the students in collective narrative practice. Then, students and faculty determine what collective practice they find most interesting. Since laying this groundwork usually takes a few months, it would be ideal to plan at least one semester in advance. Another consideration is the optimal frequency of such a project. Annually? Once a semester? One time only? Such a project could be integrated into a class that emphasizes multiculturalism, diversity, and spirituality. Balancing the social and the spiritual is an important dimension that will offer students a hands-on example of what integration looks like in agency work.

A program could also work with another department to give students the experience of collaborating with other professionals. Psychotherapy colleagues could be psychologists, social workers, and mental health counselors. It would also be interesting to work with the law school to have conversations about the effects of the legal system on social justice, and perhaps the sociology department and the medical school and medical family therapy. In any of these cases, collective narrative practice does not require a therapy background to learn.

Working with community agencies may have an isomorphic effect upon the communities in which our programs are located. Collective narrative practice sees local action as the start of social movements (Denborough, 2018).

In the end, such collaboration will have a beneficial effect for participants in the community agency as well as for students and supervisors. MFT started as an interdisciplinary profession, but we have lost our way somewhat. We need to broaden our systemic perspectives to begin with families and expand to larger systems. This approach lends itself to such an adventure, which I believe has the potential of putting MFT more focally in the view of other professionals.

Community Spirituality Across Mental Health Disciplines

The modification suggestions for this book's living web of socio-spirituality for other mental health professions have been listed at the end of each chapter. Some suggestions have been focused on the specifics of each psychotherapy profession. For this chapter, I do not believe that any revisions to the ideas in this chapter is necessary. The spiritual integration represented here connects with social justice in various community contexts. So, each mental health discipline can exercise creativity in deciding what community context best fits the training programs in psychology, social work, mental health counseling, and psychiatry.

Self, Systems, Spirit Practice

Living Spiritually in Narrative Liturgy

This Self, Systems, Spirit Practice is designed to train students how to create a collective narrative project for a class or community outreach. Students need to read the section in this chapter on the Tutu Project. David Denborough's two books on collective narrative practice can also be accessed.

View the Friday Afternoon video "Living in Stories: Embodiment in therapy through Liturgical Practice" by Chad Loftis at this link: https://dulwichcentre.com.au/living-stories-embodiment-therapy-liturgical-practice-chad-loftis/.

As part of a class on spirituality and social justice, divide students into small groups. Discuss what you see in Loftis' methodology that could apply to a community project.

Students could also read one of David Denborough's books on collective narrative practice for context.

Students meet regularly to create a collective story project that could use narrative practice in a community project.

Faculty will schedule a formal presentation for these projects after students have worked with community agencies.

Feedback from peers and faculty.

References

Almeida, R., Hernandez-Wolfe, P., & Tubbs, C. (2011). Cultural equity: Bridging the complexity of social identities with therapeutic practices. *International Journal of Narrative Therapy & Community Work, 3*, 43–56.

American Association for Marriage and Family Therapy. (2004). *Marriage and family therapy core competencies*. Author. Retrieved from https://www.coamfte.org/Documents/COAMFTE/Accreditation%20Resources/MFT%20Core%20Competencies%20(December%202004).pdf

Butler University. (n.d.). Desmond Tutu Peace Lab at Butler University. Retrieved September 20, 2021, from https://www.desmondtutucenter.org/suzanne-coyle-report/
Coyle, S. M. (2014). *Uncovering spiritual narratives: Using story in pastoral care and ministry*. Augsburg Fortress Publishers.
Coyle, S. M. (n.d.). *Welcome to spiritual narratives*. Spiritual Narratives. Retrieved August 23, 2020, from https://www.spiritualnarratives.com/
Denborough, D. (2008). *Collective narrative practice*. Dulwich Centre Publications.
Denborough, D. (2015). *Can narrative practices contribute to 'social movement'? An invitation to join a project from David Denborough*. Dulwich Centre. Retrieved August 20, 2020, from https://dulwichcentre.com.au/can-narrative-practices-contribute-to-social-movement-an-invitation-to-join-a-project-from-david-denborough
Denborough, D. (2018). *Do you want to hear a story?: Adventures in collective narrative practice*. Dulwich Centre Publications.
Dulwich Centre. (2014). *Narrative justice & the charter of story-telling rights*. Author. Retrieved from https://dulwichcentre.com.au/charter-of-story-telling-rights/
Freire, P. (2018). *Pedagogy of the oppressed*. Bloomsbury.
Ham, C. (2014). Responsibility: A commitment to an effective decision-making process. *Family Therapy Magazine*, 14–20.
Loftis, C. (2016). *Living in stories: Embodiment through therapy through liturgical practice*. Dulwich Centre. Retrieved from https://dulwichcentre.com.au/living-stories-embodiment-therapy-liturgical-practice-chad-loftis/
Madigan, S. (2011). *Narrative therapy*. American Psychological Association. Retrieved from https://psycnet.apa.org/record/2010-13685-000
Myerhoff, B. (1986). Life not death in Venice: Its second story. In V. W. Turner & E. M. Bruner (Eds.), *The anthropology of experience* (pp. 261–288). University of Illinois Press.
Payne, R. K. (2005). *A framework for understanding poverty: A cognitive approach* (6th ed.). Aha! Press.
White, M. (2005). *Workshop notes*. Dulwich Centre. Retrieved from https://dulwichcentre.com.au/wp-content/uploads/2014/01/michael-white-workshop-notes.pdf

Chapter 10
Implications of Spirituality for Faith-Based and Secular Learning Environments

Expanding therapeutic learning environments beyond the academic classroom, on-site clinic, and offsite counseling placement is a unique opportunity for MFT students to experience large systems. The original impetus for marriage and family therapy as a field was to explore new vistas to support families. With engagement with public environments, MFT students can gain a more robust understanding of the challenges contemporary families face. Such a connection fits well with one of the COAMFTE Standards Version 12.5 Developmental Competency Components—awareness, knowledge, and skill to responsibly serve diverse communities (COAMFTE Accreditation Standards Version 12.5, 2021, p. 3).

External Training Options for MFTs

Training options for MFTs are generally limited to clinical practicum experiences in on-site clinics or community mental health agencies. Learning solid clinical skills in counseling individuals, couples, and families is decidedly the "bread and butter" of training MFTs. Supervised counseling is a critical part of the curriculum as defined by COAMFTE for completing a master's in marriage and family therapy. Post-master's, the MFT graduate must complete a required number of client contact hours to become an LMFT. Both the master's program and the post-master's residency require a certain number of hours to be relational hours working with couples and families. Certainly, no substitute exists for this foundational clinical experience as the MFT looks forward to a robust career.

Students in current MFT graduate programs face a world filled with challenges and uncertainty. For the foreseeable future, we can expect that providing marriage and family therapy to clients will be a solid profession. At the same time, recent global crises such as COVID-19 and racial injustice point to the need for us all to have a set of transferrable skills that fit contexts and methods that remain unknown. To that end, it seems prudent for training programs to find places in their curriculum to provide various training settings for students. While maintaining solid clinical training is essential, adding a unique elective setting will give graduating MFTs a broader base of knowledge and skills to expand into throughout their careers.

S. M. Coyle, *Spirituality in Systemic Family Therapy Supervision and Training*, Focused Issues in Family Therapy, https://doi.org/10.1007/978-3-030-92369-3_10

To that end, we will explore a limited number of secular and faith-based contexts where MFT students might find internships. In some cases, the sheer limitation of the curriculum may not make that possible. Programs might then expand their connections to post-master's placements that are unique but still allow graduates to accrue the necessary number of client contact hours to move toward licensure. In any case, programs can provide information about unique settings for graduates to pursue these interests in the future.

Placing students in distinctive settings presents clear challenges. MFT programs need to have collaborative relationships with administrators and clinicians who work in these settings. Programs interested in placing students at community agencies with services with or without mental health offerings must initially work with the existing connections. If the program has no such institutional relationships, then the program director, faculty, and supervisors should brainstorm what relationships do exist and what program emphases fit what setting.

The next challenge will be to work with institutional administrators for the school where the program is nested. The following discussion will explore three unique contexts for MFT placements: community agencies, healthcare institutions, and churches/synagogues/mosques/temples. Distinctions between these settings will be explored alongside suggestions for connecting the setting to the standards of COAMFTE accredited programs and MFT Core Competencies (2004).

MFT Placements in Community Agencies

Placing students in community agencies and public health settings need not be an either/or when it comes to addressing spirituality with clients. Promoting a specific religious orientation with clients would, of course, be inappropriate on the therapist's initiative. It would violate several ethical understandings, most notably the unacceptable use of power and privilege.

At the same time, addressing spirituality in a general sense with clients is indeed desirable. As previously discussed, it can connect with various diversities that affect people in their everyday lives. Certainly, in community agencies, much of the work relates to diversity of some kind. A young adult who comes out as gay may need to join an LGBT support group at a community agency. For example, Jared, an MFT graduate student, attends a conservative church that believes that homosexuality is sinful. As he feels less isolated, he experiences this growing connection with other young gay adults as a strengthening of his spirituality.

At one time, public agencies and community centers often discouraged case workers and therapists from focusing on clients' spirituality. Sometimes the fear that religion would have a stultifying effect on clients was the overriding concern. And sometimes, then and today, religion can have such an impact. However, through decades of expanding spirituality into a more generous approach, spirituality, in contrast to religion, is understood in many community contexts as having the potential to support people.

For example, a snapshot of consumers of public health services in California offers insight into spiritual needs as perceived by consumers. Certainly, this survey does not offer insight into consumers of all public health services across the United States. California, however, has long been viewed as a bellwether state for mental health (Open Minds, 2015). Furthermore, the state has a diverse population that includes many racial ethnicities, cultures, ages, and types of families.

The California Mental Health and Spirituality Initiative in 2009 created a survey-based campaign to document spirituality-related needs, preferences, and the experiences of individuals and families receiving public mental health services. More than 80% of the survey's 2050 participants agreed or strongly agreed that spirituality was important to their mental health. Consumers indicated that the following spiritual practices were helpful to their mental health: prayer (73%); meditation (47%); attending religious services (40%); spending time in nature (41%); and reading sacred texts or spiritual self-help books (36%) (Yamada et al., 2020)

This information lifted up the need for community mental health agencies to take spirituality seriously in the total treatment of individuals and families. As a result of this initiative in California, Lukoff created a spiritual assessment interview called SOPP that evaluates the following areas: (1) religious/spiritual strengths and coping resources, (2) organized religion, (3) personal religion/spirituality, and (4) religious/spiritual problems (Lukoff, 2014). SOPP is currently used across California in public county mental health agencies (Yamada et al., 2020)

Even if we limit this study to California, it points to the need for community agencies to understand the role of spirituality in the lives of clients. By extension, it also emphasizes an opportunity for MFT students to understand spirituality in a community context. Agencies that offer mental health services are typically internship placement sites for students. Opportunity exists in such settings for MFTs to use systemic skills to support families with challenges in ways that recognize the uniqueness of each family.

Another study in Michigan asked persons with mental illness who used consumer-centered services such as clubhouses and consumer-run drop-in centers: "Is spirituality important to you?" and "If so, what spiritual activities do you participate in?" (Bellamy et al., 2007). Both clubhouses and consumer-run drop-in centers operate with the same values, such as hope, choice, normalization, meaningful activity, self-determination, building supports, and systems change (Mowbray et al., 2005). The Michigan study focused on persons with mental illness participating at 31 clubhouses and CRDIs. Participants utilized the following spiritual activities: (1) public participation such as church, prayer, reading spiritual books, and meditation; (2) private participation such as prayer, reading spiritual books, and meditation; (3) outside activities such as "non-religious" activities including playing sport, reading books, and other social activities; and (4) mutual support activities such as consumer-centered services, AA, and support activities when participants help peers (Bellamy et al., 2007).

The results of the Michigan study focus on suggestions for community agencies to better engage with spirituality as follows: (1) Gain a better understanding of the role of spirituality in participants' lives by integrating spirituality into assessments and individual conversations. (2) Train members and staff to facilitate spirituality/religious discussions (Bellamy et al., 2007).

Using our personal experience offers a critical context for connecting personal spirituality to spirituality that addresses public concerns. Unfortunately, not many scholarly journal articles include this unique perspective. Lukoff fills that gap in a helpful account of his personal journey advocating for spirituality in public health (2014). Developing interdisciplinary groups to discuss the importance of spirituality in the lives of consumers led to California's current emphasis on spirituality as a part of agency assessment (Lukoff, 2014).

An outcome of Lukoff's journey was the SOPP assessment mentioned earlier in this chapter. Furthermore, mental health professionals can engage with community religious leaders to determine possibilities for collaboration around spirituality. Agencies can also find creative ways to implement the standards of accrediting bodies. The Joint Commission, which accredits behavioral health and medical facilities nationwide, now emphasizes the need for spirituality as follows: "Providing education to staff regarding spiritual assessment is critical. Training staff on the appropriate content of the spiritual assessment, as well as on the different ways an assessment can be documented, is very important" (Joint Commission, 2005, p. 7).

At the same time, it can very well be the case that a program may not engage the student in understanding the agency's larger systems context. The supervisor supervises the student's clinical work in terms of the individual and/or family. The usual foci will be the student, individual or family, and hopefully, the supervisor. A more thorough focus would include the dynamics of the agency and the effects on the clinical work being conducted. If we could really expand the focus, the supervision would look at the agency's role in the community. Is the agency actively engaged with the community? Is the agency not connected with the community? If so, what could be the effect on counseling services and/or therapists?

In addition to clinical placements, programs could place students in community agencies that provide non-clinical services such as support groups. It may be impossible to place a student in a non-counseling role at a community agency due to the limitation of hours. A program could create such placements as part of a course. Typically, some state licensing boards require that MFTs have had course work on collaborating with other professions. Placing a student in a non-mental health agency could bolster learning in a class on institutional collaboration.

Alternate Group Experiences in Community Agencies

Alternate group experiences are typically not in the MFT range of clinical modalities. A dearth of training in non-counseling focused settings exists for MFTs, just as for psychologists (Cornish & Wade, 2010). Other challenges for MFTs, however, in comparison with psychologists, are not as prevalent. In contrast, MFTs are more religious as a profession. Also, as previously noted, the majority of MFTs do believe that religious discussions are appropriate if exercised within appropriate boundaries (Carlson et al., 2002).

Psychoeducational groups are an option for integrating spirituality. Recovery, HIV, cancer support, and eating disorders are all groups that offer an opportunity for MFT students to participate in in agency placements. In addition to community agency settings, many religious organizations offer a setting to pursue these training possibilities.

MFT students could offer a spiritually focused group for agency clients who want this emphasis. Faculty and supervisors could then oversee the work of the student. This would give the student experience with integrating spirituality in group work while giving the supervisor experience with focusing on spirituality.

One such example was the "Spirituality Matters Group," which was established on the Clinical Research Evaluation Facility of the Nathan Kline Institute for Psychiatric Research in New York. This was an inpatient unit for persons with persistent psychiatric symptoms. Several characteristics of the group would make it adaptable for a community agency setting. The group was led by an interdisciplinary team of three persons representing psychology, pastoral care, and rehabilitation (Revheim & Greenberg, 2007).

In the initial phase, members are introduced, and the group purpose is reviewed. This was an ongoing group that enabled old group members to orient new members. Some of the group's purpose was to equip members to use spiritual beliefs to cope with life stressors and support change. The group was described as multi-religious and nondenominational and as defining spirituality as "personal beliefs and values related to the meaning and purpose of life, which may include faith in a higher purpose or power" (Revheim & Greenberg, 2007, p. 308).

The middle phase focuses on a topic with a group activity for each session. Warm-up questions for personal sharing begin each session, and handouts and readings are distributed. A group leader is responsible for coordinating the session topic with the goals of the ongoing treatment. Group members are encouraged to share positive and negative emotions. The ending phase gives group members an opportunity to summarize the themes of group sessions that influence future goals and choices. The last session closes with a formal prayer created by group members (Revheim & Greenberg, 2007).

This spirituality group could be modified to fit an agency setting with an MFT student as one of the group facilitators. Suggested possibilities for co-facilitators include an agency staff member interested in spirituality, a community leader at a non-profit or a spiritually related organization (church, synagogue, mosque, and temple leaders, including chaplains, are possibilities), and the MFT student. Given the participating MFT student, the group could be a multiple family support group for families or couples who are interested in spirituality. A group for non-related individuals is also a possibility.

After group leaders are identified, the composition of group members will be determined. An ongoing group will allow seasoned group members to mentor new ones. It will also be possible for one student facilitator to pass the group on to the next student facilitator. The group could be named HOPE (Helping Oppressed

People's Experiences). Or one could have the group members name the group. It would be open to persons who self-identify as spiritual, denominationally religious, spiritual but not religious, and atheistic/agnostic. Criteria for group membership would be as follows: The spiritual support group welcomes people who seek meaning from life that expands from self-focus and relationships to a larger purpose.

The group's structure would be to meet for one and half hours. Prior to the session, group leaders would meet and identify some spiritual themes around hope. The purpose would be to have members share their personal experiences around life challenges and ways in which they have met those challenges. Pertinent materials such as sacred texts, self-help books, and poetry can be read, or music played during the group meeting.

Another group meeting in a community agency would be periodic roundtable discussions (Miller & Thoresen, 2003). The MFT student would organize the opportunity. A general title for the group could be "Spirit Focus" or something similar that conveys an open perspective. Each meeting would have a spiritual theme such as "hope during hard times," "finding the uplifting spirit in everyday life," or "persevering over hopelessness." Group members would share their everyday experiences following the theme. The format would follow a roundtable approach, giving the entire group opportunities to share their experiences.

In a collective narrative approach, the student facilitator would engage group members in a telling, retelling of the telling, and retelling of the retelling. Each group member would tell their story. One member of the group would retell what he or she heard from that member. Finally, the original storyteller would tell his or her response to the retelling of the retelling. Notes could be scribed by the MFT student on a large newsprint pad or whiteboard.

The study by Bellamy et al. encourages having MFT faculty and students engage with community agencies to provide preparation in spirituality in its emphasis on training (2007). To focus more directly on family dynamics, it would be interesting for an MFT student to run a genogram group in talking about participants' families. What legacy would they like to continue? What legacy would they like to leave behind? What spiritual qualities and gifts would enable the participant to carry forth both options?

These options for alternate placements for MFTs in community agencies can spark imagination in the ways that students could serve the community. An in-depth understanding of larger systems gives the MFT program an edge in collaborating with its community. Local and government politicians are another group of collaborators who can not only provide connection with non-clinical work but also offer opportunities for engaging social action on behalf of populations who are marginalized by the oppressions around racism, sexism, ableism, and agism, among the many diversities we encounter each day.

MFT Placements in Medical Settings

The importance of spirituality in medical as well as behavioral settings is seen in the Joint Commission's stress on the importance of spiritual assessment (www.joint-commission.org). Providing a biopsychosocial spiritual initial interview is also important for understanding the patient and his or her family perspective on addressing medical challenges (Hodgson et al., 2007). A helpful open- and closed-ended survey called HOPE (source of hope and meaning, whether they belong to an organized religion, personal spirituality, and the effect their spirituality may have on health and end-of-life decisions) can provide an initial overview of how the patient may or may not engage spirituality (Anandarajah & Hight, 2001). Emphasizing spirituality in patient health has positive outcomes, especially when viewed as an instrumental part of health care, particularly as it relates to end-of-life concerns (Currier et al., 2012). Medical family therapy is a growing niche for family therapists. COAMFTE accredits several master's, doctoral, and postgraduate certificate programs that specialize in medical family therapy. These programs oversee their curriculum and placement sites with rigorous guidelines that are often required to meet accreditation standards. This book considers these settings to be an option for MFT students in non-medical family therapy (MedFT) programs. Medical family therapy, however, has developed a body of literature and healthcare competencies that elevate medical settings as options for MFTs.

This extant body of MedFT literature can determine what general medical settings could be appropriate for MFT students. This discussion assumes that MFT students placed in general medical settings do not have specialized counseling skills. At the same time, general medical settings offer students in clinical programs some experience leading support groups and spiritually focused groups. Such settings also provide the MFT student with opportunities to learn how to collaborate in team groups with physicians, chaplains, nurses, and behavioral health practitioners.

Medical family therapy recognizes three approaches to spirituality in MedFT. One would be individual approaches such as prayer, religiously integrated CBT, and mindfulness-based interventions. A family approach could use lifemaps as a process. Finally, community approaches offer possibilities such as AA and psychoeducational groups (Wilson et al., 2018). Such approaches could be utilized in hospitals, psychiatric hospitals, hospices, nursing homes, and substance abuse facilities.

As spirituality is discussed as part of family therapy, many approaches lean on an individual perspective and not a systemic family perspective. In the MFT field, a relational systemic approach can be used with individuals, of course, through the systemic lens of the therapist in working with the client. At the same time, ignoring the family as a unit robs family therapy of its systemic power. Medical family therapy is a help to MFT in general in its emphasis on family, which is so important for patient support and patient compliance with protocols.

Family spirituality is much broader than individual spirituality because it reflects on and with the spirituality of the family as a unit while recognizing the individuals' spirituality in that unit. MedFT utilizes spirituality assessments for families because in caring for patients, it is important to understand what kind of family support exists. Genograms and ecomaps are also helpful for getting an overview of the family's spirituality. Finally, all families can have some form of spirituality. They may believe in God according to a religion. They may believe in some higher power. Or, for an atheistic family, they may live by an ethos of love or awe for the universe (Tanyi, 2006).

Alternate Placements in Medical Settings

As discussed, medical family therapy programs have hospital placements for MedFT students where spirituality is important in caring for patients and their families. Other placements in medical settings that utilize spirituality as a therapeutic modality also exist for general MFT students. These settings involve Clinical Pastoral Education in psychiatric hospitals and general hospitals, nursing homes, and hospices.

Group experiences can be created in nursing homes that engage the MFT student, the resident, and the family. In fact, focusing on the family unit in this setting could possibly alleviate the isolation that nursing home residents often experience. Not quite home and not quite a hospital, it is a challenging combination for the resident who may miss his or her independence while yearning for connection with family or community of choice. Some different group experiences are possible in this setting.

Organizing a family support group in a nursing home can be greatly beneficial for the resident's family members who provide care for their loved one. A title such as "Spiritual Support for Caregivers" could offer family members a place to share their struggles as well as discuss what spiritual resources give them resilience. The program would likely need to connect with the social worker at the nursing home to identify the ins and outs of getting this group off the ground. It could be possible to have a spiritual support group for residents. If the facility has a chaplain, however, it is likely that they would lead the group.

Hospice settings typically have a chaplain to address end-of-life concerns. But an MFT student could serve a need for the family in terms of the spiritual and family dynamics that emerge as death approaches and dealing with subsequent issues. As we know, settling an estate can raise concerns about who gets what and family loyalty. Family loyalties have both systemic and spiritual dynamics. They tend to intensify as stress on the family increases.

A quite workable placement in a hospice setting would be to set up a multi-family group with the chaplain at hospice. The MFT student could focus on spiritual issues with the family in collaboration with the chaplain. Spiritual themes in a family focus on forgiveness, hope, and mutuality. A series of questions for the family group could be as follows: (1) Forgiveness—In what ways does your family work to forgive one another? What are some of the obstacles to that happening? Can you remember sometime in the past when you were able to forgive? How could you bring that forward to the present? (2) Hope—What are your hopes and dreams for your family in the future? What do you believe your family member (person in hospice) would hope for your family? Might you be able to talk with them about this? (3) Mutuality—Who in this family carries the load of caring? How might the rest of you help shoulder that load? (Coyle & Davis, 2017). The MFT students and chaplain could also ask the families if they have a favorite sacred text, poem, or meditation that could be shared with other families. This offering could be done at the beginning or end of a family's time with the group. A memorial ritual could be shared with the whole group when a hospice patient dies.

In addition to a group activity, the MFT student could serve as a consultant to the chaplain on family dynamics. Both leaders could work with a single family in a family session. Or the MFT student could visit the hospice patient with the chaplain to explore any concerns he or she may have for the family. The visiting care team could ask if the patient if he or she has any wish for the family after his or her death. This kind of collaboration could certainly deepen family resilience in a time of loss.

MFT Placements in Religious Settings

Churches in the United States have a long history of providing supports to their communities. The beginning of Sunday School was an effort to provide education for the community before local schools were common (Larsen, 2008). Churches began to organize orphanages after the Civil War to care for children left without caregivers or parents unable to support them. Marriage enrichment began in the 1950s after the post-World War II boom provided housing and addressed marriage challenges that sometimes resulted from the war as veterans returned.

Since the 1980s, religious institutions have increasingly become aware of the need for support groups to help members meet life challenges. These support groups cover marriage enrichment, divorce, teen challenges, grief, and substance recovery. AA groups typically meet at congregations that provide space and no interference. Religious organizations that provide support groups and meeting spaces run the gamut from religiously conservative to liberal. Church/synagogue/mosque staff typically facilitate these groups as part of their community outreach. In addition, some groups are run by participants in the group with the support of the religious institution's permanent staff.

In the author's experience, staff-run groups take extra care to provide an open environment to people who espouse a religious and spiritual belief and those who self-identify as agnostic or atheistic. Groups are typically quite clear with participants about the specificity of religious belief or absence of belief. Some groups, such as marriage enrichment groups, may look at marriage through a religious lens because family spirituality is an important dimension of marriage. Participants would have an opportunity to know about the spiritual orientation of a marriage support group from the description of the group.

Finally, Clinical Pastoral Education as a part of the Association for Clinical Pastoral Education is a possible MFT student placement that covers the medical and religious settings. The purpose of the Association is to affect people's lives through the provision of spiritual care education. ACPE may provide spiritual health education as a part of postgraduate education or other education delivery methods (ACPE, 2020). CPE is basically supervised chaplaincy in a hospital setting. Credentialed CPE educators supervise student chaplains who provide spiritual care to hospital staff and patients. The CPE experience includes peer groups and individual supervision. Most CPE settings are in hospitals and sometimes in psychiatric facility settings.

Alternate Placements in Religious Settings

Several alternate placements in religious organizations are possible for MFT students. An essential contribution of the student in religious settings would be to identify family spirituality as an adjunct addition to individual spirituality. Depending on the beliefs of the religious community, one or the other emphasis may be central to the activities of the formal religion. The student can help the religious group identify its commitments to sustaining the spiritual life of both individuals and families. MFT programs will be able to contact local congregations/synagogues, mosques, and temples to explore areas of care that that religious organizations may want to support.

A common group for such religious organizations is a divorce support group for people who have gone through a divorce or for children of a divorced couple. The program director would make contact and begin a placement process. Some congregations might be eager to host MFT students for such a group. Religious institutions that have conservative theological beliefs about divorce may find it especially difficult to sustain their members as they go through the process. If things go well, it is likely that the program can provide placements for students in the future.

Another possibility is for the program to work with religious organizations to place students in marriage enrichment programs. The Gottman Institute, EFT, and Imago all offer training in marriage enrichment along with manuals that participants can use. The Gottman Institute and Imago also have parenting options that programs can use with trained students. Some of these programs have the spirituality component integrated into the training. If not, the student can add some questions after the session that would emphasize spirituality.

Some religious organizations also offer grief support groups that an MFT student could possibly join to contribute a systemic family perspective, either with an already established group or by beginning a new group. The existing literature on death, dying, and loss could offer the MFT student a good starting point for a group that could be co-led with other students or a staff member at the religious institution. This type of support group would have the potential to become an ongoing group.

Placement in CPE at hospitals also offers possibilities. The MFT program would be wise to connect with seminaries in their community to explore whether MFT students could be placed through the seminary to an area CPE program. MFT programs nested in seminaries would already have that option. CPE is attractive because chaplains are uniquely trained to be able to respond to different spiritualities without imposing their own beliefs on patients.

Future Possibilities

Promising possibilities for placing MFT students in alternate faith-based and secular community settings require creativity on the part of the MFT program. The author's experience is that students are often able to have both connections and ideas that can blossom into concrete realities. This means that program directors, faculty, and students need to continually stay connected with their communities. Alumni are also great resources for community possibilities. Sometimes, a volunteer pilot project can morph into opportunities for community funding.

The COVID-19 pandemic introduced new possibilities through technology and telehealth. Opportunities for telehealth in businesses and schools as an online version of an EAP program could offer MFTs unique placement possibilities. As students undergo specialized training in telehealth, psychoeducation groups and support groups are possibilities alongside more traditional individual, couple, and family therapy.

Other possibilities for telehealth might be peer-to-peer support for mental health professionals. This option could be offered in clinical practice groups as a perk for potential employees. Certainly, MFT trainees could be supervised in this kind of placement. In turn, such a placement could offer future therapists a new niche in their future professions.

It may seem to an overloaded program director that this extension of work is just too much to take on. Making these kind of community connections, however, often pave the way for postgraduation jobs for students. It also lays the groundwork for increasing client referrals in on-site clinics.

Some of the CTS MAMFT program's most successful student placements were created through personal and alumni connections. Currently, the program has MFT students in a medical family therapy placement at the Indiana University School of Medicine, ongoing for 5 years, and at the local Veterans Administration hospital for 10 years. These placements clearly provided direct client hours and not alternate hours as this chapter discusses. However, these placements came through alumni and personal connections, which illustrates the importance of marketing one's program.

Spirituality in Alternate Learning Environments Across Mental Health Disciplines

Many of the suggestions in this chapter regarding niches to infuse spirituality in clinical practice apply equally to family therapy as well as psychology, social work, mental health/professional counseling, and psychiatry. The contribution of family therapy to other mental health disciplines would be a systemic view of a diverse spirituality. As such an approach develops, more collaboration among professional psychotherapy may more easily occur. The result would be more robust mental health resources.

Self, Systems, Spirit Practice

Situating Spirituality in Alternate Leaning Environments

Students training to be licensed psychotherapists may often have little time for developing therapeutic skills outside a clinical practice setting. Sometimes the assumption is that clinical therapy skills just automatically transfer to other settings. This is not true. So, this practice is designed to be used in master's and doctoral learning environments so that those systemic therapy skills can be sharpened to enable using them in alternate environments.

Virtual/Role Play for Skills in Alternate Care Environments

Pre-practice readings Students read one of the following books: David Denborough's *Do You Want to Hear a Story? Adventures in Collective Narrative Practice* or Stavros; Torres' *Conversations Worth Having: Using Appreciative Inquiry to Fuel Productive and Meaningful Engagement.* These approaches utilize the therapist's natural skills in a setting other than the therapy room.

Module in course or mini workshop Faculty/trainers can implement this training as a module of mini workshops. It would be helpful prior to graduation or placement in a community context, which is not straight therapy.

Process Didactic/experiential components of training will give participants a better understanding, at the basic level, of how spirituality can/cannot inspire them to engage more fully in a community setting.

1. Students meet in small group to discuss the reading they chose. The facilitator asks the following question: What caught your attention in the reading?

2. Have a general discussion.
3. Facilitator asks students what community setting among the following are they most excited about: general hospital, psychiatric hospital, substance abuse support center, community agency, church outreach.
4. Students break into the group, general hospital, etc. they chose.
5. Like-minded students discuss two areas: (a) What skills do you think that setting demands? and (b) What did you learn from the reading that could help you in that setting?
6. Students meet in large group to brainstorm for next step with facilitator.
7. Over the next semester, like-minded students meet in their interest group to learn more about that setting. This could be visiting the community settings and even exploring a placement in that setting.

References

ACPE. (2020). *Article 2: Identification and purpose*. Author. Retrieved from https://www.manula.com/manuals/acpe/acpe-manuals/2016/en/topic/article-2-identification-and-purpose

American Association for Marriage and Family Therapy. (2004). *Marriage and family therapy core competencies*. Author. Retrieved from https://www.coamfte.org/Documents/COAMFTE/Accreditation%20Resources/MFT%20Core%20Competencies%20(December%202004).pdf

Anandarajah, G., & Hight, E. (2001). Spirituality and medical practice: Using the HOPE questions as a practical tool for spiritual assessment. *American Family Physician, 63*(1), 81–89. https://doi.org/10.1016/s1443-8461(01)80044-7

Bellamy, C. D., Jarrett, N. C., Mowbray, O., MacFarlane, P., Mowbray, C. T., & Holter, M. C. (2007). Relevance of spirituality for people with mental illness attending consumer-centered services. *Psychiatric Rehabilitation Journal, 30*(4), 287–294. https://doi.org/10.2975/30.4.2007.287.294

Carlson, T. D., Kirkpatrick, D., Hecker, L., & Killmer, M. (2002). Religion, spirituality, and marriage and family therapy: A study of family therapists' beliefs about the appropriateness of addressing religious and spiritual issues in therapy. *American Journal of Family Therapy, 30*(2), 157–171. https://doi.org/10.1080/019261802753573867

Commission on Accreditation for Marriage and Family Therapy Education. (2021). *COAMFTE Accreditation standards: Graduate & post-graduate marriage and family therapy training programs Version 12.5*. Author. Retrieved from https://coamfte.org/documents/COAMFTE/Accreditation%20Resources/COAMFTE%20Standards%20Version%2012.5%20-%20Published%20August%202021%20-%208.26.21%20(with%20links).pdf

Cornish, M. A., & Wade, N. G. (2010). Spirituality and religion in group counseling: A literature review with practice guidelines. *Professional Psychology: Research and Practice, 41*(5), 398–404. https://doi.org/10.1037/a0020179

Coyle, S. M., & Davis, C. J. (2017). Christian couples and families. In S. Kelly (Ed.), *Diversity in couple and family therapy: Ethnicities, sexualities, and socioeconomics* (pp. 203–230). Praeger.

Currier, J. M., Kim, S. H., Sandy, C., & Neimeyer, R. A. (2012). The factor structure of the Daily Spiritual Experiences Scale: Exploring the role of theistic and nontheistic approaches at the end of life. *Psychology of Religion and Spirituality, 4*(2), 108–122. https://doi.org/10.1037/a0027710

Hodgson, J., Lamson, A. L., & Reese, L. (2007). The Biopsychosocial-spiritual interview method. In D. Linville & K. M. Hertlein (Eds.), *The therapist's notebook for family health care:*

Homework, handouts, and activities for individuals, couples, and families coping with illness, loss, and disability (pp. 3–12). Haworth Press.

Larsen, T. (2008). When did Sunday schools start? *Christianity Today*. Retrieved from https://www.christianitytoday.com/history/2008/august/when-did-sunday-schools-start.html

Lukoff, D. (2014). From personal experience to clinical practice to research: A career path leading to public policy changes in integrating spirituality into mental health. *Spirituality in Clinical Practice, 1*(2), 145–152. https://doi.org/10.1037/scp0000016

Miller, W. R., & Thoresen, C. E. (2003). Spirituality, religion, and health: An emerging research field. *American Psychologist, 58*(1), 24–35. https://doi.org/10.1037/0003-066x.58.1.24

Mowbray, C. T., Collins, M. E., Bellamy, C. D., Megivern, D. A., Bybee, D., & Szilvagyi, S. (2005). Supported education for adults with psychiatric disabilities: An innovation for social work and psychosocial rehabilitation practice. *Social Work, 50*(1), 7–20. https://doi.org/10.1093/sw/50.1.7

Open Minds. (2015). *California as a national policy bellwether for health & human services.* Author. Retrieved from https://openminds.com/wp-content/uploads/MIReport-California-bellwether-080615.pdf

Revheim, N., & Greenberg, W. M. (2007). Spirituality matters: Creating a time and place for hope. *Psychiatric Rehabilitation Journal, 30*(4), 307–310. https://doi.org/10.2975/30.4.2007.307.310

Tanyi, R. A. (2006). Spirituality and family nursing: Spiritual assessment and interventions for families. *Journal of Advanced Nursing, 53*(3), 287–294. https://doi.org/10.1111/j.1365-2648.2006.03731.x

The Joint Commission. (2005). *Evolving with care*. Author. Retrieved from https://www.jointcommission.org/about-us/evolving-with-care/

Wilson, J., Hodgson, J., Jones, E., & Wilson, G. (2018). Medical family therapy in spiritual care. In T. Mendenhall, A. Lamson, J. Hodgson, & M. Baird (Eds.), *Clinical methods in medical family therapy* (pp. 463–495). Springer.

Yamada, A. M., Lukoff, D., Lim, C. S., & Mancuso, L. L. (2020). Integrating spirituality and mental health: Perspectives of adults receiving public mental health services in California. *Psychology of Religion and Spirituality, 2*(3), 276–287. https://doi.org/10.1037/rel0000260

Chapter 11
Future Directions

Spirituality in systemic family therapy has focused on research topics about spirituality and specific courses on spirituality in training program curricula. If spirituality is to have a beneficial effect on marriage and family therapy training, however, then an expansion into other areas of the training program is essential. The previous discussion has lifted up new approaches to spirituality, which will now be expanded into future directions for the field. Future directions that will serve spirituality in systemic family therapy include the following: 1) spirituality courses in MFT program curricula; 2) spiritually as applied in supervision; 3) expanded research on spiritually integrated systemic family therapy; and 4) expanded collaboration with communities of interest on spiritually integrated systemic family therapy.

Spirituality Course in the MFT Program Curriculum

In integrating spirituality in a family therapy training program, the place to begin is creating a course in spirituality/religion/theology for the curriculum. Such a course would fit under the COAMFTE Version 12.5 Eligibility Criterion D: Diversity and Inclusivity Policies (COAMFTE Accreditation Standards Version 12.5, 2021, p. 9). A common approach in accredited family therapy training programs is to offer one course in spirituality or no course at all. And the starting point for teaching that course is to have adequately trained faculty. At some schools, these courses are taught by family therapy scholars, most of whom have had no formal training in religion or theology. Still other schools hire faculty who have had some formal training in religion or theology through university and seminary academics. In conversations with colleagues, some faculty who self-identify as spiritual have told me that they believe that their personal faith equips them to teach this course on spirituality in the family therapy curriculum. Their preparation is often reading religious and spiritual writing and constructing reflexive questions for discussion. Prior to creating a course in spirituality, the program needs to have adequately trained faculty to teach it.

So, how can MFT faculty acquire adequate training in spirituality/religion? Some faculty in MFT training programs are already trained in both theology/

S. M. Coyle, *Spirituality in Systemic Family Therapy Supervision and Training*, Focused Issues in Family Therapy, https://doi.org/10.1007/978-3-030-92369-3_11

religion and family therapy. These faculty offer expertise in both fields and can be a resource for their colleagues. However, it is often difficult for academic faculty to admit that they are not knowledgeable in all areas. While they may be resistant to learning from their colleagues, there are options. Training programs can hire someone in geographical proximity who is trained in both theological studies and family therapy, sharing that adjunct faculty member. Online teaching is also an option. Another possibility in a university would be to team teach the course with a faculty member from the family therapy department and a faculty member from a religion department. A program could also have a team-teaching duo: one faculty member from the family therapy department and the other from a local college, university, or seminary. Another option would be to invite an MFT faculty member at another training program who is trained in religion/theology to assist in teaching through a webinar format or teleconferencing platform.

Regardless of who teaches the course, it is critical to have someone who has training in religion or theology. We would not expect to have a person who is not knowledgeable about MFT teach a family therapy course. How would we expect anything different for a spirituality/religion course? The other approach in training MFT faculty at a basic level in religion/theology would be to create workshops at the AAMFT Annual Conference that faculty could attend. Another option would be to meet with other faculty through teleconferencing for conversation and training in religion/theology.

Referencing theology alongside religion raises a concern that is barely mentioned in MFT literature. The discussion focuses on religion and/or spirituality. A general review of the literature reveals that MFT scholars focus primarily on spirituality, not religion. Religion is, of course, at times mentioned in MFT literature. And it may really be misguided to eliminate religion from the discussion because there is an inherent connection between religion and spirituality.

Yet another glaring oversight is not discussing theology. We would be amiss as we discuss future directions for spirituality in systemic family therapy not to discuss theology. As earlier discussions indicated, theology is "faith seeking understanding." It is not just individual spirituality. It is not the objective study of religion as an academic area. Different types of theology that open themselves to different spiritual perspectives, such as liberation theology and process theology. At its heart, theology focuses on personal reflection on human experiences and how they connect with God or a transcendent reality. Sounds a bit like the methodology of systemic reflection on family and community concerns, right? So, perhaps a future direction for MFT would be to read and discuss theology as an area that could strengthen spiritual integration in the field.

The next step, of course, would be to create the spirituality course. This book, as well as journal articles, offer some solid examples of spirituality courses that may be used as springboards for a course that is a contextual fit in a particular training program's curriculum. Engaging students in the creation of such a course would allow for it to be tailored to the students' interests. SurveyMonkey surveys are an excellent tool to poll students in a safe way about their desires for such a course.

Students and faculty could be resistant to a spirituality course, so reducing that possibility by engaging students at the outset would pave the way for a more successful experience for both professor and students.

Spiritually Integrated Supervision

Systemic family therapy has long emphasized rigorous training in supervision. Following a systemic perspective, MFTs have innovated unique approaches in supervision such as live supervision, which sets it apart from other psychotherapy professions. Our required supervision courses are rigorous and infuse our cutting-edge systemic approach into supervision with students. A recent development in MFT supervision is incorporating multiculturalism into systemic supervision. One of the Developmental Components in the COAMFTE Version 12.5 is "Awareness, knowledge and skill to responsibly serve diverse communities" (COAMFTE Accreditation Standards, Version 12.5, p.3). Competent supervision then demands that systemic supervisors understand all the diversity concerns.

Integrating the multicultural dimension into MFT supervision is not unique when compared to supervision in other psychotherapy professions. Multiculturally informed supervision is now the norm in all mental health professions from psychology to social work to mental health counseling. As previously discussed in this book, spirituality/religion is one of the diversities listed in the MFT core competencies. But where is spirituality practiced in multiculturally integrated supervision? It does not show up in the MFT literature. And it seems that it does not appear in systemic family therapy training either.

This seeming omission is quite distressing. Systemic supervision has long been an important component of MFT training and practice. Not explicitly addressing spirituality in multicultural supervision diminishes an otherwise robust approach to diversity for MFTs. My argument is that for spirituality to be integrated into a training program, it must be integrated into supervision.

Yes, it is my contention that spirituality should be included in multicultural supervision. But that inclusion must be explicit. Many times, spirituality is understood as some amorphous reality that just happens without any articulated objective. My argument throughout this book is that spirituality must be addressed intentionally and robustly if the field of MFT is serious about spiritual integration in COAMFTE accredited programs. An intentional approach of integrating spirituality into systemic supervision must be created and practiced.

The model created in this book is the living web of socio-spirituality, a dynamic model that employs a theologically informed methodology in a systemic context. It balances two concepts that have validity in both the areas of spirituality and systemic practice: immanence and transcendence. Through the discovery of immanence and transcendence comes the possibility of hope, which conveys credence in both spirituality and systemic practice. Specific spiritually integrated approaches using the living web of socio-spirituality have been outlined. The all-important aspect of how to integrate spirituality in systemic supervision is shown in a diagrammatic fashion.

A future direction for spiritually integrated supervision is to test the living web of socio-spirituality in both practice and research. Other approaches are indeed possible, such as implementing new models for spiritually infused supervision in group practices outside the academic guild. A call goes out to AAMFT Approved Supervisors to test the living web of socio-spirituality as well as other approaches. Supervisory experiences can then be written for publication in peer-reviewed journals. Furthermore, demonstrations of these approaches can be done in conference workshops. Both journal and workshop presentations will stimulate professional discussion that can situate systemic supervision in MFT training programs for spiritual integration.

Expanded Research in Spiritually Integrated Systemic Family Therapy

Research on spirituality in systemic family therapy has increased since the 1990s. Much of this research has focused on people's attitudes and beliefs about spirituality in family therapy. More recent research has examined outcomes from an MFT course with a spirituality focus (Williams-Reade et al., 2018). This book concentrated on self of therapist concerns aligned with spirituality and spiritual interventions in systemic family therapy. Where do we go from here?

At this point, a future direction for robust integration of spirituality in MFT requires that we focus on how to develop an infusion of spirituality in family therapy programs. We, as educators and consumers of family therapy training, need to know what spiritually aligned approaches have effective outcomes in accredited programs. This information will require more research studies on spirituality in systemic family therapy as well as individual program evaluation of student responses to the integration of spirituality in their studies.

Programs that already have training components focusing on spirituality can contribute to the field by initiating ongoing research on how effective this curriculum is for their students. This research can be both quantitative and qualitative. Then, sharing this research with other MFT training programs is essential. Certainly, one way to share this research is to publish in peer-reviewed journals.

However, there are other paths forward that open the conversation about spirituality in a more interactive way. Collaborating with MFT training programs can expand the integration of spirituality in training through workshops at regional and national MFT conferences. Teleconferencing platforms offer more options through webinars. Furthermore, research training programs can be shared and assessed regionally with other training programs.

Expanded Collaboration with Communities of Interest on Spiritually Integrated Systemic Family Therapy

Increased collaboration with various communities of interest concerning spirituality is an important future direction for systemic family therapy. Students, faculty, and supervisors can likely be defined as the most immediate communities of interest as well as graduates and counseling clients. Then, we would define community non-profits and organizations. It is here that I would argue that MFT training programs can productively expand groups for conversations.

Further collaboration with these communities of interest would focus on how civic organizations address the spiritual needs of families. Family is the emphasis here. MFT programs need to expand a typically individualist approach in work with oppressed people to a family focus. Families are the business of MFTs. We need to embrace it. So, what would this look like?

This expanded collaboration would include community agencies, hospitals, hospices, nonprofit networks, and religious organizations such as churches, synagogues, temples, and church related non-profits. Training programs might include spiritual integration with these communities of interest through what may be an already established institutional advisory group.

Concentrating on the spiritual foci in these agencies and on how MFT students can support them would be a good approach. In hospitals: How can MFT students work with the chaplaincy department? In hospice: Does the team need volunteer MFT students to support families? In religious organizations: How can MFT students provide workshops for families and their spiritual needs? In community agencies: How can MFT students provide spiritual support groups open to persons of all beliefs?

Moving Forward

Families of every race, ethnicity, class, and socioeconomic status can engage with systemic family therapy. Members of these families engage with their diversities of ability, age, gender identification, and sexual orientation. Put together, systemic family therapy has a huge responsibility to support these people with a robust spiritual foundation. We cannot shirk this responsibility.

Our society is currently rife with challenges around diversity. The political environment sometimes takes advantage of our unique characteristics to profit from those differences rather than sustaining our similarities. People cling to divisive traditions, rather than integrate their complementary diversities. As the political environment continues to polarize us all, really understanding our uniqueness through diversity would help chip away at the rigid cultural boundaries that divide.

Diversity is sometimes understood as something that only fits a politically liberal agenda. Thus, people with conservative sensibilities may resist conversations around race, ethnicity, class, and socioeconomic status. Yet, our skin color, body shape, and where we live are dimensions of what it means to be human.

Combining diversity and justice with spirituality has the potential to rise above equally dividing religious convictions to find a common area where we believe that all humans are spiritual. By using spirituality as a foundation for inviting God into people's lives, we have the possibility to address human pain with hope.

We need not fret about whether we are too rigid and dictatorial through our spiritual integration. Instead, we must find new and creative ways that spirituality can be steady and open. Systemic family therapy has the capacity to do lead creatively. Hopefully, this book can be a springboard for such endeavors and provide encouragement for others who engage in spiritually integrated work.

Future Directions Across Mental Health Disciplines

Many of the foci in this chapter above look to future directions. Moving forward for systemic family therapy also applies to mental health disciplines. Each of us in our own profession seeks to develop a robust identity that draws people to it. Yet, we compete with others. My last note to colleagues in other mental health disciplines is to embrace collaboration and recognize ways in which larger systems embrace spirituality and social justice.

Final Words

Our journey to the spiritual integration of systemic family therapy began with unique understandings of spirituality as well as religion. From there, the discussion presented the living web of socio-spirituality as an integration tool that emphasized stories and spiritual experience. Finally, practical ways to operationalize this tool resulted in an openness to changing paradigms. These changing paradigms emphasize recognition of spiritual life and how that is experienced every day.

The practices presented in this book give both trainers and trainees options to explore their chosen spiritualities and theoretical leanings while still having a flexible yet structured living web of socio-spirituality. It is such a living, breathing frame that is essential in world yearning for a robust spirituality that recognizes humans as flawed yet creative beings pushing toward the divine, whatever that means for each person. Let us breathe! Let us live! Let us move forward!

Self, Systems, Spirit Practice

Future Directions for Spiritually Integrated Practice

Organize a large group in your program using a modified appreciative inquiry approach.

Discuss the multiple ways students envision systemic family therapy.

Have participants rank the three changes they would make to the MFT program at your institution.

Then, take the discussion results, and in a faculty meeting, make changes in your MFT program that embrace those future directions.

References

Commission on Accreditation for Marriage and Family Therapy Education. (2021). *COAMFTE Accreditation standards: Graduate & post-graduate marriage and family therapy training programs Version 12.5*. Author. Retrieved from https://coamfte.org/documents/COAMFTE/Accreditation%20Resources/COAMFTE%20Standards%20Version%2012.5%20-%20Published%20August%202021%20-%208.26.21%20(with%20links).pdf

Williams-Reade, J. M., Lobo, E., & Gutierrez, G. (2018). Integrating spirituality into MFT training: A reflexive curriculum and qualitative evaluation. *Journal of Marital and Family Therapy, 45*(2), 219–232. https://doi.org/10.1111/jmft.12314

Appendix A: Living Web of Socio-spirituality

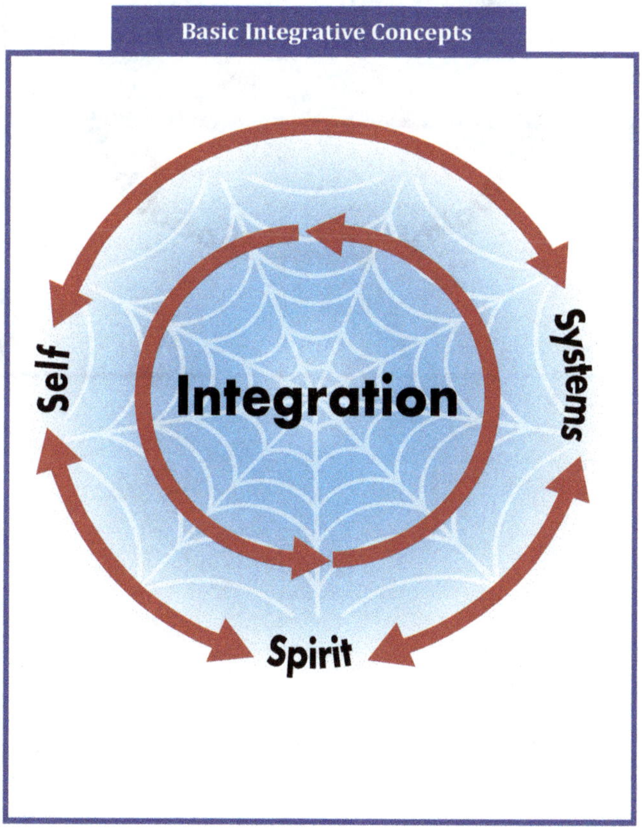

S. M. Coyle, *Spirituality in Systemic Family Therapy Supervision and Training*, Focused Issues in Family Therapy, https://doi.org/10.1007/978-3-030-92369-3

Living Web of Socio-Spirituality
Basic Foundation
Social Justice
Spirituality
Socio-Spirituality
Spirituality
Social Justice

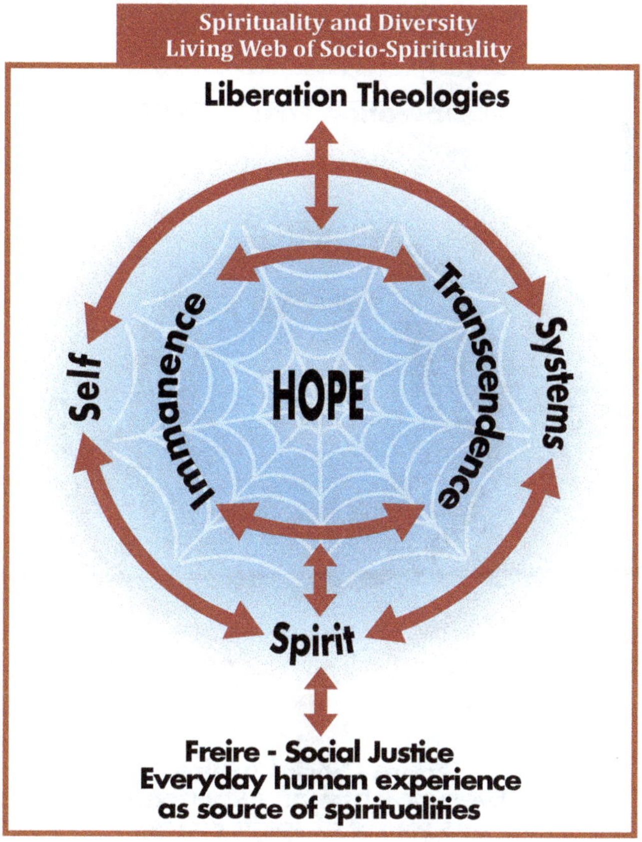
Spirituality and Diversity
Living Web of Socio-Spirituality
Liberation Theologies
Self
Immanence
HOPE
Transcendence
Systems
Spirit
Freire - Social Justice
Everyday human experience
as source of spiritualities

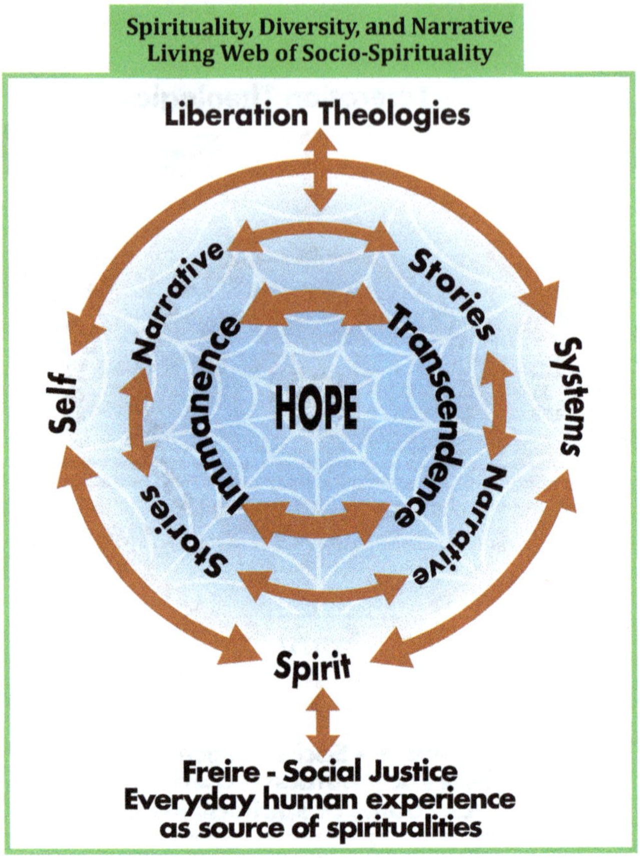
Spirituality, Diversity, and Narrative
Living Web of Socio-Spirituality
Liberation Theologies
Narrative
Stories
Immanence
Transcendence
HOPE
Self
Systems
Stories
Narrative
Spirit
Freire - Social Justice
Everyday human experience
as source of spiritualities

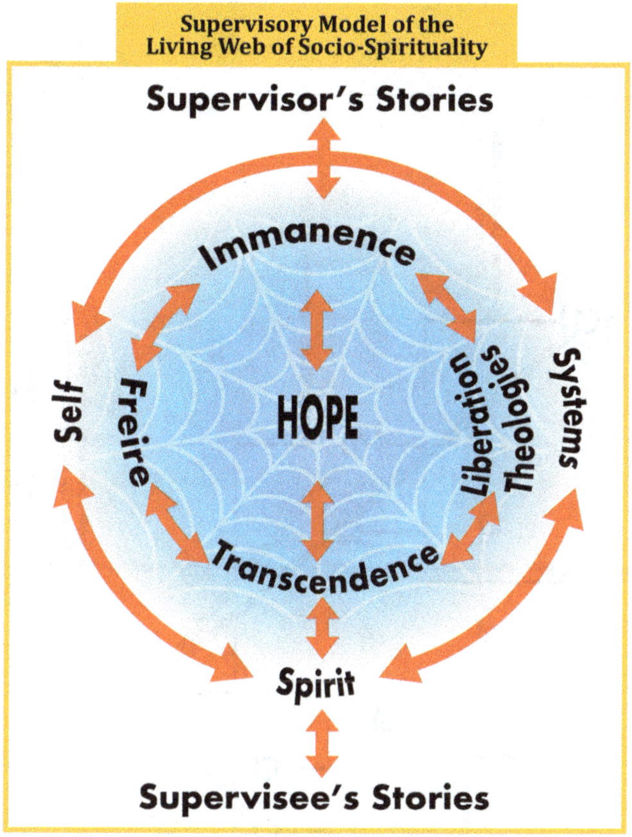
Supervisory Model of the
Living Web of Socio-Spirituality
Supervisor's Stories
Immanence
Self
Freire
HOPE
Liberation
Theologies
Systems
Transcendence
Spirit
Supervisee's Stories

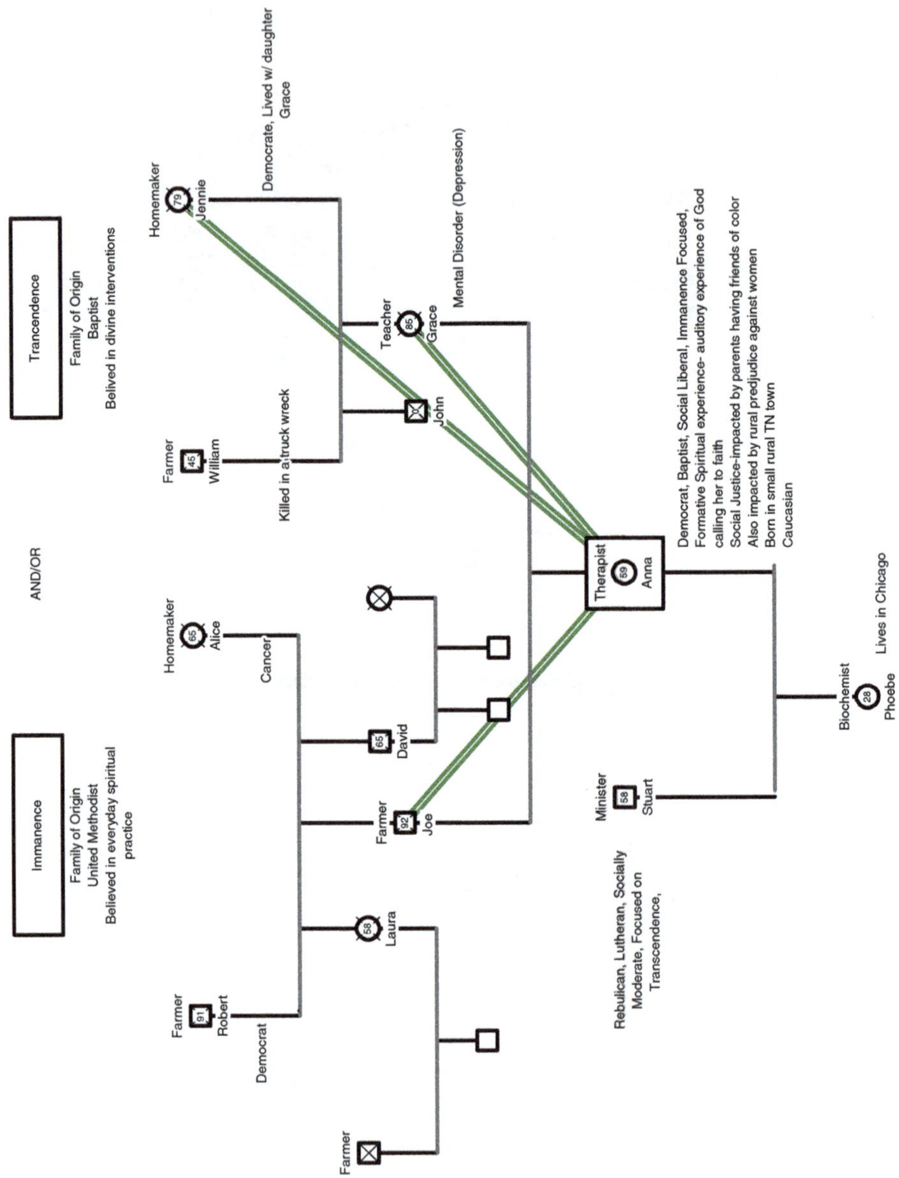

Trancendence
Family of Origin
Baptist
Belived in divine interventions
AND/OR
Immanence
Family of Origin
United Methodist
Believed in everyday spiritual practice
Homemaker
79
Jennie
Democrate, Lived w/ daughter Grace
Farmer
45
William
Killed in a truck wreck
John
Teacher
85
Grace
Mental Disorder (Depression)
Homemaker
65
Alice
Cancer
65
David
Farmer
92
Joe
58
Laura
Farmer
91
Robert
Democrat
Farmer
Therapist
59
Anna
Democrat, Baptist, Social Liberal, Immanence Focused,
Formative Spiritual experience- auditory experience of God calling her to faith
Social Justice-impacted by parents having friends of color
Also impacted by rural predjudice against women
Born in small rural TN town
Caucasian
Minister
58
Stuart
Rebulican, Lutheran, Socially Moderate, Focused on Transcendence,
Biochemist
28
Phoebe
Lives in Chicago

Appendix B: "Integration of Self, Systems, and Spirit" Syllabus

CHRISTIAN THEOLOGICAL SEMINARY

Course Information

- Summer 2021
- Prerequisites: T 500 Intro to Theology and P 520 Intro to MFT Theory or P 522 Intro to MFT Practice
- Zoom—Thursdays—May 27, June 3, June 17, June 24 at 6–9 pm; Saturdays—May 29, June 5, June 19 at 9 am to 12 pm
- Course location—Synchronous and asynchronous
- Course format—Populi, VoiceThread, Zoom

Instructor(s) Information

- Suzanne M. Coyle, Ph.D., LMFT
- Phone—(317) 931-2349; scoyle@cts.edu
- Office hours—Virtual Zoom hours Tuesdays, 6–9 pm, May 25, June 1, June 8, June 15, June 22
- www.spiritualnarratives.com

S. M. Coyle, *Spirituality in Systemic Family Therapy Supervision and Training*, Focused Issues in Family Therapy, https://doi.org/10.1007/978-3-030-92369-3

Course Description

This course integrates theological/spiritual reflection with systemic theories and professional formation. Students begin the course by focusing upon their professional and personal development through self of the therapist emphases. As students identify self of therapist concerns, they then begin to identify their worldview. Then that worldview is connected with relational systemic concepts that evolve into methodological considerations of integrating self, systems, and spirit. Finally, students are introduced to ways in which learnings from this course can be applied to practice settings and the Capstone Presentation.

Course Objectives

The objectives for this class are tailored according to the student responses to the SurveyMonkey enquiring about student learning goals for this class. The following are the course objectives:

1. Explore understandings of spirituality, religion, and theology and the ways in which they are similar and different.
2. Explore personal and professional self of therapist concerns through experiential and reading assignments.
3. Explore relational systemic concepts and ways in which they connect with MFT models of therapy.
4. Explore methodologies of integrating self, systems, and spirit.
5. Apply learning from the class to relational systemic clinical practice.
6. Integrate learnings toward a mock MFT Capstone Paper or other paper.

MAMFT Student Learning Outcomes (Highlighted SLOs Are Covered in This Course)

1. SLO #1—Students will demonstrate clinical skills through theoretical and clinical knowledge through MFT literature and research in a practicum setting.

Assessments

   (a) 100% of students evaluated each semester of practicum on the MFT Trainee Evaluation—Supervisor Report will receive an average of 3; minimum benchmark is 80%.
   (b) 100% of student evaluated at their Capstone Presentation will receive an average of 3 on the MFT literature and research criterion on the Capstone Evaluation Rubric; minimum benchmark is 80%.

2. SLO #2—Students will demonstrate the ability to assess, conceptualize, and plan systemic treatment of individuals, couples, and families.

Assessment

   (a) 100% of students will achieve a minimum average of 3 on a Likert scale of 1–5 on Treatment Plan Rubric in P 520 and Case Conceptualization Plan

Rubric in P 522; Clinical Assessment Rubric, Case Conceptualization Plan Rubric, and Treatment Plan Rubric are completed for P 621, P 623, and P 746 upon completion of the course with a minimum benchmark of 80%.

3. SLO #3—Students will demonstrate the ability to complete entry into the Marriage and Family Therapy profession.

Assessment

(a) Students graduate within the advertised length of program.
(b) Program will maintain a job placement rate of 80%.
(c) 70% and more of graduates sitting for the national exam will pass.

4. SLO #4—Students will demonstrate the ability to utilize a social justice ethic through Professional Formation Cohort Groups.

Assessments

(a) 100% of students will achieve a minimum average of 3 out of 1–5 Likert scale on "Assessment of Cultural Competency" at the end of the Professional Formation Cohort Group "Culture"; 80% minimum benchmark.
(b) 100% of students will achieve a satisfactory rating on Professional Formation Cohort Groups "Gender/Sexual Orientation/Sexuality" and "Spirituality" at the end of the cohort groups: 80% minimum benchmark.

5. SLO #5—Student will demonstrate ability to reflect theologically/spiritually.

Assessment Mechanism:

a) Theological reflection criteria in written paper and oral presentation on the Capstone Presentation Rubric
b) Theological reflection criteria in written paper in P 617 Integration of Self, Systems, and Spirit on the Mock Capstone Rubric

Benchmarks:
80 % of students must achieve an average of 3 on a 5-point Likert scale on each assessment mechanism.

Target:
100% of students must achieve an average of 3 on a 5-point Likert scale on each assessment mechanism.

SLO # 6—Students will demonstrate ability to integrate theological/spiritual reflections in a relational systemic context.
Assessment Mechanism:
a) Integration of theological and systemic perspectives criteria in written and oral presentation of Capstone Presentation Rubric
b) Integration of theological systemic perspectives criteria in written paper in P 617 Integration of Self, Systems, and Spirit on the Mock Capstone Rubric

Benchmark:
80% of student must achieve an average of 3 on a 5-point Likert scale on each assessment mechanism.

Target:
100% of student achieve an average of 3 on a 5-point Likert scale on each assessment mechanism.

Licensure and Accreditation Standards

Marriage and Family Therapy Licensure

This course meets partial course requirements for marriage and family therapy licensure in Indiana and other states.

Marriage and Family Therapy Core Competencies

The marriage and family therapy (MFT) core competencies were developed through a collaborative effort of the American Association for Marriage and Family Therapy (AAMFT) and interested stakeholders. The competencies represent the minimum that MFTs licensed to practice independently must possess. This course addresses the following core competencies:

Domain 1: Admission to Treatment

1.1.1 Conceptual—Understand systems concepts, theories, and techniques that are foundational to the practice of marriage and family therapy

1.2.1 Perceptual—Recognize contextual and systemic dynamics (e.g., gender, age, socioeconomic status, culture/race/ethnicity, sexual orientation, spirituality, religion, larger systems, social context).

1.3.1 Executive—Gather and review intake information, giving balanced attention to individual, family, community, cultural, and contextual factors

Domain 2: Clinical Assessment and Diagnosis

2.2.3 Perceptual—Develop hypotheses regarding relationship patterns, their bearing on the presenting problem, and the influence of extra-therapeutic factors on client systems

Domain 4: Therapeutic Interventions

4.3.2 Executive—Deliver interventions in a way that is sensitive to special needs of clients (e.g., gender, age, socioeconomic status, culture/race/ethnicity, sexual orientation, disability, personal history, larger systems issues of the client)

4.4.1 Evaluative—Evaluate interventions for consistency, congruency with model of therapy and theory of change, cultural and contextual relevance, and goals of the treatment plan

Domain 5: Legal Issues, Ethics, and Standards

5.4.2 Evaluative—Monitor attitudes, personal well-being, personal issues, and personal problems to insure they do not impact the therapy process adversely or create vulnerability for misconduct

5.5.2 Professional—Consult with peers and/or supervisors if personal issues, attitudes, or beliefs threaten to adversely impact clinical work

Course Materials and Texts

Required Readings[1]

Bidwell, D. (2018). *When one religion isn't enough: Lives of spiritually fluid people*. Beacon Press.

Cheon, H. S., & Murphy, M. J. (2007). The self-of-the-therapist awakened: Postmodern approaches to the use of self in marriage and family therapy. *Journal of Feminist Family Therapy, 19*(1), 1–16.

Coyle, S. M. (2013). *Re-storying your faith*. John Hunt Publishing.

Griffith, J., & Griffith, M. (2003). *Encountering the sacred in psychotherapy: How to talk with people about their spiritual lives*. The Guilford Press.

Hecker, L., & Sori, C. (2012). *The therapist's notebook, Vol. 2: More homework, handouts, and activities for use in psychotherapy (Haworth Practical Practice in Mental Health)*. Routledge. (Selections from this reference)

Rober, P. (1999). The therapist's inner conversation in family therapy practice: Some ideas about the self of the therapist, therapeutic impasse, and the process of reflection. *Family Process, 38*(2), 209–228.

Robinson, E. A. (2014). *Exploring theology*. Augsburg Fortress Publishers.

Simon, G. M. (2006). The heart of the matter: A proposal for placing the self of the therapist at the center of family therapy research and training. *Family Process, 45*(3), 331–344.

Smith-Acuna, S. (2011). *Systems theory in action: Applications to individual, couples, and family therapy*. John Wiley.

Timm, T. M., & Blow, A. J. (1999). Self-of-the-therapist work: A balance between removing restraints and identifying resources. *Contemporary Family Therapy, 21*(3), 331–351.

[1] Students need to read a theology book of their choosing they have not previously read.

Recommended Readings

Bidwell, D. (2016). *Spirituality, social construction and relational processes: Essays and reflections*. The Taos Institute.

Coyle, S. M. (2014). *Uncovering spiritual narratives: Using story in pastoral care and ministry*. Augsburg Fortress Publishers.

Townsend, L. (2009). *Introduction to pastoral counseling*. Abingdon Press.

Course Assignments/Requirements

(May send some assignments to professor by e-mail as designated with the following in subject box: P 617 (last name) name of assignment)

Prepare papers in Times Roman 12-point font. Go to https://wordcounter.net/words-per-page to compute your number of pages. Format all written papers in APA format.

- Populi discussion counts for 25% of grade—Students will select one reading from the self of therapist, systems (one chapter), spirituality/theology assignments, and integration methods. The following questions will be addressed: (1) What in the reading catches your attention? (2) How does it affect you as seek to pull together self, systems, and spirit? GRADING: Receive 5 points if submitted before due date. 2 points deduction if late. 0 points received if not completed. DUE weekly through June 23 on Wednesdays, 12 noon.
- VoiceThread discussion on Coyle PowerPoint lecture for 25% of total grade—Students respond weekly to the Coyle PowerPoint lecture with three comments for each week.
- PowerPoint. GRADING: 5 points per week. 2 points deduction if late. 0 points received if not completed. DUE weekly on Thursdays, 12 noon.
- Creative Arts Project counts for 20% of grade—A detailed description of the requirements for this paper will be distributed to students. DUE June 19.
- Mock MFT Capstone Paper counts for 30% of grade DUE June 23. Students can submit a draft of the paper. DUE June 12. (Professor will read and give feedback by June 19.)
- CTS Grading
  - Grades will be determined by the number of points accumulated out of a total of 100 possible points.

A	94–100 points	**C:**	73–76 points
A−:	90–93 points	**C−:**	70–72 points
B+:	87–89 points	**D+:**	67–69 points
B:	83–86 points	**D:**	63–66 points
B−	80–82 points	**D−:**	60–62.99 points
C+:	77–79 points	**F:**	0–59.99 points

– CTS Grading Scale operates on a 4.0 grading system:

A 4.0	A– 3.7	B+ 3.3	B 3.0	B– 2.7	C+ 2.3
C 2.0	C– 1.7	D+ 1.3	D 1.0	D– 0.7	F 0

– Student Workload *(see below for instructions)*

Assignment	Estimated time needed to complete	Due date	Points/percentage of grade
Readings	42 h	See course schedule	P/F
Self of therapist in Populi	2 h	Week of May 24	5%
Systems reflection in Populi	2 h	Week of May 31	5%
Spirituality/theology reflection in Populi	2 h	Class of June 17	5%
Integration methods in Populi	2 h	Classes of June 19 and June 24	5% each week
Creative arts project	20 h	June 19	20%
Mock MFT Capstone Paper of integrative paper in practice setting	40 h	July 10	30%
Coyle lecture/PowerPoint/videos in Voice Thread	22 h	May 24 to June 23	25% total with 5% each week
Totals	Approx. 135 h		

– General guidelines as to workload expectations with regard to reading and writing:

- **Reading:** For relatively dense reading, assume as few as 10–15 pages/h; for relatively accessible reading, assume as much as 20–25 pages/h.
- **Writing:** Assume about 2–3 h/page for research papers or final essays; and about 1–2 h/page for reflection papers or journal entries.

Due Dates and Extension

Assignments will be deducted as posted in the Student Workload above for Populi and VoiceThread assignments. For Creative Arts Project and Mock MFT Capstone Paper, 1 point will be deducted for every day past the due date.

Requests for extension must be requested no later than 24 h prior to the due date of the assignment.

Attendance

Seminary policy requires that students miss no more than 25% of class time. For our online class, that means that *students cannot miss more than 5.3 h of Zoom time*. You will not receive credit for the class if you miss more than those hours unless extenuating circumstances make it necessary for you to make special arrangements prior to the missed hours with the professor.

Course Schedule

The class will utilize the following pedagogical approaches:

Lecture/Discussion/Readings in Zoom and VoiceThread—Class lectures will assume that students have read the assigned readings. Discussion will require knowledge of the reading. This knowledge includes knowing what you do not know about the readings. Come to class prepared with questions for discussion. *MFT Core Competencies*: 1.1.1, 1.2.1, 1.3.1, 2.2.3, 4.3.2, 4.4.1, and 5.5.2.

Populi Discussions—Students will discuss the following questions each week on self, systems, spirit, and integration methods: (1) What in the reading catches your attention? (2) How does it affect you as seek to pull together self, systems, and spirit? *MFT Core Competencies*: 1.1.1., 1.2.1, 1.3.1, 2.2.3, 4.3.2, 4.4.1, and 5.5.2.

Experiential Exercises—Each Zoom class will begin with an experiential exercise designed to prepare students to assimilate issues about self, systems, and spirit in their personal and relational identities. *MFT Core Competencies*: 1.2.1, 5.4.2, and 5.5.2.

Spiritual Formation Conversation—Students have the option to meet with the professor for a 30-min conversation in Zoom to assess the their worldview as a foundational step for assimilating self, systems, and spirit. The professor will work with each student to contextualize their learning according to their spiritual worldview. Groups will also meet in breakout rooms during Zoom for peer conversation. *MFT Core Competencies*: 1.2.1, 5.4.2, and 5.5.2.

Reflecting Teams of Self, System, and Spirit—Students will be assigned to reflecting teams named Self, Systems, and Spirit through Zoom breakout rooms and Populi discussions with attention to gender, racial ethnicity, and life experience to the degree it is possible. *MFT Core Competencies*: 1.2.1, 2.2.3, 4.3.2, 4.4.1, and 5.5.2.

Creative Arts Project—The project can be done individually or with peers. This creative arts project will illustrate the challenges in methodological integration of self, systems, and spirit. For example, it could be a light-hearted skit, a presentation of appropriate art, composed music, and or a combination of things. *MFT Core Competencies*: 1.2.1 and 4.4.1.

Detailed Course Schedule

Populi Posts DUE Wednesdays, 12 pm; VoiceThread Comments
DUE Thursdays, 12 pm.

Self

Week of May 24

Readings: Cheon and Murphy; Rober: Simon; Timm and Blow.
Populi Discussion: Self of Therapist
VoiceThread Discussion: Coyle PowerPoint
DUE: Populi Posts and VT Comments

Systems

Week of May 31

Smith-Acuna; Read one chapter from Hecker and Sori for Zoom discussion; Populi Discussion: Systems
VoiceThread Discussion: Coyle PowerPoint
DUE: Populi Posts and VT Comments

Spirit

Class of June 17

Readings: Robinson; Griffith and Griffith; Read one chapter from Hecker and Sori for Zoom discussion; your selected theology book.
Populi Discussion: Spirituality/theology
VoiceThread Discussion: Coyle PowerPoint
DUE: Populi Posts and VT Comments

Integration Methods

Class of June 19

Readings: Bidwell; Coyle (three chapters), *Supervision in Systemic Family Therapy Supervision and Training* (forthcoming) Springer Nature; Coyle, *Re-storying Your Faith*
Populi Discussion: Integration methods
VoiceThread Discussion: Coyle PowerPoint
DUE: Self-reflection about your learning from Re-storying Your Faith for 3 bonus points. DUE June 19 Creative Arts Project
DUE: Populi Post and VT Comments

Integration Methods

Class of June 24

Readings: Re-read primary sources and any recommended readings for Mock Capstone Paper
Populi Discussion: Integration methods
VoiceThread Discussion: Coyle PowerPoint
DUE: Populi Post and VT Comments
DUE: Mock Capstone Paper JULY 10

ADA

Students with Disabilities

If you anticipate the need for reasonable accommodations to meet the requirements of this course, you must register with the Office of Student Disabilities and Accommodations. Contact Karen Kelm, SDA Coordinator in the SDA Office, at 317/931-2330 or email kkelm@cts.edu. Students are required to provide documentation of disability to SDA Office prior to receiving accommodations.

Appendix C: Spirituality Integration Resources

Table 5.1 Supervisory assessment—modified Hodge (2005)

Initial brief spiritual assessment	Supervisory spiritual assessment	Connection with living web of socio-spirituality
1. I was wondering if you consider spirituality or religion to be a personal strength?	1. I am wondering if your spirituality or approach to spirituality affects your work with your clients?	1. Supervisee/supervisor spiritual stories connect with client through awareness of immanence/transcendence
2. In what ways does your spirituality help you to cope with the difficulties you encounter?	2. In what ways might it be helpful?	2. LWSS understands spiritual stories focused on the social context of supervision to counter social injustice
3. Are there certain spiritual beliefs and practices that you find particularly helpful in dealing with problems?	3. In what ways might it be hindrance?	3. Freire's understanding of oppression uncovers ways knowledge needs to be shared in order to be liberating
4. I was also wondering if you attend a church or some other spiritual community?	4. In what situations might you suggest to clients a spiritual resource or community of faith?	4. Acknowledges the socio context that connects with spirituality and lives of supervisee and client
5. Do resources exist in your faith community that might be helpful to you?	5. Would you ever do this?	5. Supervisees' values can uncover their spiritual stories that lift up oppression
Citation:	Citation:	Citation:
Hodge, D. R. (2005). Spiritual assessment in marital and family therapy: A methodological framework for selecting from among six qualitative assessment tools. *Journal of Marital and Family Therapy, 31*(4), 341–356. https://doi.org/10.1111/j.1752-0606.2005.tb01575.x	Coyle, S. M. (2021). *Supervisory Assessment* (modified Hodge, 2005). IBSA	Coyle, S. M. (2021). *Supervisory Living Web of Socio-Spirituality*

S. M. Coyle, *Spirituality in Systemic Family Therapy Supervision and Training*, Focused Issues in Family Therapy, https://doi.org/10.1007/978-3-030-92369-3

Table 5.2 Supervisory questions in a socio-spirituality model

Self—What can you tell me about yourself that would enable me to fully appreciate you? I hear that you (enjoy singing, etc., some skill, or personal quality). How might this skill/quality draw forth your inner self? Your relational selves with others?
Self/Socio-spirituality—As you envision your client's story, which of your relational selves makes the strongest appearance?
Systems/Spirituality—You need to focus now upon which relational self best connects with your client's story. What possibility of spirituality does that self see in your client?
What story of hope does your client have now?
How do you see yourself sustaining that hope in your client?
What might be the obstacle? How might you speak to those obstacles?
Spirituality/Social justice—As you identify your client's problem story, how has or has not your client been able to envision a hopeful future?
What would need to change in that story for them to engage that hopeful future?
Are there systemic obstacles to this hope that your client would live to change?
How might that happen?
How will you sustain your client in that arduous journey?
Are there social justice efforts you might engage outside the therapy room?

Table 6.1 Spiritual competencies

Spiritual literacy
Spiritual competencies in knowledge of profession
1. Develop knowledge of the spiritual/religious literature that gives a foundation to understanding the role of spirituality/religion in clients' lives.
2. Develop knowledge of ways in which a specific diversity connects with a specific spirituality.
Spiritual competencies in practice of therapy
1. Understand knowledge of different religions and non-theistic spiritualities that lends itself to clinical practice.
2. Understand the difference between healthy spirituality/religion and destructive spirituality/religion.
Spiritual competencies in human diversity and social structure
1. Understand the intersectionalities of various diversities and how they may connect with spirituality.
2. Learn how to administer some spiritual inventories and the possible connection to social structure.
Spiritual competencies in professional identity
1. Understand how spirituality/religion differs from emotions and feelings.
2. Discover the difference between professional functioning between a chaplain, minister, and MFT in addressing the client's spirituality.
Spiritual sensitivity
Spiritual competencies in knowledge of profession
1. Develop a personal theoretical approach to addressing a client's spiritual/religious concerns.
2. Understand ways to enable clients to bring their spirituality up to date to correlate with their changing worldview.
Spiritual competencies in practice of therapy
1. Demonstrate skill in helping families respond to spiritual crises.
2. Develop spiritually integrated interventions that connect with one's own spiritual worldview.
3. Demonstrate skills integrating spiritual and social justice practices in addressing diversities.
Spiritual competencies in human diversity and social structure
1. Engage in antiracism training to increase one's sensitivity to clients' race, ethnicity, and class.
2. Seek out supervision that focuses on diversity and social structure.
Spiritual competencies in professional identity
1. Deepen one's own spirituality through personal therapy, spiritual formation, and spiritual practices.
2. Explore one's family of origin in the area of spirituality and diversity.

Table 8.1 Re-storying spirituality exercise

Telling of the Story (interviewee): Think about a formative spiritual experience and share it with us. (A formative spiritual experience is defined as a spiritual experience that you know is true for you and serves as a source of strength. It takes you beyond self and relationships to something that is bigger than you.)
Questions: How does this story support you?
Re-telling of the Story (other members): What part of the story resonates for you? Re-telling of the Re-telling of the Story (interviewee): How does this re-telling of your story resonate for you? (Coyle, 2019).

Table 8.2 Spirituality and self of therapist

Q1:	I am able to identify my own spiritual narratives.
Q2:	I am able to identify the spiritual values and/or stories I hold dear.
Q3:	I have intentionally reflected on my spiritual narratives as they connect with my conducting therapy.
Q4:	I am able to identify how my spiritual values connect with those of my clients.
Q5:	I am able to identify how my spiritual questions connect with the clinical questions of a case.
Q6:	I am able to identify the ways in which the spiritual values and/or stories of my clients resonate with me.
Q7:	Awareness of my own spiritual narratives affects my ability to thicken my clients' spiritual narratives in therapy.

Appendix D: Self, Systems, and Spirit Practices

Self, Systems, and Spirit Practice—Chapter 2

What Is Spirituality?

This practice is designed to generate a series of questions about spirituality. Those questions will be used to create a collaborative environment for therapeutic encounters. The different perspectives that emerge are expected to enrich one another. This naming exercise is related to narrative practice. The process of naming carries the potential for giving hopes and dreams a name that brings our present into the future.

Naming the Group

The group divides into sub-groups of four to six people. The first step for each subgroup is to gather together with the purpose of assigning their group a name that conveys some aspect of spirituality to the individual members of the group and then to agree upon a name that conveys the collective understanding of a quality of spirituality.

- The facilitator determines the length of time for the group to select its name. It is suggested that a one-and-a-half to 3-h timeframe is set.
- For example, people could suggest the name of a spiritual leader like Buddha, Jesus, Confucius, etc.
  Or, another example would be to identify a quality of spirituality like peace, love, etc. Finally, another example would be to select a random word like Lake Placid, etc.
- The group then shares their group name with the other groups.

S. M. Coyle, *Spirituality in Systemic Family Therapy Supervision and Training*, Focused Issues in Family Therapy, https://doi.org/10.1007/978-3-030-92369-3

Naming Spirituality

- The facilitator asks each individual of each sub-group to write a definition of spirituality that speaks to them.
- The individuals of each sub-group share their definitions with the whole group.
- Then, each sub-group works with their individual members to come up with a definition on which the whole group can agree.
- The sub-groups meet in a large group to discuss the outcomes of their collaboration.

Naming Possibilities

- The facilitator asks each sub-group to discuss Chap. 1. The question for consideration: "What catches your attention?"
- The sub-groups summarize their answers for discussion.
- Finally, the sub-groups and then the whole group identify some possibilities for their group from the definition of spirituality and discussion of the chapter.
- Some suggested possibilities might be the following: (1) Discuss how the definition of spirituality could impact the curricular structure itself; (2) Work to integrate an awareness of the understanding of spirituality in the clinical practicum experience; and (3) Students might study different religions and discuss how spirituality could emerge from that study.

Self, Systems, Spirit Practice—Chapter 3

Diversity and Spirituality in the Living Web of Socio-Spirituality

This practice is designed for peer groups of students and/or supervisors. According to a pre-assigned rotation, participants bring a clinical case for discussion and supervision. As an alternative, pre-practicum students can select a clinical case from a systemic family therapy textbook. The process for the session is as follows:

- The facilitator distributes copies of Fig. 3.1: Living web of socio-spirituality to all the participants.
- The session may begin with the discussion of Chap. 3. An alternate approach is for the facilitator to summarize the chapter contents.
- The group participants identify the aspects of diversity/social justice and spirituality they see in the clinical case.

Then, the facilitator asks either sub-groups or individual participants the following questions:

1. As you make a treatment plan for the clients in the case study using the living web, what topic would you first engage the client in considering during the session?
2. How would you move from that point to a proximate goal for the session and to a contribution to a longer-term therapeutic outcome?
3. How would you respond to the client's problem story?
4. How would you use the living web to encourage the client to develop a future story using spirituality to address social injustice?

Group Feedback: Sub-groups discuss their experience of the process in the large group.

Self, Systems, and Spirit Practice—Chapter 4

Looking at the Living Web of Socio-Spirituality

This practice is designed for peer groups of students and/or supervisors. According to pre-assigned rotation, participants bring a clinical case for discussion and supervision. As an alternative, pre-practicum students can select a clinical case from a systemic family therapy textbook.

The facilitator distributes copies of Fig. 4.1: Living web of socio-spirituality to all the participants The session may begin with the discussion of Chap. 4. An alternate approach is for the facilitator to summarize the chapter contents. Group participants identify the aspects of the living web of socio-spirituality in the clinical case. Then, the facilitator asks sub-groups or individual participants the following questions:

1. What aspects of the living web of socio-spirituality catches your attention?
2. How might you further develop that attention catching aspect?
3. How does that attention catching aspect apply to the clinical case?
4. How would you change the living web of socio-spirituality?

Self, Systems, Spirit Practice—Chapter 5

Seeking Socio-Spirituality in Supervision

This practice is designed for peer groups of supervisors. According to pre-assigned rotation, participants bring a clinical case of supervision for discussion. The facilitator distributes copies of Fig. 5.1: Supervisory model of the living web of socio-spirituality to all the participants.

The session may begin with the discussion of Chap. 5. An alternate approach is for the facilitator to summarize the chapter contents. Group participants identify the aspects of the living web of socio-spirituality in the supervisory case. Then, the facilitator asks sub-groups or individual participants the following questions:

1. What aspects of the supervisory model of the living web of socio-spirituality catches your attention?
2. How might you further develop that attention-catching aspect?
3. How does that attention-catching aspect apply to the supervisory case?
4. How would you change the supervisory model of the living web of socio-spirituality?

Self, Systems, Spirit Practice—Chapter 6

Creating a Spiritually Integrated Curriculum

One of the biggest challenges in creating a spiritually integrated curriculum in a training program is achieving “buy-in” with faculty and students. The following suggestions will lay the groundwork for a successful curriculum change.

1. Create a survey for faculty and students to complete to ascertain what the desired goals are.
2. Organize a brainstorming session for the faculty; brainstorming for students.
3. Take the feedback from the students to the faculty at a separate meeting.
4. Create a curriculum team of faculty and a student representative.
5. Interview MFT program leadership at schools that have a spiritually integrated curriculum.
6. Create a trial curriculum.
7. Create a survey for faculty and students.
8. Integrate the feedback into the final draft for administrative approval.

Self, Systems, Spirit Practice—Chapter 7

Discovering Creativity in Teaching Spirituality

Creating a spiritually integrated course for a clinical training program should be just that creative. So, how do faculty engage in a creative process with competing administrative, publishing, and teaching deadlines? Set aside time for a mini-workshop of 2 or so hours. The following are suggestions that will take a morning or afternoon, whether virtually or face-to-face.

Mini Workshop

Pre-meeting

- Gather one to three resources that nurture your own spirituality however you define it. Review those resources. What catches your attention?
- What are some questions to consider in small groups?

Dreaming

Show a series of abstract pictures such as clouds, swirls of color, nature photo, etc. Have music playing in the background.

- What gives you energy to dream dreams?
- How big are your dreams about your clinical training program?
- Describe a visual image of a dream about a spiritually integrated course?
- Group discussion

Hurdling

- Now, in your mind's eye, see yourself running toward a track and field hurdle. What do you have to get over the hurdle?
- Do you envision hurdles to overcome in achieving that dream?
- Group discussion

Journeying

- Describe what dreams and hurdles you will take with you on the journey to create a course with a spiritual emphasis
- Group discussion
- How might your spiritual resources you gathered prior to this future journey sustain you?
- Group discussion

Brainstorm where, as faculty, will you go from here?

Self, Systems, Spirit Practice—Chapter 8

Possibilities for Further Research

Invite a group of private practice clinicians, agency clinicians, faculty, supervisors to explore the possibilities for researching spirituality in systemic family practice.

Several discussions can be held:

- What determines trainees' sense of competence in clinical practice?
- In what way does spirituality determine that sense of competency?
- What is a challenging aspect of integrating spirituality in clinical practice?

Self, Systems, Spirit Practice—Chapter 9

Living Spiritually in Narrative Liturgy

This Self, Systems, Spirit Practice is designed to train students how to create a collective narrative project for a class or community outreach. Students need to read the section in this chapter on the Tutu Project. David Denborough's two books on collective narrative practice can also be accessed.

View the Friday Afternoon video "Living in Stories: Embodiment in therapy through Liturgical Practice" by Chad Loftis at this link: https://dulwichcentre.com.au/living-stories-embodiment-therapy-liturgical-practice-chad-loftis/

As part of a class on spirituality and social justice, divide students into small groups. Discuss what you see in Loftis' methodology that could apply to a community project.

Students could also read one of David Denborough's books on collective narrative practice for context.

Students meet regularly to create a collective story project that could use narrative practice in a community project.

Faculty will schedule a formal presentation for these projects after students have worked with community agencies.

Feedback from peers and faculty.

Self, Systems, Spirit Practice—Chapter 10

Situating Spirituality in Alternate Leaning Environments

Students training to be licensed psychotherapists may often have little time for developing therapeutic skills outside a clinical practice setting. Sometimes the assumption is that clinical therapy skills just automatically transfer to other settings. This is not true. So, this practice is designed to be used in master's and doctoral learning environments, so that those systemic therapy skills can be sharpened to enable using them in alternate environments.

Virtual/Role Play for Skills in Alternate Care Environments

Pre-practice readings Students read one of the following books: David Denborough's *Do You Want to Hear a Story? Adventures in Collective Narrative Practice* or Stavros; Torres' *Conversations Worth Having: Using Appreciative Inquiry to Fuel Productive and Meaningful Engagement*. These approaches utilize the therapist's natural skills in a setting other than the therapy room.

Module in course or mini workshop Faculty/trainers can implement this training as a module of mini workshops. It would be helpful prior to graduation or placement in a community context, which is not a straight therapy.

Process Didactic/experiential components of training will give participants a better understanding, at the basic level, of how spirituality can/cannot inspire them to engage more fully in a community setting.

1. Students meet in small group to discuss the reading they chose. The facilitator asks the following question: What caught your attention in the reading?
2. Have a general discussion.
3. Facilitator asks students what community setting of the following are they most excited about: general hospital, psychiatric hospital, substance abuse support center, community agency, church outreach.
4. Students break into the group, general hospital, etc. they chose.
5. Like-minded students discuss two areas: (a) What skills do you think that setting demands? and (b) What did you learn from the reading that could help you in that setting?
6. Students meet in large group to brainstorm for next step with facilitator.
7. Over the next semester, like-minded students meet in their interest group to learn more about that setting. This could be visiting the community settings and even exploring a placement in that setting.

Self, Systems, Spirit Practice—Chapter 11

Future Directions for Spiritually Integrated Practice

Organize a large group in your program using a modified appreciative inquiry approach.

Discuss the multiple ways students envision systemic family therapy.

Have participants rank the three changes they would make to the MFT program at your institution.

Then, take the discussion results, and in a faculty meeting, make changes in your MFT program that embrace those future directions.

Index

S. M. Coyle, *Spirituality in Systemic Family Therapy Supervision and Training*, Focused Issues in Family Therapy, https://doi.org/10.1007/978-3-030-92369-3